PLEASURE
PRIV

CW00739653

David Stare

Für Pat,
mit besten Grüßen,
Claudia Sternberg

IN THE
WRONG
PLACE

AT THE
WRONG
TIME

AM
FALSCHEN
ORT

ZUR
FALSCHEN
ZEIT

PLEASURE, PRIVILEGE, PRIVATIONS

Lofthouse Park near Wakefield, 1908-1922

Edited by
Claudia Sternberg and David Stowe

In the Wrong Place at the Wrong Time

Am falschen Ort zur falschen Zeit

Leeds 2018

Published by

In the Wrong Place at the Wrong Time
Am falschen Ort zur falschen Zeit

A British German
World War One Centenary Project
supported by
AHRC-WWI Public Engagement
Centre for Hidden Histories,
University of Nottingham
and
Legacies of War
at the University of Leeds

https://ruhlebenlofthouse.com

Copyright © Claudia Sternberg and David Stowe
and the authors 2018

All rights reserved.
No part of this publication may be reproduced
without prior permission from the editors.

ISBN 978-1-9995827-6-0

Every effort has been made to trace copyright holders and to obtain
their permission for the use of copyright material. The editors
apologise for any errors or omissions and would be grateful for
notification of any corrections that should be incorporated in future
reprints or editions of this book.

Printed in the United Kingdom
by Biddles Books Ltd

CONTENTS

Part IV: Military Life and Culture

Germany

Postwar

Postscript

Preface

It gives me great pleasure to write a Preface to this important book, which looks at the Lofthouse Park internment camp near Wakefield. I first came across this institution in the middle of the 1980s, while researching and writing my PhD thesis which appeared as *The Enemy in Our Midst: Germans in Britain during the First World War* (Oxford: Berg, 1991).

Internment became a key feature of the marginalisation and persecution of the German community in Britain during this period, which included anti-German riots, property confiscation and deportation. I discovered that Lofthouse Park acted as one of the network of camps used to house male enemy aliens of military age in Britain, with the head camp in Knockaloe on the Isle of Man. In particular, I found the book by Paul Cohen-Portheim focusing on Wakefield, which this volume examines, a profound and accurate insight into the realities of First World War internment in Britain. In fact, the camp in Wakefield, together with the one in Knockaloe, as well as those elsewhere in the United Kingdom, simply served as part of a global system of incarceration, with camps in existence throughout the British Empire from Holsworthy near Sydney to Banff in Alberta. While most internees experienced incarceration in the country in which they lived, others experienced transportation from one part of the world to another.

This fascinating book edited by Claudia Sternberg and David Stowe drills down to the reality of life behind barbed wire by focusing on life in Wakefield, presenting us with a series of documents, including case studies of individuals who spent time within the camp, and a history of the institution written by David Stowe. The volume helps to fill a gap in the history of an institution which profoundly impacted upon individual lives and also helps us to understand internment during the Great War.

Panikos Panayi

April 2018

Thanks and Acknowledgements

In the context of the wider project that gave rise to this publication, we have worked with and learned from many individuals and institutions.

We would like to thank John Beckett, Larissa Allwork and Mike Noble of the AHRC-WWI Engagement Centre for Hidden Histories at the University of Nottingham for their support of *In the Wrong Place at the Wrong Time/Am falschen Ort zur falschen Zeit* and the inspiring sharing opportunities that the Centre provided. We also wish to thank Alison Fell, Jessica Meyer, Ingrid Sharp, Gareth Dant and the wider group of colleagues at Legacies of War, Special Collections and the School of Fine Art, History of Art and Cultural Studies at the University of Leeds for their help and cooperation over the course of the First World War centenary years.

We are very grateful to Claire Pickering and John Whitaker at Wakefield Library and Museum for supporting our research and giving this Wakefield publication a Wakefield location for its first presentation. This thanks is extended to Lucy Moore and her colleagues at Leeds Museums and Galleries for giving their time and sharing their expertise and resources on various occasion.

A special thanks goes to Peter Liddle for his First World War collection at Leeds University Library and more specifically for his fateful remark in early 2015 that the civilian internees of the *Engländerlager* Ruhleben (and, as we propose, by extension those of Lofthouse Park) are worthy of further attention. We are grateful to Panikos Panayi and Matthew Stibbe for their indispensable research on internment, but also for their collegial exchange and hands-on engagement with our project and participants in Leeds and Lofthouse.

Two Heritage Open Days held at Lofthouse Gate Working Men's Club in 2016 and 2017 proved very successful. This was due in no small part to funding from the Centre for Hidden Histories and the Committee and Staff of the Lofthouse Gate W.M.C. who define the very meaning of the term hospitality. It is with the same warmth and generosity of spirit that we would like to thank Keith and Sue (Stewards), Don, Jane and Margaret and other members for helping to make the two open days very special.

The response was also very encouraging, and the editors would like to thank the local people who came forward with their own stories and memories of growing up in the 'Park' in the 1940s and 1950s. It was a pleasure to meet Roger Byard and some of the 'Lofthouse Boys' who had known each other since childhood. Roger's contribution to the book is worthy of note where he was able to supply a drawing of the building which was used as the Commandant's quarters during the First World War. We also heard from Eric who took an active part in the celebration of the Queen's Coronation at Lofthouse Park as a young boy in 1953. Other visitors brought objects from their personal archives which had not hitherto been seen by the public and were connected with family history, the camp or the long-gone tram service between Leeds and Wakefield.

Further support from the wider local community was found in the help we were given from Outwood Community Video and the Wakefield & District Family History Society. The contact here has proved of enormous benefit where images of Lofthouse Park have been donated and where time has been given freely. In respect of this, we are most grateful to Michael Hooley and Chris Welch, and to Stella Robinson who has gone above and beyond the call of duty in volunteering her time in the interest of further research and promoting the book. We are also grateful to Peter Duffy Ltd for the permission to access the grounds within the old perimeter of Lofthouse Park Camp which have not yet been built on.

We are indebted to those German and Austrian residents of Yorkshire and descendants with German heritage who followed our invitation to talk about being German in Britain from the vantage point of the present. We thank Jessica Bradley and Louise Atkinson for joining us on this occasion and taking the findings forward in creative ways, as Louise has also done when mapping Lofthouse Park. Help provided by members of the German Lutheran Church, the German Saturday School Leeds (DSSL) and Anglo-German circles and societies was much appreciated.

We thank Claire Corkill and Chris Kolonko for giving us additional insights from an archaeological point of view and Tina Richardson and Tim Waters for their psycho/geographical take on Lofthouse Park as a historical site without any physical remains.

Additionally, we thank Yvonne Cresswell, Zoë Denness, Christoph Jahr, Alison Jones, Carmen Mann, Stefan Manz and members of the Anglo-German Family History Society for their input during a variety of encounters, among others on the Isle of Man and in Hawick in Scotland. Our thanks goes also to Anne Buckley of the Skipton POW Project at Leeds University, with whom we share the endeavour to explore a vanished Yorkshire-based First World War camp, for exchanging findings and experiences.

Our appreciation also goes out to a host of young people who were prepared to find out about the history of Lofthouse Park and get involved in numerous ways. Among these are the young curators of the Preservative Party at Leeds City Museum and Leeds University students who attended *ARTF3008/5008M Beyond the Trench*, a module dedicated to collaborative projects on the history, remembrance and critical heritage of the First World War. We also thank the pupils of Carl-Friedrich-von-Siemens-Gymnasium in Berlin for embarking on a long journey to walk the streets of Lofthouse, explore – with the help of Nigel Grizzard – Bradford's Little Germany and look at the First World War archives in Leeds. This partnership was made possible by the Jugendgeschichtswerkstatt Spandau, Uwe Hofschläger and his team, Tom Greulich, Martina Batteux and Michael Franz and further supported by the Stadtgeschichtliches Museum and Archive Spandau.

Our Lofthouse Park research has also benefitted from the input and development of learning resources by Eva Göbel and Gertie and Paul Whitfield. Their constructive reworking of the material helps to put the research to further use in German and British education. We are grateful to the DSSL for enabling a trial run with the material and to the Association of German Saturday Schools in the UK (VDSS) for allowing us to introduce this topic to this supplementary school network.

We would also like to acknowledge the importance of the following libraries and archives for our research: Archiv der Rechtswissenschaftlichen Fakultät der Universität Kiel, Bradford Local Studies Library, Leeds Local Studies Library, Middlesbrough Local Studies Library, Sunderland Local Studies Library, Wakefield Local Studies Library, Imperial War Museum, ICRC Historical Archive (Geneva), Special Collections at the University of Leeds, The National Archives, West Yorkshire Archive Services (Leeds and Wakefield), Manx National Heritage, Staatsbibliothek zu Berlin – Preußischer Kulturbesitz, Staats- und Universitätsbibliothek Bremen, Sammlung der Berlinischen Galerie and Europeana 1914-1918.

David Stowe would like to personally thank Ruth Allison for her help with the text and the additional information she has supplied, and Oliver Wilkinson for stepping in at short notice and agreeing to write the chapter on military prisoners of war. The editors are also grateful to Peter Päßler and Alan Roberts for information on the German war dead in the records of the Volksbund Deutsche Kriegsgräberfürsorge e.v. and the Commonwealth War Graves Commission relating to Cannock Chase.

Claudia Sternberg extends her personal thanks to Brenda Hollweg for her editorial support and is very grateful to both her and Monroe Sternberg for their unfailing patience over the past years. This book is also dedicated to the memory of Hans Sternberg who passed away while this publication was under way.

Foremost we thank the contributors of this volume – Ruth Allison, Emily Bagshaw, Franz Götz, Eberhard Haering, Henning Ibs, Hilke Langhammer, Corinna Meiß, Alan Muddiman, Richard Oswald, the *Postal Historian*, Oliver Wilkinson, Carol Wright and Karl-Heinz Wüstner – for their commitment to bringing to this publication historical scholarship, family narratives, personal insight and invaluable archival material.

Our final thank you goes to anyone whose information we did not include or whose generous offer of support we were not able to take up due to limited capacity and the demands of our 'daytime jobs.

Introduction

Background and Context

The idea for a book that would explore and recover the history of Lofthouse Park, a Yorkshire amusement park turned internment and prisoner-of-war camp during the First World War, emerged in the context of a wider project. *In the Wrong Place at the Wrong Time (IWPWT)* was set up as a public engagement project affiliated with Legacies of War, the University of Leeds First World War Centenary hub. It was conceived from the outset as a comparative, collaborative and bilingual British German exploration and received funding and support from the Centre for Hidden Histories at the University of Nottingham. The Centre for Hidden Histories was one of five engagement centres that had been created in 2014 with funding from the Arts and Humanities Research Council (AHRC) to engage with and support communities as they sought to commemorate and reflect upon the century-long legacy of the First World War.

Up and running since 2015, *IWPWT* has worked with historians, descendants, local residents, educators, university students, pupils, young people, artists, museums and libraries in Britain and Germany on the topic of World War One internment of civilians across the two countries.[1] The project had been sparked in Special Collections at the University of Leeds and more specifically in the Liddle Collection, the Library's vast First World War collection of books, objects, recordings and official and private documents.[2] Among the materials connected to over 6,000 individuals, a sizeable sub-collection relates to the experience of British and British colonial civilians who had been interned as 'enemy aliens' in Ruhleben Camp in Spandau near Berlin from 1914 to 1918. Within the circles of Anglophone First World War *aficionados*, the *Engländer-lager* Ruhleben is relatively well known and over the years has attracted attention in the British media. In Germany, however, the Ruhleben Camp has had no generally accessible representation and is virtually unknown to the Spandauers and Berliners of today. More emphasis, if any, has been on information about prisoner-of-war camps maintained by Germany and the institution of forced labour during the First World War. Therefore the first public display in Spandau dedicated to Ruhleben Camp was an exhibition at Zitadelle Spandau (29 November 2017 to 2 April 2018), created by the Youth History Workshop Spandau (*Jugendgeschichtswerkstatt Spandau*) and pupils from Carl-Friedrich-von-Siemens-Gymnasium, a local secondary school, in collaboration with *In the Wrong Place at the Wrong Time*. The young people and their team had visited Leeds, the Liddle Collection and Lofthouse before they completed their work.[3]

But the paradox of concurrent proximity and absence was by no means unique to the case of the Ruhleben Camp in Germany. In the rich and diverse Liddle Collection at Leeds, a single file was found that contained a photocopied article about Lofthouse Park Camp, a major World War One site located only eight miles away from the Library.[4] the only other source was a recording with a Hungarian internee; it must have fallen foul of technical issues, because it was cut off just as the interviewee mentioned his time in Wakefield.[5] We had to cast our net wider, but very little could be brought to light in the first instance. Our question, 'Did you know that 1,500 Germans and Austro-Hungarian civilians and 1,000 officers and orderlies were held in Wakefield from 1915 to 1919?', also drew a blank; only occasionally did we come across someone who was vaguely aware of the existence of a local prisoner-of-war camp.

Just as with Ruhleben, the reason for knowing more or less about local wartime history is a matter of personal and communal interest, but also aligns with memory culture more widely. In a workshop held with pupils from a West Yorkshire secondary school, the young people were tasked to peruse primary source material relating to British airmen, infantrymen, nurses – and Ruhleben internees. They easily recognised the former, but it took more time until the students had figured out the logic of internment. When asked whether Britain in turn might have interned German or Austrian civilians in a similar fashion, the young people were adamant and united in their conviction that this could never have been the case. They were astonished to learn that, in November 1917, 29,511 'enemy aliens' were interned in Britain.[6] Among older people, internment of Germans on the Isle of Man during the Second World War was something more familiar, but the history of earlier internment and any location closer to home also came as a surprise.

While we found that internment practices during the First World War were not generally well known, they had of course caught the attention of historians, who have studied and scrutinised the large-scale operation of alien registration, detention and repatriation.[7] Manx National Heritage and a number of volunteer-led initiatives on the Isle of Man have developed important resources for research; they also present *in situ* and online displays of their sites and collections.[8] Other projects include Stobs Camp near Hawick in the Scottish Borders.[9] The Anglo-German Family History Society has published accounts of internment experiences and provides guidance for family history research and how to follow up on German ancestors and possible wartime disruptions.[10] In historical research, Paul Cohen-Portheim's memoir *Time Stood Still: My Internment in England, 1914-1918* (London 1931) makes a regular appearance in the literature on civilian internment.[11] But more often than not, Cohen-Portheim's central location – Lofthouse Park near Wakefield – is only treated as a placeholder for the bigger story that wants to be told. While it may be argued that camps resembled each other and were closed spaces, suppressing encounters with the outside world, it nevertheless surprises that the centrality of this text did not trigger location-specific curiosity.

But what about the other internees? The Ruhlebenites represented in the Liddle Collection were well-to-do businessmen, engineers, scientists, academics or young men of means who took an active part in the organisation and cultural life of the camp. They preserved the records of their community building under adverse circumstances, wrote books and diaries, kept souvenirs and gifted all these to an archive for future reference. Lofthouse Park was a 'privilege' camp; the majority of internees and later military officers had a social background similar to that of the Ruhlebenites represented in the archive. Many came from the successful bourgeoisie or the aristocracy; others were colonial administrators, international traders, professional specialists, academics, acclaimed musicians or artists. But apart from Cohen-Portheim, none of these men seemed to have felt inclined to share their experiences.

Why this was the case is open to speculation. The defeat of 1918 and subsequent changes in Germany and Austro-Hungary – which included the Kaiser's abdication, the abolition of both the monarchy and the nobility, revolutionary turmoil, civil unrest, constitutional renewal and the Versailles Treaty – may have been a disincentive to publish stories of internment and/or forced repatriation. In the longer term, and perhaps more importantly, the Second World War dominated experience, memory and critique. The Holocaust and here the concentration of civilians for the purpose of genocidal extermination has been an overwhelming challenge and shaped the understanding of 'the camp' that was the central legacy of the Second World War. This may also explain a limited interest of German scholarship in the history of internment of Germans abroad. A further point to consider is that the Holocaust and the *Gleichschaltung* (synchronisation) of all aspects of society under Hitler make family history research more charged and possibly less desirable than in Britain.

But it was not just the internees and officers detained whose presence in Wakefield had left no mark. We also realised that information was scarce about the local infrastructure as well as the logistics of goods and people that developed around the camp. Building habitable compounds, maintaining security and organising arrivals and departures could not have been achieved without sufficient staff and leadership. Dealing with the physical, psychological and medical needs of thousands of displaced men who had jobs, families and responsibilities, while at the same time adjusting to the militarisation of everyday life outside the camp, were also challenges we wanted to acknowledge.

Motivated rather than discouraged by a lack of material and scholarship on Lofthouse Park, we embarked on searches for traces, objects and knowledge in archives and libraries. We also organised two Heritage Open Days at Lofthouse Gate Working Men's Club in 2016 and 2017 and explored the area of the former camp on foot, looking for clues and inspiration. We liaised with local studies libraries and local history societies, invited experts and mixed and mingled Britons and Germans and those in between.

And indeed after a while not only archival sources, but also local knowledge and hitherto unknown objects began to emerge. Due to the nature of displacement, connections also started to appear without a link to Yorkshire. Once these findings had reached a critical mass, the decision was taken to consolidate them in a publication about Lofthouse Park, 1908-1922, encompassing its days of pleasure and amusement, its years as a site of detention, its dismantlement and the final moment of dereliction.

It was clear from the beginning that we would join forces as editors and do so in the spirit of the *IWPWT* project, combining the steadfastness of a Yorkshireman with a track record of innovative research into various aspects of the First World War with the sensibilities of a German *Anglistin* with a research interest in migration and diaspora and the representation of war. The set-up ensured not only lively debate but also checks and balances as we began to tap into our sources as well as the knowledge base and archives of our fellow authors.

Sources and Chapters

A cursory look at some of the documents held in the National Archives at Kew resulted in about thirty names being identified in connection to Lofthouse Park during the preliminary stages of research. These names included, among others, several doctors and members of the German aristocracy. Further research through online archives such as the International Committee for the Red Cross (ICRC) revealed more names, with the figure standing at around five-hundred Lofthouse Park detainees having been identified at the time of going to press.

Another positive outcome was the finding of more than 100 men of Austro-Hungarian birth. This is significant because the number of Austro-Hungarian internees at Lofthouse Park accounted for only 10-12 per cent of the total population, and it thus enabled us to look at the group in more specific terms. The case of the Austro-Hungarians is dealt with in more detail in the last section of David Stowe's opening chapter which looks at the context of Lofthouse Park in its transformation from amusement park to internment camp.

A central theme throughout Stowe's chapter is that of space and the re-ordering of space in the changes that took place at Lofthouse Park during the transition of 1914. This includes the disciplinary space of the camp and its regulation and governance, especially where seen in terms of self-governance and internal organisation, and the committees which were formed to represent individual and group interests. Changes also became manifest in the restrictions which were imposed by the authorities and the curtailment of liberties and freedom of movement. In short: same space, different uses.

Lofthouse Park comprised three compounds and was staffed by part-time voluntary soldiers of the National Reserve and then the Royal Defence Corps. The role of both is examined in the context of the Royal Defence Corps and its origins in the National Reserve. The Royal Defence Corps' at the end of the war had significantly changed. This is examined in Chapter 18, with further insight offered into the daily routine from official documents and other accounts and including an account of a former soldier who had served at Lofthouse Park. That part of the chapter title, '24 on/24 off', reflects the duties carried out before the changes took place.

The main focus of Chapter 19 by Ruth Allison is Commandant Gregory Sinclair Haines, who was in charge at Lofthouse Park between 1916 and 1918. Haines is generally associated with two incidents in which his character was questioned. The first was in 1915 and involved allegations over a failed business venture which proved to be untrue. The second related to the court-martial of an officer from Lofthouse Park in 1918 who had accused Haines of allowing special visiting rights to a female friend of Baron Leopold von Plessen in which they were left unattended. Similar allegations were made regarding visits to Counts von Metternich and Nettelbladt. What has been forgotten about Haines, however, is that he was a prison reformer who was held in high esteem by both prisoners and prison officials alike. He was also a man of considerable experience in both the management of civilian and military prisoners. His reputation is something that Allison sets out to rehabilitate in this chapter.

The use of Lofthouse Park as a military prisoner-of-war camp in 1918-19 is given due attention in Chapter 20 by Oliver Wilkinson, which also looks at a number of escape attempts in this period. This might be seen in Wilkinson's treatment of serial escaper Heinz E. Justus and the innate drive in soldiers like Justus to try and escape. One way in which Wilkinson looks at this is in terms of the psychological impact this drive had on men like Justus and the mental breakdown he suffered. Justus was later sent to a West Didsbury hospital where he was recorded as a 'mental case'. This does raise the question of the willingness on the part of the authorities to label soldiers like Justus 'mad' and 'bad'. Wilkinson also looks at the protests made by German naval officers at Lofthouse Park and claims of mistreatment in Scotland after the sinking of the German High Seas Fleet at Scapa Flow in 1919.

Albert H. Brugger was another member of the escaping club. The German officer and prisoner of war was also the author of *Meine Flucht aus dem Kriegsgefangenen-Lager Lofthouse Park near Wakefield*, published in Berlin in 1937. The story of the attempted escape by Brugger and his accomplice Leutnant von Waldenburg is read by Claudia Sternberg in Chapter 21 as a contribution to the genre of escape narratives, but also as a text that presents interesting snapshots of city life in Britain in November 1919. Most importantly, however, Brugger's text needs to be understood in the context of the time of its publication. It combines adventure with nationalist and anti-Semitic discourse, thus serving as an example of the confluence of First World War reminiscence and National Socialist rhetoric.

During most of its existence, however, Lofthouse Park provided a home of sorts to civilians and not soldiers. *Time Stood Still*, Paul Cohen-Portheim's recollections and critical assessment of his time as a civilian internee at Lofthouse Park, is essential reading for those interested in the experience. Chapter 11 is dedicated to the cosmopolitan painter and writer of German and Austrian Jewish heritage, and Claudia Sternberg provides more details about the author and his seminal text. Biographical information about Cohen-Portheim is relatively sparse, but the chapter also points to the prolific author's wider work and his popularity in the interwar years.

Paul Cohen-Portheim was one of many internees who engaged in creative activities. As in other camps of a similar nature, the men could not be forced to work and had to fill their time. Many internees had skills to share, either as professionals or amateurs. Others used their time to acquire skills and took up some of the many opportunities to learn. Chapters 16 and 17 by Claudia Sternberg provide insights into the effort and enthusiasm that was invested in musical and theatrical performances and the making of art and artisanal pieces. Chapter 12 by Emily Bagshaw introduces *Lager-Bote*, the camp magazine produced by Lofthouse Park internees. It contains articles, reviews, poetry and advertisements and allows further insights into the cultural life in the camp. Keeping occupied in these ways eased the mind of internees and helped to ward off 'barbed wire disease', as did physical activities and sport.

The collaboration with researchers in Germany also brought forth a rich source of materials from regional and state archives, to which may be added personal and family collections. The influence is strong in chapters by Franz Götz, Eberhard Haering and Henning Ibs and their respective accounts on the artist Max Schnös (Chapter 8), the engineer Richard Cornelius Bechtel (Chapter 3) and doctoral student of law, Hermann J. Held (Chapter 13), who was a prominent lecturer in the camp's 'barbed wire university'. It is noticeable too in the contributions from Corinna Meiß on Gustav Georg Wiesener (Chapter 9), and Karl-Heinz Wüstner who expands on previous research on German pork butcher migrants to look at some of those who were interned at Lofthouse Park (Chapter 10). One of the themes addressed in Wüstner's chapter is that of 'statelessness' and the problems encountered by many when repatriated.

More recently is the addition of Hilke Langhammer's chapter on the Celler Schloss, a gentlemen's camp in Celle, Germany, and a useful comparison where privilege is associated with Lofthouse Park.[12] Yet there is evidence of privation too. Richard Oswald's chapter on his great grandfather, Richard Oswald Siebenhüner, who was a hairdresser in Leeds when the war broke out, is one of dignity in the difficult circumstances he found himself when he was arrested and sent to Lofthouse Park in 1914. He was helped by his wife Ottilia. He was also supported by the Quakers (Society of Friends) who visited the camp, and who assisted the family financially when he was later transferred to the Isle of Man.

The theme of family continues in Chapter 5 in Alan Muddiman's account of John Henry Brickmann, who was also a married man. Brickmann had come to Middlesbrough from Memel in East Prussia sometime after 1891, and had worked at the same engineering firm since 1894 when he was arrested at the outbreak of war and interned as an 'enemy alien'. Brickmann died at the Leeds Infirmary in 1916. The official cause of death was given as cerebral haemorrhage, but, although not confirmed, the possibility remains that John Henry Brickmann was a victim of foul play when a car ploughed into a group of internees who were on exercise from the camp. Muddiman's story is also the story of Annie Elizabeth, John Brickmann's widow, who had to reapply for British citizenship after her husband's death because she was regarded as German since her marriage to an unnaturalised foreigner.

More insights into the bonds between interned men and their families can be gained from Chapter 14. Here an unnamed (upon request) postal historian showcases examples of his collection of Lofthouse Park correspondence which reveals not only some of the internees' family and business concerns, but also the complexity of censorship and the wartime postal system. As a counterpoint to the many stories of individuals who were forcefully moved to rather than chose to be in Yorkshire at the time, Chapter 2 by Carol Wright gives an indication of the ways and lives of families who were rooted in the places along the Leeds-Wakefield tram route in the early part of the twentieth century.

There are eight sections and twenty-five chapters in total, written by fifteen authors, with contributions from British and German academics, independent scholars and researchers, descendants and local and family historians. In addition to this there are several short sections. Some of the themes covered here include food and rations, faith and religion (Chapter 15) and extracts from reports and inspections at the camp. Thus in terms of structure the book is divided into a number of separate, yet interconnected themes which includes family histories, several additional case studies, a section on camp life and culture and the transition from civilian to military prisoner-of-war camp in 1918. The dismantling of the camp after the war is considered in Chapter 23, along with the deaths of six civilians and two German officers between 1915 and 1918. The deaths are covered by David Stowe and Claudia Sternberg in Chapter 25. Stowe also looks at the process of alien registration in the case of Leeds in Chapter 24.

In short, the research in this book represents a move in many respects from the singular experience of Paul Cohen-Portheim, as outlined in his *Time Stood Still*, to a more inclusive narrative of internment which draws on the use of personal accounts and archives, letters and photographs, postcards and drawings, and the bringing together of a range of different primary source materials, including newspapers, the camp journal, concert and theatre programmes, as well as the use of official reports and documents. The emphasis on the empirical and explanatory in the chapters also complements the visual and non-written sources where these chapters are illustrated. Taken together, what is offered is a new and encompassing account of the multiple experiences of internment and POW imprisonment in the context of Lofthouse Park and the First World War.

From the Past to the Present
Wartime camps are transitory, makeshift places which come and go with war and the logic of war. Hardly ever mapped, they are closed-off places hidden in plain sight during their existence and quickly forgotten once they are gone. By putting Lofthouse Park back on the map during the centenary years of the First World War, we wish to contribute to historical scholarship with a micro-history that is highly localised and yet also global due to individual biographies as well as the underlying conflict and the imperial powers embroiled in it. An additional aim of *In the*

Wrong Place at the Wrong Time has been to invite reflection beyond the war years and on the more abstract and transcending themes that have emerged.

While Lofthouse Park as a prisoner-of-war camp tells the straightforward story of belligerence and the necessary containment of captured 'enemies', the narrative of civilian internment in both Britain and Germany is more ambivalent and does not easily align with commemorative schemata. In British stories of the Great War, the focus is frequently on the 'contribution' that individuals or communities have made to the war effort. Contributions can take shape at the front or home front; when it comes to combat, the notion of sacrifice rather than aggression dominates. The constructive resilience of the British internees at Ruhleben Camp can be subsumed under this formula, but the rounding up neighbours, tradesmen, colleagues or business partners as well as the confiscation of possessions, the tearing apart of families and forced repatriation are uncomfortably at odds with ideas of Britishness. For Germans, who tend to take a distanced and non-identificatory approach to stories about Germany at war, facing up to one's own wartime hostilities meets less resistance. What appears to be harder to incorporate, however, is the idea that a negative experience could have been 'suffered' and not just 'inflicted'.

A further challenge is to assess internment itself. What are we to make of these men who did not – in fact, never – bore arms in the war that had changed their fate? Are they to be pitied? Or are their privations petty and negligible because they remained in safe quarters while others put their lives at risk, including their own family members? Why did some men not speak about their time of internment after the war? Why was the experience written out of some family histories? Does the internees' insistence on cultural, educational and intellectual pursuits at the height of military devastation point to war as an aberration? Or are internment camps filled with men of fighting age islands of futility that undermine male prowess and national pride? Are the wives who had been assigned their husband's nationality victims of a patriarchal order that denied them their patriotic rights? Or do they epitomise the arbitrariness that lies behind ascriptions of national qualities and dispositions? Should we identify with the interned men and their families because their mobility, mixed marriages, transnational employers as well as their interest in travel and cultural exchange resemble contemporary realities and lifestyles? Or should we disregard the case of internment altogether because numbers were small and insignificant compared with those of the mobilised masses who were in the thick of it for reasons that were equally outside of their control?

The construction of 'enemy aliens' in 1914 required the closing of borders, the reconfiguration of national identity and the renewal of demarcations between 'us' and 'them' that had previously been irrelevant, unmarked or inconsequential. Civilian internees were frequently used by either side for national propaganda and as a means to influence neutral countries. They were also brought to the table as 'bargaining chips' in wartime negotiations. The dangers of presentism and sweeping comparisons notwithstanding, it is pertinent to take the long view on British German relations and European mobility at the present time. The official commemorations of the Battle of the Somme on 1 July 2016 and the EU Referendum on 23 June 2016 lay only seven days apart. Although the centenary events and the question of the European Union ran their separate course, these parallel timings are instructive because the discourse of national identity tends to crystallise at certain critical moments.[13]

The new European other, or 'EU migrant', has not only been framed in Britain within the language of mass immigration, but also triggered the reappearance of terms like 'registration' and 'deportation' in the press.[14] When Prime Minister Theresa May singled out the 'citizen of nowhere' at the Conservative Party Conference in October 2016, she added the 'cosmopolitan (elite)' to the newly formed group of non-belongers.[15] For Anglophile Germans, Brexit came as a culture shock because it clashed with a sense of togetherness that had solidified, mainly in West Germany, through many cultural links, but also military ones. When 20,000 British troops and families left Germany in 2015 as part of a full withdrawal to be concluded in 2019, 70 years had gone by since the end of the Second World War and the Berlin Airlift of 1948/9.[16] New cultural uncertainties are felt, but not necessarily analysed historically. It is no stroke of chance, however, that the British Council, the country's most transnational institution, runs a year-long 'UK/Germany Season' in 2018, the centenary year of the First World War Armistice, to explore and celebrate cultural connections.[17]

In order to allow discussions of the past in light of the present, the publication of this book goes hand in hand with a student-curated exhibition about Lofthouse Park, also entitled *Pleasure, Privilege, Privations*, for Wakefield Library at Wakefield One (28 April – 7 July 2018). Together with linguist Jessica Bradley and visual artist Louise Atkinson, interview sessions were held with descendants and more recently arrived Germans and Austrians who live in Yorkshire today to find out more about family memory and experiences of being German in Britain. Furthermore, *In the Wrong Place at the Wrong Time* cooperated with Ruhleben and internment expert Matthew Stibbe and educators Gertie and Paul Whitfield at Whitworks and adapted learning resources about

Lofthouse Park and Ruhleben for the use in German
Saturday Schools. This network of supplementary schools
caters to German-speaking families in the UK and helps to
retain and develop German as a community language in
Britain.

By bringing together a host of authors from Britain and
Germany and allowing the two languages to speak to each
other, we have returned Lofthouse Park to the map for
those with an interest in the history of the First World War,
the benefits and vagaries of migration, and the precarious
role that the civilian occupies at times of war.

Claudia Sternberg and David Stowe

April 2018

From Pleasure to Detention:
The Making of Lofthouse Park Camp near Wakefield

David Stowe (Leeds)

Introduction

The site of the former internment camp at Lofthouse Park stands on the main Leeds to Wakefield road between Lofthouse Hill and Lofthouse Gate and is roughly equidistant between the two cities. The focus of this chapter is the site's beginnings as an amusement park and its use as a civilian internment camp after the outbreak of war in 1914. Despite the large number of internees and staff who lived and worked in the camp, they were not a single homogenous mass, but individuals whose stories highlight the differences between them and the frictions that sometimes arose.

The majority of the civilians interned at Lofthouse Park were German. However, a number of Austro-Hungarian subjects are identified in a later section of this chapter. It is through identification that we are able to see their experiences more clearly in the context of captivity and internment. The Austro-Hungarians are an oft-overlooked group as a whole in the history of internment in Britain. This is also true of the German and Turkish-born internees where they are found at Lofthouse Park, and includes the committees which were formed to look after group interests, which is also examined in this chapter.

I. Lofthouse Amusement Park

Lofthouse Park Internment Camp had its origins in an amusement park. The park originally covered a part of the

Charlesworth Estate. It was bought from Captain Herbert
Charles Metcalfe, the Chief Constable of the West Riding,
by the Yorkshire (West Riding) Electric Tramways
Company Ltd in June 1906. The intention was to turn part
of the extensive grounds into a permanent pleasure park
for the area. It was also about investment. A tram park was
built to serve the new park when it opened in June 1908,
with reduced admission to the park redeemed against the
price of a return ticket from Leeds or Wakefield. The cost
of the total outlay was estimated to have been in the region
of £32,000.[1]

Billed as 'Fairyland' and the 'Amusement Park, Aerodrome and Fun City of Yorkshire' in a later incarnation, its
promoters began advertising for showmen in April 1908.
The main architectural focal point was the Pavilion with its
60-foot gilded twin towers and the adjoining Winter
Gardens. The Pavilion housed a Dance Hall and a Theatre
which could accommodate up to 1,500 people.[2] The dance
floor was made of 4-inch maple boards.[3] There was also a
fully licensed bar and a varied programme for the visitors
with sketches and performances given twice a day in the
tents. The large huts at the side of the Pavilion were used
for sideshows. Other attractions included a skating rink, a
bowling green, a maze and a romantic dell at the far side
of the park. There was also a bandstand with space for
open-air concerts. The *Yorkshire Evening Post* offered the
following description of Lofthouse Park in anticipation of
its opening on 3 June 1908:

> In the laying out of the grounds at Lofthouse Park the
> promoters of the scheme appear to have followed the
> plan adopted in the case of similar ventures in various
> parts of the country. A large concert hall or pavilion [...]
> occupies a central position, while all around are scattered
> the paraphernalia of a fair. There are all manner of
> sideshows, including variety and pierrot entertainments,
> bioscope pictures, a village of natives from the Philippine

Islands, everything in fact, to keep the fun rolling
continuously through the day.[4]

Set within sixty acres, the entrance to the amusement park
was marked by a decorative arch which was lit up at night
by coloured electric light bulbs. Just inside the entrance
was a stone circular lodge with a shale covered drive and
ornamental flower beds leading to the main attractions. To
the left of the entrance was a private drive leading to the
large house, which was later used by the commandants in
charge of the internment camp.

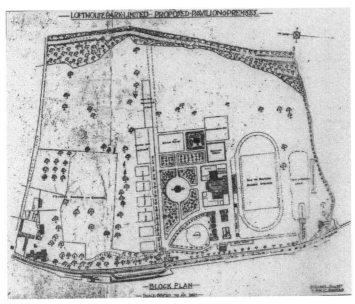

Fig. 1.1: Block Plan: Lofthouse Park Limited, Proposed Pavilion
& Premises, c. 1906 (with kind permission West Yorkshire
Archive Service Wakefield, Ref. A14).

The park was enclosed by a large stone wall some six or
seven feet high and two feet thick on the side of the tram
route and the main Leeds to Wakefield road, while its
boundaries to the south were largely defined by the stream
or brook running alongside Canal Lane at Lofthouse Gate.

The power for the amusement park was supplied by the park's own electric sub-station facing the entrance on the Leeds Road.[5] Interestingly, an aerial railway is shown in the proposed layout from 1906 (Fig. 1.1), with plans to build an athletics ground behind the Pavilion, and a number of tennis courts in the northern part of the amusement park.[6]

The aerial railway is mentioned in Ronald Rhodes's *Going Back a Bit* and his recollections of Lofthouse Park as a young man before and during the war:

> There were [...] two 'Aerial Flights', each consisting of two thick steel cables, from which the 'riders' were launched. On one of these 'Flights', the rider hung, suspended by his hands, from a 'T' shaped piece of metal with a pulley wheel attached, which, running along the cable by force of gravity, carried the 'rider' the best part of a hundred yards to the opposite end platform. This was 'two way traffic', as the 'Twin cable' carried another passenger the opposite way.[7]

Some of the people connected with the theme park included Signor G. De La Camera, who had previously been at Brighton and was the conductor of the Corporation Band.[8] He was also musical director for a number of years at Lofthouse Park. Stanley Blight was the Director of the Lofthouse Park Choral Union, which held its rehearsals and concerts in the Pavilion, and included performances based on works such as Samuel Coleridge-Taylor's 'The Death of Minnehaha', William Cowper's 'John Gilpin' and some of the choral works of Charles Harford Lloyd.[9] Music played a big part in the events at Lofthouse Park, with guest bands such as the regimental band of the East Yorkshire Regiment being asked to perform in the purpose-built bandstand in the centre of the Park.[10]

Lofthouse Park also had its own cinema and, as previously mentioned, a fully-licensed bar. In an interesting case in August 1910 the manager of the bar was summoned to appear before the courts at Wakefield. He had been charged under the Children's Act (1908) for allowing children under fourteen years of age to be on licensed premises during the sale of intoxicating liquor. As reported in the *Yorkshire Evening Post*, the premises had been visited by the police during the afternoon and early evening of 1 August after several complaints of children being on site. However, the case was dismissed when it was contended that the premises did not come under the Children's Act, and that the bar was therefore exempted in much the same way as refreshment rooms at railway stations.[11] The catering and buffet at Lofthouse Park was managed by Spiers and Pond, of London.[12]

Fig. 1.2: Lofthouse Park Bandstand (Outwood Community Video, Ref. L59).

Bank Holidays proved very popular at Lofthouse Park, with an estimated 15,000 people visiting during the holiday weekend in August 1910. One of the main attractions was a flying exhibition and balloon ascent, with aviator George Barnes and 'Captain Fleet' making a parachute descent from the balloon. Admission was sixpence for adults and threepence for children.[13] The thrill of flight was a particular crowd pleaser, as evidenced in an exhibition given by Harold Robinson in May 1913, which was also well attended. The exhibition coincided with the new Yorkshire Aerodrome, which formed part of the Blackburn Aeroplane Company, founded by Harold and Robert Blackburn. The aircraft hangar for the Yorkshire Aerodrome was erected in the south portion of Lofthouse Park. The exhibition was reported in *Flight* as follows:

> On Whit Monday and Tuesday, Mr Harold Blackburn gave exhibition flights before a large crowd of Leeds and Wakefield people. He flew a new 50 h.p. (horse-power) Gnome Blackburn which was in the air for the first time on Monday. Rising rapidly to height of 1,000 feet, he circled round the Aerodrome and the surrounding country. There was a strong gusty wind blowing at the time and occasionally when flying against the wind, his machine appeared to be almost at a standstill. Two fairly long flights were made on the Tuesday, flying on one occasion across country in the direction of Wakefield. On Friday he made a tour right round the outskirts of Wakefield. Keeping all the time at about 2,000 ft, so that from any quarter of town a clear view of the machine was obtained. A perfect *vol plane* into the Aerodrome terminated the flight.[14]

Despite the promotion of big attractions, including boxing tournaments, military bands and the twice-weekly firework display organised by 'James Pain and Sons, Pyrotechnist to the King and Queen', Lofthouse Park was struggling by 1914. There had been some attempt to re-invent the amusement park as 'The Fun City of Yorkshire', as found in advertisements published in *The Era* and the *Leeds Mercury*, in which attractions like the 'Big Zoo and Animal Congress' and a 'Street of Cairo in Oriental Splendour' were promoted as part of the experience of visiting the Park.[15] The Park had also undergone a change in management in this period, and on 12 June 1914 an appeal was made on behalf of the staff to help some of their colleagues who were in financial difficulties and found themselves stranded. The appeal was printed on a handbill and circulated in the neighbourhood. It read:

> An Appeal. Lofthouse Park, today at 3 p.m. and to-night at 7 p.m. For the benefit of the staff, the above Park will be open to-day. Admission: Afternoon 3d., evening 6d. Grand Serpentine and coffee dance. Illuminated dances. 'Billy, the horse with the human brain,' from the London Coloseum, will appear during the interval. The whole of the proceeds, without any deduction whatever, will be divided for the relief of the band and staff, many of whom are stranded and unable to reach their homes.[16]

Lofthouse Park was sold by public auction at Wakefield on the evening of 19 June 1914. The bidding started at £3,000 and stopped at £5,500. The sale included the mansion, its grounds, the extensive shrubberies, the ornamental and kitchen gardens, and the adjoining grounds of the Park.[17] Its life as an amusement park had come to an end. Lofthouse Park was requisitioned shortly after the outbreak of war as a compound for German prisoners.[18]

II. Lofthouse Park Camp

Work began in getting the former amusement park ready in September 1914 when 200 Royal Engineers of the 2nd (West Riding) Field Company started work erecting barbed-wire fences, electric standards and spotlights. The pavilion, skating rink and the buildings which had been previously used for sideshows were adapted for use as dormitories and the grounds were extensively altered. The shrubs and trees in the centre of the park were cut down. The military authorities had also prepared an extended compound where the civilians could exercise, and the finishing touches were being put to a canteen which was used as a general store where the civilians could buy provisions. Lofthouse Park received its first fifty internees on 22 October 1914.[19] The transformation from amusement park to internment camp had taken six weeks.

Among the first of the civilian internees to arrive were a number from London, Cambridge, Hull and Nottingham. York Castle also features amongst some of the later arrivals, where many of the civilians from the North and North East of England had been held since being arrested. The civilians were taken first to Wakefield Westgate Station, before being lined up in double file and marched to special tramcars for conveyance to Lofthouse Park. The arrival of the first internees aroused much interest in the local press, which was not without dramatic effect where the *Yorkshire Evening Post* reported that the tramcars were 'guarded fore and aft by soldiers with fixed bayonets.'[20] Lieutenant-Colonel Gordon-Cumming was Commandant at Lofthouse Park, and Major Fullerton was in charge of the military guard in October 1914.

Although it was initially expected that the camp would house around one thousand internees, this number grew to almost 1,500 by the end of 1915 and involved the building of three enclosures or compounds.[21] Each of the three enclosures held about five hundred men, and each enclosure was separated by gates and a barbed wire fence, with the internees needing permission and a pass to move between the compounds. The first compound to be erected was South Camp, which was built around the Pavilion. A part of the Pavilion was converted into living quarters, and wooden huts were added as more civilians were brought to Lofthouse Park. A hospital block was also built at the end of the compound. This was followed by the building of North Camp, which can be identified by its large wooden huts and corrugated iron buildings. The last of the three enclosures was West Camp, which was also the smallest. West Camp was 'home' to Paul Cohen-Portheim from August 1915 until he was repatriated to

Holland in February 1918.[22] Cohen-Portheim was the author of the internment memoir *Time Stood Still*, which was published in 1931, and recounted his experiences at Knockaloe Camp and Lofthouse Park during the war.

Fig. 1.3: Lofthouse Park: A View of the Grounds (*German Prisoners in Great Britain*, Bolton and London: Tillotson, [n.y.], p. 47)

Lofthouse Park was generally regarded as a 'privilege camp.' It was a fee-paying camp where those who could afford to pay the 10 shillings (50p) a week to stay there were offered better accommodation and facilities.[23] The camp later comprised a bank, theatre, school, libraries, a barber shop and tailors. There was also a YMCA hut, a football pitch, four tennis courts, athletics track, a bowling green, a well-equipped gymnasium and a Turkish sauna.[24] In some cases, several men were given permission to purchase and erect their own huts, although this was stopped in 1915 when the War Office prohibited more of the huts to be put up. Each hut cost between £20 and £30.[25] These were the chalet-style huts built in the South Camp, which predate the building of West Camp by several months. There were probably no more than twenty of the chalets in total at Lofthouse Park Camp.

By far the most common type of huts were the medium-size wooden living huts and the larger corrugated-iron type with more than seventy five of them used for accommodation at Lofthouse Park.[26] Add to this the various buildings such as the camp hospital, the recreation hut, the post office, the canteen, the carpenter's and shoemakers' huts, the kitchens (of which there were three with thirty-four cooks and assistants for each of the compounds in 1916), a laundry, a tailors' workshop, two wash-houses, a brick-built boiler house, a guard house, the accommodation for the guards and the messing arrangements for the non-commissioned officers, and the number of buildings in use at Lofthouse Park comes close to almost one hundred.[27] The hospital block was one of the larger buildings at Lofthouse Park Camp. Seventy feet in length, it could accommodate up to fifty patients and was staffed by one British doctor, one German doctor, four RAMC orderlies and six orderlies drawn from the civilian internees in 1915. An isolation ward was later added.[28]

It is interesting to note that the building of West Camp was originally intended for the use of German military personnel.[29] This would account for the building of a third and separate compound in 1915. Also of interest is the recommendation that a pail system be used instead of water closets in the building of the additional compound.[30] Its repurposing for the use of civilian internees ties in with the arrival of civilians from other camps and the recall and re-internment of civilians who had been previously released on parole. This includes the re-arrest of Count Paul Wolff Metternich in July 1915 and his subsequent internment in Lofthouse. Metternich had been arrested on honeymoon shortly after the outbreak of war and interned at Newbury, but was released when the camp closed in December 1914.[31]

What is telling about the hasty construction of West Camp is the number of men who could not afford to pay for extras when they were transferred from Dorchester in 1915. Of the 221 men who were housed in the west compound, only thirty-five were able to pay for extra food to supplement the basic rations given to the internees. It was a similar situation in the South Camp where between eighty or ninety men were forced to sleep in the former skating rink because they were unable to afford better accommodation.[32] Added together, the numbers represent approximately a quarter of the population who were unable to pay for extra food or better housing arrangements. The skating rink and former dance hall doubled-up as a dining hall during the day.

Fig. 1.4: Lofthouse Park: The Main Street (*German Prisoners in Great Britain,* Bolton and London: Tillotson, [n.y.], p. 48).

In terms of its size and composition, the population at Lofthouse Park had increased more than three-fold since the beginning of 1915, with the total number of internees standing at 1,449 at the end of the year.[33] The increase in numbers reflects the wider trend in general where mass internment is considered from the start of the war. This is especially so after the sinking of the *Lusitania* in May 1915. As Panikos Panayi shows in *Prisoners of Britain,* the number of civilians interned in Britain had almost doubled between September 1914 and 1 May 1915, with an increase from

10,500 to 20,000 civilians being interned in the first nine months of the war.[34] This figure had reached 32,440 by November 1915.[35]

The prescribed number of internees at Lofthouse Park would remain fairly static up until 1917 and 1918, when there was a sharp decrease in numbers. This was due in part to the transfer or repatriation of around four hundred civilian internees in this period. The official figures stood at just over a thousand in May 1918.[36] However, it is important to remember that the traffic between Lofthouse Park and other internment camps was also two-way, with records showing that at least nine 'stewards' were transferred from Douglas Camp to Lofthouse Park on 4 December 1916, and a number of other men transferred from Douglas to Lofthouse *en route* to Holland in January 1918. Amongst those transferred from Lofthouse Park to Knockaloe Camp were Johann Buck, Magnus Burghard, Paul Fink and Otto Tribensee, with other internees being received at Douglas and Knockaloe before being transferred to mainland camps in London, Ripon, and Spalding towards the end of the war.[37]

The same records also show that Theo Franke, Nicol Gollwitzer, Otto Hochweber and Arnold Katzenstein were allowed to pay for their own transfer from Douglas to Lofthouse Camp in 1915. Other persons of particular interest here are Professor G.A. Bredow, who was a sculptor, and assisted in the plays which were produced at Douglas, and Frederick Dunbar. Dunbar was transferred from Lofthouse Park to Douglas Camp because he was believed to have been involved in a plot to escape from Lofthouse Park Camp. The nine stewards transferred from Douglas to Lofthouse Park in December 1916 were Wilhelm Dose, Karl Gorden, Hans Hozlowski, Matthias Klang, Willy Lieker, Max Pfluke, Karl Schaas, Hugo Wanner and Robert Weiss.[38]

As can be seen, there existed a complex system at play in the management and movement of people between the camps. On the whole, however, the prescribed number of internees had remained much the same at around the 1,400 to 1,500 mark and had done so since the end of 1915 up until early 1918. These figures would include the 1,032 Germans and '113 Austrians and 4 Turks' mentioned in a report carried out by the United States Embassy on behalf of the German Government in January 1916.[39]

One of the Turkish internees was Sabri Mahir, who was a champion middle-weight boxer. Mahir had fought Lucien Humbert at Carlton Hill Barracks in Leeds in May 1914.[40] It seems likely that he was arrested at around the same time as two other sportsmen, Otto Froitzheim and Oscar Kreuzer, who had recently played in the Davis Cup in the United States.[41] The two tennis players were returning to Europe from New York when their ship was intercepted by the Royal Navy and the men arrested and interned at Gibraltar.[42] Count Beissel, Ernst Glahn and Max Klein are among some of the other civilians who had been interned at Gibraltar's Windmill Hill Camp and transferred to Lofthouse Park in April 1915. Glahn and Klein had been arrested on the *SS Emir*.[43] A number of military and civilian doctors feature amongst those captured too. Froitzheim, Kreuzer, Beissel, Glahn and Klein, were repatriated in February 1918.[44]

Lofthouse Park also saw the arrival of a number of men from the German colonies at this time. Many of the civilians had been arrested in Nigeria, Togoland, the Cameroons and the Gold Coast.[45] Concerns that the change in climate might be injurious to the health of the men can be found in a petition retired Major Kremnitz sent to the US Ambassador (Walter Page) in September 1915, in which he suggested that the men might be transferred to a warmer place such as Guernsey where the climatic conditions would be more favourable.[46] Kremnitz had been released from Lofthouse Park earlier in the year due to his age and was writing from Berlin. In a separate petition, Max Campe described the accommodation at Lofthouse Park as 'entirely inadequate' on his release in 1915.[47] Campe had been released on health grounds. He went on to say:

> The huts are made of light wood, with no protection against the weather; colds (catarrh lungs, fever) were of everyday occurrences; there were days on which 20 to 25 men were ill. He himself was released on account of lung trouble contracted in captivity. Even during the summer the prisoners from Africa had suffered from cold there; and the pneumonia and death of Volley were to be attributed to the same cause.[48]

The response to Campe's grievance is of particular interest, with the reply that the huts in Wakefield Camp were well heated – in many cases overheated – and that the general health of 'prisoners had improved since their admission.' It was also said that Max Campe had suffered from a communicable disease, not lung trouble.[49]

What is perhaps most revealing about the examples given above, is not so much the nature of the grievance, but the number of petitions which the US Embassy had to deal with on a regular basis. In dealing with similar correspondence, Walter Page had received almost two hundred petitions from internees who had been taken prisoner in West Africa and transferred to Lofthouse Park.[50]

Of immediate importance though is Max Campe's reference to 'Volley'. This is Otto Volley, one of eight civilians who died at Lofthouse Park between 1915 and 1918. His death, and that of Karl Bauck, John Henry Brickmann, Johannes Deistel, Walter Drautz, Herman Krauss, Karl Uberholz and Paul Walbert, is dealt with more fully in a later chapter of the book, as are the camp life and daily routines at Lofthouse Park, which form the basis of the next section.

III. Camp Life and Routine

The daily routine began with the twice-daily roll call, as each hut was assembled and counted separately. This was followed by breakfast at 8.00 am, lunch at 1.00 pm and evening meal at around 6.00 pm. The lights were put out at 10.30 pm. More specifically, the day started at 6.00 am for those who worked in the camp as cooks and stewards.[51]

For Paul Cohen-Portheim, the twice-daily roll call was 'grotesque', as was censorship, the restrictions imposed on the movement between compounds and being treated like children and not grown men when the lights were turned out after 10.00 pm.[52] Cohen-Portheim's cynical view of the system is evident throughout *Time Stood Still*, and probably not without reason; where the 'absurd' is stated, it does have to be said.[53] Even working on the most basic estimate, the twice-daily head count in the west compound amounts to more than two thousand times for each individual during the 1,000 and more days some of the men spent at Lofthouse Park between March 1915 and 1918.

The head count was only part of the routine, and there existed at Lofthouse Park a system in which the camp was both organised and (self-)regulated from above and within. In terms of internal organisation, each camp elected a chief captain and an assistant chief captain, and each hut elected its own captain and adjutant, with each hut thus being represented and able to vote in the captains' meetings. The chief captains were responsible for the camp business and represented the internees in bringing complaints and requests before the Commandant and liaising with officials, such as the camp inspectors. Karl Schmidt was the Chief Captain of South Camp in December 1915, and Wilhelm Mitan acted as Assistant Chief Captain on behalf of this compound.[54]

There were six commandants at Lofthouse Park. These were: Lieutenant-Colonel Ludovic Seymour Gordon-Cumming (1914-15), Major Ernest Thomas Lloyd (1915), Lieutenant-Colonel George Cattell (1915-16), Lieutenant-Colonel G.S. Haines (1916-18), Archibald Henry Tylden Rouse (1918-19) and Lieutenant-Colonel Robert William Hawthorn Ronaldson (1919-20). Gregory Haines had been in charge at Newbury, Jersey and Stratford before coming to Lofthouse Park in 1916. George Cattell had been Commandant at Dyffryn Aled in Wales and was also Commandant at Rouen POW Camp in France. He later joined the YMCA and served as a volunteer on the Western Front. Lieutenant-Colonel Ronaldson had previously served with the Highland Light Infantry, suffering gunshot wounds to the left knee when his battalion was in action at Richebourg St. Vaast in January 1915. Ronaldson was also Commandant at Skipton Camp for a short time.[55]

In terms of governance, the running of the camp was not without controversy, especially where the question of camp discipline was raised in the House of Commons in July 1915, and whether the internees were allowed to go to Leeds without an escort.[56] There may have been some substance to this, although the escape of Alfred Klapproth and Frederick Wiener in May the same year had forced a tightening up of security in general, with the internees only allowed to leave the camp under strict supervision since that time.[57] Klapproth and Wiener's escape is told in more detail in Chapter 7 of this book, including what happened to Wiener after he had successfully made his way back to Austria and rejoined his unit as a reserve officer. There were several other attempts to escape, mainly in the post-war period when Lofthouse Park served as a camp for military prisoners.

The expansion of the camp in 1915 had also seen more rigid measures imposed with the construction of a third compound and additional sentries placed on the gates connecting the three compounds. However, it was not uncommon to see groups of internees going on walks with their guard escorts in the early period of the camp, although the mood of the public did change somewhat after the events on the Somme in 1916 and the British casualties started mounting. The initial response, however, was one of amusement and opportunity for some of the younger people in the locality; civilian internees would scatter coins for the children to pick up or earn money by running errands.[58]

As mentioned in the previous section, Lofthouse Park had its own bank where internees were allowed to withdraw up to £3 per week.[59] This could be spent on buying additional food such as extra meat, fish, vegetables and fruit to supplement the camp diet in some cases. Some of the wealthier civilians were able to order luxury items in Leeds and Wakefield, and although of more modest means, Paul Cohen-Portheim was able to buy a camp bed, a tin jug and basin as well as some material for curtains from a Leeds firm which visited the camp whenever a new batch of civilian internees arrived.[60] Oscar Froitzheim, the champion tennis player, wrote to a friend in the United States in December 1915, that Lofthouse Park was '[N]othing rosy [...] although we can buy almost everything we can wish for except alcoholic beverages.' He added: 'Money has risen to almost ten-fold its worth.'[61]

The use of alcohol clearly did play a part in the regular routine and culture of camp life. In a claim to recover the return of 210 dozen empty wine and spirit bottles in May 1916, Leeds County Court heard that Hebblethwaite and Perham supplied Lofthouse Park Camp with between fifty to eighty dozen bottles of wine and spirits each week. The return claimed on the bottles was valued at one penny per bottle.[62] This works out at just over £10 for the 2,520 empty bottles which had not been returned, or roughly the equivalent of three weeks' supply of wine and spirits. Hebblethwaite and Perham, who were cigar and wine merchants based in Albion Street, Leeds, also supplied claret, port, hock, whisky and brandy to the camp. Although 210 dozen empty bottles may sound excessive, the contract would have been approved by the authorities at Lofthouse Park Camp.

Fig. 1.5: Lofthouse Park: The Recreation Room (*German Prisoners in Great Britain*, Bolton and London: Tillotson, [n.y.], p. 51).

There were two canteens at Lofthouse Park, including a bar in the South Camp. The profits of the bar and canteen were handed over to the Camp Committee to pay the cooks and hospital orderlies, with cash payments being made to the camp gardener, storeman and postman in 1918. Some of the profits were used for hiring instruments for the camp orchestra, with payments being made to both Hopkinsons and Balmforth's in Leeds for the hire of musical instruments, and also the printing of programmes and stationary. Monies were also paid to Mr Andrassy for the hire of chairs in the Visitors' Room in the Winter Gardens and the hut used in the West Camp (see also the table at the end of this chapter).[63]

Fig. 1.6: Lofthouse Park: The Canteen (*German Prisoners in Great Britain*, Bolton and London: Tillotson, [n.y.], p. 50).

The inherent wealth of Lofthouse Park presented opportunities where local business and individual enterprise was concerned, and there grew something of a local economy around the camp almost from the beginning. Some of the local businesses in and around Lofthouse at this time included Joseph Gill, who had a chain of shops and a bakery, and John Sharphouse, who was a grocer.[64] The camp was also supplied by Thomas Collinson and Sons, who advertised both locally and in the camp journal *Lager-Bote* as high class caterers.[65] J. Norman Brook Greenwood was employed by the firm as a Military Canteen Assistant at Lofthouse Park before he enlisted in the King's Own Yorkshire Light Infantry in December 1915. He had enlisted at the nearby Stanley Council School. His father Herbert Greenwood was also employed by Collinson Caterers at Silkstone Military Camp, Barnsley.[66]

The potential for corruption was present too. Two members of the National Reserve were charged with stealing a quantity of sugar, tea, pepper, gravy salts and meat, and a contractor was charged with receiving stolen goods in 1915. The theft came to light because a guard had seen the two soldiers, one of them a butcher and the other a cook, place a brown paper parcel in the refuse cart and cover it with cabbage leaves when the contractor had arrived on his daily rounds to collect the refuse and pig swill. The contractor was stopped and had his cart searched by Captain Thomas P. Tew, and the two soldiers and refuse man were subsequently arrested and charged. The total value of the goods was a little over eight shillings (40p). The three men received a one-month prison sentence when they appeared before the Wakefield City Court in June 1915. The contractor was later released on appeal.[67]

In many respects the camp seemed to have it all. Yet in spite of what might be seen as comforts, and complaints from the local government board at Rothwell that some of the internees were 'eating their heads off' and should be put to work,[68] it does need to be remembered that the men were held behind a sixteen-feet deep fence of barbed wire and in some cases suffered the privations that go with confinement. This included an increased tendency to mental health problems or 'barbed-wire disease,' as it was then becoming recognized.[69]

Although there are only a few known cases of mental health problems at Lofthouse Park, records do show that some men were referred to hospital for observation and treatment. Leonard Holman, for example, was transferred to the West Riding Lunatic Asylum in February 1915 and spent three years there before being repatriated in May 1918, while George Vogelmann was treated at the County Asylum at Bracebridge and Colney Hatch in Middlesex. Other cases include Leopold Bissinger, who was admitted to the West Riding Lunatic Asylum for observation in August 1918, and Hans Brunner who was diagnosed with 'Neurasthenia' in December 1917. Arthur Thielen was described as suffering from 'Neurasthenia' and 'Hysteria' when he was admitted to hospital at the same time.[70] Sadly, there were also two suicides at Lofthouse Park Camp. To what extent the deaths of Herman Krauss in April 1915 and Walter Drautz in July 1918 may be fully attributed to camp life is difficult to say with any real degree of certainty, but the length of confinement, the separation from loved ones, the inability to fulfil professional obligations, the loss of active income, the ongoing war and the uncertainty about when or if one might be repatriated would not have helped where the impact of internment was felt by some.[71] This much is recognised in one of the last inspections to be carried out at Lofthouse Park before the civilian internees were mostly transferred to the Isle of Man. The following extract is taken from Lieutenant-Colonel Lunbled's report on behalf of the Swedish Legation and the Austro-Hungarian internees in September 1918.

> I noticed during my visit that the interest in entertainments and sports was considerably decreasing, e.g. the tennis playing grounds had not been used for the past three months, whereas formerly they had been in great request. I found the men all more or less nervously excited, neurasthenic, exaggerating everything, considering slight worries as deep distress, and small inconveniences as great suffering.[72]

Lundbled's recommendation in this case was the suggestion that every prisoner should be forced to undergo hard, physical work for their own sake and that of their health. It would also serve as a distraction. The number of Austro-Hungarian civilian internees held at Lofthouse Park in September 1918 was 91.[73]

IV. Austrian and Hungarian Internees

Austro-Hungarians accounted for about one-tenth of the civilian population at Lofthouse Park Camp. It is possible to identify many of the internees of Austro-Hungarian birth through the records of the International Committee for the Red Cross (ICRC) or, where named, in some of the inspections carried out by the Swedish Legation acting on their behalf. The names of the following men were taken from a petition signed by fifteen Hungarian civilian internees in November 1915:

Alex Pollacsek. No. 1991. Hut 4. Elemer Pollacsek. No. 1991. Hut 4. Aurel Lazar. No. 2087. Hut 10. Andor Kemeny. No. 2059. Hut. 4. Erno Brummer. No. 2089. Hut 2. Eugene Neiger. No. 2077. Hut 6. Stephen Szekeres. No. 2088. Dore Guttman. No. 2082. Hut 14. Max Gelberg. No. 1897. Hut 17. Vincent Bohar. No. 1874. Hut 2. George Fuhrman No. 1102, Eugene Szekely No. 1341, Marcel W. Fodor No. 384, Stephen Muller No. 596, and Stephen Revesz No. 715, Hut 2 also.[74]

Similarly, the ICRC records for Lofthouse Park show that a large percentage of the Austro-Hungarians were born in Galicia and lived in the Cheetham Hill and Red Bank area of Manchester, with Verdon Street featuring prominently amongst the names given in the records.[75] Of the 111 civilians listed, more than eighty per cent had been born in Galicia, with a number of family connections being made. These include Barnet and Rubin Allweiss, Hyman and Soloman Klinghoffer, Stefan and Wasyl Solar as well as Israel and Mendel Teitelbaum, whose place of birth is given as Krakow, Boryslaw, Chelczyca and Baranow.[76] It is worth noting that there had been a large Jewish presence in the Cheetham Hill and Red Bank area of Manchester since the mid- to late-nineteenth century. The areas of Moss Side and Whalley Range feature in the records too.[77]

Lofthouse Park was also home to a number of (reserve) officers, amongst them Anton Gerl and Anton Woiset-schlager, who had claimed commissioned rank and officer status on their capture.[78] Gerl and Woisetschlager had seen active service on the Russian Front, where they had been captured and sent to a prisoner of war camp in Siberia from which they escaped. Gerl was later interned at Hong Kong by the British, before being transferred to Liverpool Camp in New South Wales, Australia.[79] Anton Woisetschlager was captured on the Danish merchantman *Virginia* in January 1916. He too was interned in Australia, and it is likely that both men arrived at Lofthouse Park via a similar route, with a short period of internment at Alexandra Palace before their transfer to Lofthouse Park.[80] Confirmation of their claims to officer status was sought by the British in 1917, with the reply from the Swedish Legation in Stockholm that Gerl and Woisetschlager were *Offiziers-Aspiranten* who held the rank of Ensign, and were thus entitled to be treated as subaltern officers. The Officer-Aspirant, as defined in the reply to the British authorities, had passed the necessary educational qualifications and was entitled to be promoted to the rank of an officer of the reserve. The Officer-Aspirant had also served as *Einjährig-Freiwilliger* (one-year volunteer) and was able to carry out the duties of a subaltern. The rank was about status and social standing in many respects too. This included the allowance of four shillings a day to be paid as a prisoner of war, or the equivalent of 28 shillings per week (£1.40).[81]

Although their status was confirmed by the Austro-Hungarian Ministry of War, the request that both men be treated as commissioned officers was rejected by the British on the grounds that the prisoners were not taken in active operations and therefore not entitled to the same pay or treatment as an officer. There appeared to be some pressure from the German Government too where the definition of officer status was concerned in the case of *Offiziers-Aspiranten*.

It was also said in the reply from the British that

> [i]ntimation has been received from the German
> Government that they so not regard such men as officers
> or entitled to officers treatment, and His Majesty's
> Government do not feel able to differentiate between
> prisoners of the same rank in the German and Austro-
> Hungarian Forces.[82]

The rank of Anton Gerl is given as *Fähnrich* in other correspondence, including a two-page petition Gerl sent to the British authorities in November 1917, outlining the differences in the use of the terms 'Ensign' and 'Fähnrich' and claiming that the Russians acknowledged the rank of the 'Fähnriche' and even the lower rank of 'Kadetten'.[83] Cadets Max Krausz and Paul Reiser are also recorded among the Austro-Hungarian officers captured as non-combatants who were held at Lofthouse Park Camp.[84] Despite their previous service on the Russian Front, it was thus as non-combatants that Gerl and Woisetschlager were defined.

Fig. 1.7: Lofthouse Park: The General Sleeping Quarters (*German Prisoners in Great Britain*, Bolton and London: Tillotson, [n.y.], p. 51).

The Austro-Hungarian internees were represented by an Austrian and Hungarian Prisoners' Committee at Lofthouse Park, whose members acted as official representatives of the Austro-Hungarians and their interests. In many respects this worked in much the same way as the rest of the camp where the Austrians and Hungarians belonged to and supported some of the same organisations as the German internees, although separate committees did exist for finance, the kitchens, canteen, school and other internal camp matters.[85] It is also likely that additional sub-committees were formed. The number of Jewish internees at Lofthouse Park would suggest, for example, that separate provisions were made for dietary laws where these were requested.

The 'Privilege Camp' at Douglas on the Isle of Man provides a useful comparison here where separate provisions were made and a kosher kitchen formed one of three main kitchens at this camp. The kosher kitchen at Douglas comprised a manager in charge of three cooks, two attendants, two butchers and two supervisors or *shomrim*. A special meat storeroom was also provided. The *shomrim* ensured that the food and meat was prepared according to Jewish dietary laws. The total number of Jewish civilians interned in Camp I (Privilege) and Camp II (Ordinary) at Douglas stood at just over 600 in May 1917, of which 440 had requested special dietary needs in accordance with Jewish dietary laws. The population at Douglas Camp stood at approximately 2,500 in 1917.[86]

It is notable that the internal organisation at Lofthouse Park in the South and West camps differed from that of the North Camp, with a kind of institution set up in the latter called the LV or *Lager-Vertretung* and only four members holding the power.[87] There is some evidence to suggest that much of the North Camp was organised along pre-war German class lines, with not a little friction between the three compounds. Paul Cohen-Portheim's

observations of camp life are instructive here. A brief
summary might read as thus:
North Camp was superior and inclined to snobbish-
ness. It was Prussian and national. Some of the men were
titled and belonged to the German nobility. One of the
huts was called die *Grafenhütte* (Counts' Hut). It was the
'Mayfair' of Lofthouse Park. South Camp was the least
conventional. Some huts were smaller, some huts were
larger. The dominant theme of the camp was 'colonial' and
many of the men were from the German colonies in
Africa. It was less neat and tidy in 'Bohemia'. West Camp
was essentially middle-class. Most of the men were of
moderate means and a mix of middle-aged businessmen
and younger (bank) clerks, who seemed to dominate. 'The
Bankbeamtenhütte [Bank Clerks' Hut] was to the West Camp
what the *Grafenhütte* was to the North'.[88]

In terms of internal representation, Otto Kohn and
Karl Rücker were very much at the forefront of activity
where Austro-Hungarian interests were concerned. This
can be seen where concerns were raised about repatriation,
the exchange of prisoners and the scale of rations,
particularly where the cooking of horseflesh was raised in
1918. The question of transfer or repatriation to a neutral
country was brought up by Kohn and Rücker in April and
May 1918 in response to press reports that the British
Government had entered into negotiations with Germany
regarding the exchange of prisoners with no mention of
the Austrians and Hungarians.[89] Understandably, Kohn
and Rücker's concerns focused on the pace of repatriation
and the 'prospect of remaining the only civilian prisoners
in Great Britain'.[90] There was also talk of 'disappointment'
and 'anxiety', as found in the following extract sent to the
British Foreign Office on 31 May 1918:

> As matters stand at present we must assume that our
> German fellow-prisoners, and eventually Turks and
> Bulgarians, will be sent home, while Austrians and

Hungarians are confronted with the prospect of remaining the only civilian prisoners in Great Britain. There can be no doubt that our sufferings have been especially aggravated by the bitterness due to the differential treatment experienced by our countrymen in this country and of British subjects in Austria-Hungary. It would mean carrying this anomaly, and with it our miseries, to the extreme limit, should the proposed agreement not be extended to us. Already now the mental condition of many is causing anxiety, and the disappointment of our hopes in this case would be conducive to tragic consequences [...].[91]

The scale of rations referred to was revised in this period to bring it into line with the compulsory ration scheme which had been brought into place in areas like London and the Home Counties, and then nationwide. The amended scale can be found in the example given under Army Council Instruction No. 623, which was issued on 2 June 1918.[92] The decision to issue horseflesh three times a week instead of the same quantity of beef brought about further complaints, with Count Herman Wrangel of the Swedish Legation being asked by the British to investigate and report his findings, which he did at the end of June 1918. The following comments relate to Lofthouse Park.

As was to be expected, this regulation has caused great discontent amongst the prisoners in certain of the internment camps for civilians. Already, on 13 June, the Austro-Hungarian Committee at Lofthouse Park informed me of this new regulation, stating that the internees in all the compounds had formed the unanimous decision not to eat horse flesh under any conditions.[93]

There was a further claim that the new scale of rations fell short of the medically allowed minimum and that the horse flesh would prove indigestible if poor quality. Some compromise seems to have been reached following the request for Count Wrangel to visit Alexandra Palace, where it was agreed that some of the Austrian and

Hungarian internees there were prepared to eat the meat if of good quality, and that the 'necessary ingredients such as fat, flour, vinegar and onions in sufficient quantities were provided on the days horse flesh was given.'[94] It was a compromise which seems to have been met with approval at Lofthouse Park where horse flesh remained part of the diet several months later.[95]

Although the complaints seem fairly trivial, at least on the face of it and in the wider context of the war and rationing, food was a constant source of anxiety among many of the internees.[96] It was also something that was recognised by Kohn and Rücker in their attempts to get better treatment for the internees, which also included the request to re-establish the old visiting hours which had been reduced to 'one quarter of an hour' in July 1918. The reply from the authorities was that it was not possible 'to modify existing regulations, but the Commandant will be authorised to extend in special cases the visits of friends who have come a long distance.'[97]

Sometime later in 1918, the decision was taken to move the internees to the Isle of Man. There was a change of command too, with Lieutenant-Colonel Rouse taking over the running of the camp from Gregory Sinclair Haines.[98] Among the civilians already mentioned, Erno Brummer, Georg Fuhrman, Max Gelberg, Eugene Neiger, Stephen (Istvan) Revesz and Stephan Szekeres were transferred to No. 8 North Camp, Ripon. Spalding Camp also features in the places where some of the civilians were sent and from where they were later repatriated.[99]

The evacuation of Lofthouse Park Camp took place in October 1918. The order to evacuate the camp is republished in Appendix 1. It was almost four years to the day since Lofthouse Park Camp first opened.

The camp itself, however, was reassigned a new use. Retaining its 'privilege' status, Lofthouse Park became a military prisoners-of-war camp for officers and was in operation in this capacity until its dismantlement in 1920. After that, the few remaining structures on the site of the former amusement park fell into disuse. Finally, a fire in 1922 destroyed the Pavilion, which had been a landmark building for visitors, internees and prisoners alike during the location's pre-war, wartime and post-war days.

Report on Visit to Lofthouse Park Camp, 1915

Lofthouse Park, near Wakefield, which I visited on 13 February, had been an unsuccessful 'pleasure park'. Among the buildings is a skating rink with large recreation rooms in one of which there is a stage which the prisoners are permitted to use. The camp had been opened in October, but at the time of my visit there were only 225 prisoners in it. New barracks are being built on the side of a hill, which will greatly increase its capacity. Hot food is served four times a day. The real Germans in the camp complained because beef was given to them in one form or another every day. Most of the people in the camp are men who have been in England for many years and opportunities are given to them to see their wives (most of whom are British by birth). In the hospital there are several men who wished to have special treatment, but who spoke well of the doctor in charge. The water closets are satisfactory at present, but I was told that the pail system was to be used with the new part of the camp. There are shower baths with hot and cold water. The buildings are heated by stoves and lighted by electricity.

John B. Jackson, Camp Inspector, 1915.

Army Council Instruction No. 623 of 1918
War Office 2 June 1918

Prisoners of War Amended Scale of Rations

Bread	9 ounces	Daily
Broken Biscuits	4 ounces	Daily
Meat: Beef or Horseflesh	4 ounces	3 days a week
Bacon (Chinese)	1 3/5 ounces	2 days a week
Salt-cured, smoked or pickled herrings	10 ounces	2 days a week
Tea or	¼ ounce	Daily
Coffee	½ ounce	-
Sugar	1 ounce	-
Salt	¼ ounce	-
Potatoes	20 ounces	-
Other vegetables	4 ounces	-
Split peas or beans	2 ounces	-
Oatmeal	1 ounce	Rice may be issued in lieu if full ration not obtainable
Jam	1 ounce	Daily
Cheese	1 ounce	Daily
Pepper	1/100 ounce	Daily
Maize Meal	½ ounce	Daily

1. Weekly: Either 8 ounces salt-cured, smoked or pickled herrings and 2 ounces oatmeal; or 4 ounces salt-cured, smoked or pickled herrings, 2 ounces of oatmeal and 2½ ounces of broken biscuit.

2. When men are not employed on work, the following items of the daily ration will be deducted unless the medical officer advises to the contrary in any particular case:

Bread (4 ounces), Oatmeal or rice (1 ounce), Cheese (1 ounce), Maize meal (½ ounce)

3. It is pointed out that the principle expressed in para. 8 of A.O. (Army Order) 369 of 1915, viz., that supplies not actually required for consumption by troops will not be drawn, applies equally to prisoner of war rations.

4. No foodstuffs may be purchased by prisoners of war except such as may be sold in their canteen; neither will they be permitted to receive as presents from anywhere in the United Kingdom, Channel Islands, Dominions, or Colonies any article of food, but no restriction is placed on the contents of parcels from allied and neutral or hostile countries as regards to foodstuffs. 0103/2/2442 (Q.M.G.6)

Source: TNA FOR 383/360. Army Council Instruction No. 623 of 1918 (2 June 1918).

Lofthouse Park: Rebate Account for April 1918

Payments

To Whom	On What Account	Bank	Cash
Andrassy	Hire of chairs for Visitors' Room and hut in West Camp	£15. 10. 3	-------
Dunhill and Son	Hire of Organ, Tuning	£2. 10. 0	-------
Rothwell Gas Co.	Gas for cooking in South Camp: Quarter ending 31-3-1918	£47. 18. 0	-------
Major Porter	Special Tram Fares	-------	£1. 12. 0
Hopkinsons	Hire of Musical Instruments	£7. 7. 0	-------
Lt. Stoton	Expenses in Parcel Office	-------	£4. 8. 0
Hopkinsons	Hire of Organ	£1. 5. 0	-------
Balnforth	Hire of Musical Instruments	£3. 14. 3	-------
Command Paymaster	Deficient and damaged stores for Repatriation and internment in Holland	£14. 12. 9	-------
Command Paymaster	Clearing drains and work in North Camp	£17. 12. 8	-------
Mr Jowett	Repairs in North Camp Bath Room	£4. 7. 0	-------
Major Porter	Shoes for Hospital Night Orderly (thin)	-------	- 7. 6
South Camp	Fatigue Work	-------	£2. 7. 6
Bean & Halliday	Programme for Exhibition West Camp	£4. 2. 0	-------
Major Porter	Petty Cash	£2. 0. 0	-------
Major Porter	Hospital Orderlies, Gardener, Storeman, Postman	£491. 0. 1	£20. 0. 0
	Cash in Bank		£-17. 6. 5
	Cash in Hand	£611. 19. 3	£30. 1. 9.5

Source: TNA FO 393/360 (1918), Report on Wakefield Camp (Swedish Legation), 20 June 1918. Exhibit A.

Family Ties: Lofthouse-cum-Carlton and Robin Hood

Carol Wright (Rothwell and Leeds)

This chapter will look at the lives of two families who lived near Lofthouse Park before and after the First World War. Although not prominent like the Charlesworth or Armitage families, who owned the mines in the area and the quarry and brickworks close to Lofthouse Park, the Dobsons and Milners would have been well known within their own circles and the close-knit communities of Lofthouse-cum-Carlton and Robin Hood. Using information from census records, photos and other documents, it is possible to look at where they lived, the work they did and some of the social and leisure activities they would have been involved in. These glimpses of everyday life exemplify how local families progressed through times of peace and war while the narratives that constitute the greater part of this publication unfolded, both elsewhere and in this particular section of the West Riding in the first decades of the 20th century.

My great grandfather was Lewis Dobson, who was born in 1875, and lived in Robin Hood. Lewis Dobson had started work when he was around twelve years old and had already been working for twenty years when Lofthouse Park opened as a theme park in 1908. The 1911 Census shows that Lewis (36) was then living at 6 Pawson Street, Robin Hood, with his wife Ann Elizabeth (33) and their first child, Lucy Allison Dobson, aged 9 months.[1] A second daughter was born in August 1912. This was my grandmother, Edith Mary Dobson, with Hilda Margaret Dobson born in 1916, and Oswald Dobson in 1919. Ann Elizabeth would have been over 40 when her son was born. Oswald was known as 'Ossie' throughout most of his life. Lewis Dobson's occupation is given as a 'coal hewer' in the 1911 Census.[2]

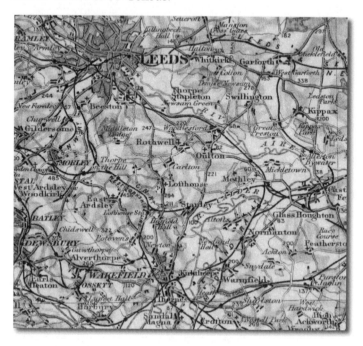

Fig. 2.1: The area between Leeds and Wakefield, with Lofthouse in the middle section. Excerpt from Ordnance Survey of England and Wales, Revised New Series, 1903, Sheet 7, Scale 1:253440 (© Great Britain Historical GIS Project 2004-17).

Lewis Dobson and Ann Elizabeth Allison married in 1907 at the church of St Nicholas in West Tanfield, near Ripon.[3] In addition to caring for her young family and husband, Ann attended the Robin Hood United Methodist Church, and was awarded a book for regular attendance in 1920-21. There were Methodist chapels in Robin Hood, Lofthouse and Outwood, in addition to other church congregations. The life and events at chapel were an important social activity. There was fun too, as seen in some of the playlets which were performed by members of the United Free Methodist Church.

In terms of the wider Dobson family, Lewis Dobson had two brothers, Percy and Horace Clifford. Both were still single and living at the family home in Ebenezer Street, Robin Hood, in 1911. Percy (30) and Horace Clifford (23) are described as 'coal servants' in the 1911 Census and were working as labourers in the mines. Their father was also working as a coal servant.[4] Benjamin Dobson still had four years to work before he could claim the old age pension of 5 shillings per week (25p), which was only awarded to those aged 70 and over. Benjamin Dobson had married Sarah Ann Milner, daughter of George Milner, in 1866.

Fig. 2.2: The Dobson family c. 1918 (Wright Family Archive).

George Milner (1821-95) was described as an engineer man or furnace man in the census returns from 1871 to 1891. He had worked in an iron foundry, in what must have been a physically demanding occupation, until he was 69 years of age. His son George (b. 1856) is listed in the census returns as a 'stone mason', and perhaps worked in quarries owned by the Armitage family or another local employer. The Milner family were living next door to the Dobson family in 1871, which shows further evidence of close community links and how they had developed.[5] My grandmother Edith was interested in her family history, keeping documents relating to births, marriages and deaths, newspaper clippings and so on, and was able to tell me as a youngster that the Milners were related to us.

Lucy and Edith Dobson were aged four and two when the First World War broke out, and it is hard to know how aware they would have been of the conflict. Their parents, however, would have witnessed the conversion of Lofthouse Park from an entertainment venue on their doorstep to a site of encampment that became out of bounds for the local population. I remember my grandmother saying that as a child she would tell the Germans off, but later, when I was learning about the World Wars, that they were people just like us. Lewis Dobson was working as a colliery deputy at the start of the war and was in a reserve occupation.

Some insight into the war can be found in the recollections of Gwen Moorhouse in an interview for the Rothwell and District Record in July 2002. Mrs Moorhouse was born in 1910:

> I don't remember the war starting but I do recall a Zeppelin coming over. I also remember my father coming home saying the war was over and putting our flag out. I can also remember hearing that Scarborough and Whitby had been bombarded by a German battleship coming close in, and both of the castles in Scarborough and Whitby had been hit.[6]

Leisure time was important and could well have included a visit to Lofthouse Park as a special treat. Other activities included sports, music and study. Lofthouse had its own cricket team, and cross-country running was a popular spectator activity. There were also regular brass band competitions and performances from ensembles such as the Rothwell Temperance Band. Roller skating was another favourite pastime before the war.

Fig. 2.3: Young roller skaters at Lofthouse Park (Outwood Community Video. Ref. L 35).

Additionally, the Mechanics' Institute in Wakefield in Wood Street provided a seat of learning and self-improvement through education. Progress in work was equally encouraged, as can be seen in Lewis Dobson's application for the post of underground official and a letter of recommendation he received from the Middleton Estate & Colliery Company in April 1922.

In the years following the First World War, the Dobson family were to suffer cases of serious illness and bereavement. Firstly, Hilda Dobson caught scarlet fever and received treatment at the St. George's Hospital in nearby Rothwell. Then tragedy struck the family when Ann Elizabeth Dobson was diagnosed with cancer and passed away in 1930 at the age of 53. Three years later, Lucy Allison Dobson succumbed to tuberculosis infection. This was before the inception of the National Health Service, and the medical costs would have been borne by the family, possibly with the help of an insurance policy or subscription to a hospital fund.

My grandmother Edith was now the oldest child and helped raise her younger brother Oswald in the absence of his mother. More happily, Edith Dobson married Tom Nelson in Wakefield in 1938. Tom Nelson was born at Springfield Place, Hunslet, in 1913, and then lived at No. 2 Queen Street, next door to the Queens Hotel at Stourton. The Queen's Hotel public house is still there today. During their courtship he would walk from Hunslet over the Parnaby Tops to visit Edith, who lived at Middleton Avenue in Rothwell Haigh. Hilda Dobson married Edward Gill at Lofthouse in 1940, and three years later Ossie Dobson married Beryl Cooper. They would all start families of their own despite the further distress and trouble of the Second World War.

Fig. 2.4: Edith Nelson and Grandson Paul c. 1991 (Carol Wright Family Archive).

My grandfather Tom Nelson went on to work as a medical attendant in collieries close to Lofthouse Park. He was at Newmarket when the Lofthouse Colliery disaster happened in March 1973. I remember being at my grandparents' house when he came home on his scooter bike to let my grandmother know that he would have to go and assist with any survivors from the rescue effort. Seven miners lost their lives when the coalface they were working was flooded and the men became trapped. My grandparents Tom and Edith passed away in 1986 and 1994.

I would like to dedicate this chapter to Private Fred Smales, who was killed in action on 7 July 1916 serving with the 1st/4th King's Own Yorkshire Light Infantry. Fred was the son of Alfred and Jane Ann Smales, and brother of Alice Smales, of Outwood near Wakefield. He was 21 years of age. Fred Smales is commemorated on the Thiepval Memorial to the Missing. Alice Smales later married John Abbott Bartle (1903-79), who had worked at Lofthouse Colliery since the age of thirteen, in August 1926.

Richard Cornelius Bechtel: An Internment Odyssey in and out of Yorkshire

Eberhard Haering (Bremen)

Richard Cornelius Bechtel was born in Baltimore, Maryland, on 12 October 1878. He was the second of four children of the German merchant Carl Heinrich Cornelius Bechtel and his wife Emma Clementine Stachow. Richard Bechtel attended an American school; at home the family spoke German. The Bechtels left the United States for business reasons in September 1894, and returned to Bremen in Germany, the father's hometown.

Fig. 3.1: Richard Bechtel in his mid-twenties in Berlin, February 1903 (Bechtel Family Archive).

After passing his *Abitur* (A-levels), Richard gained his first technical experience in 1898 as an intern at the newly built grain mill Rolandmühle, which was managed by his father. Here he assembled a steam engine and then put it into operation. Later Richard completed his professional training as a mechanical engineer, probably in Berlin. In 1910 he married Auguste Schneider, who came from East Prussia. The couple moved to Wellington, Shropshire, in 1911, where Richard worked for the large engineering company Lilleshall Co. Ltd.

As a non-naturalised German resident in England, Richard Bechtel was a registered 'enemy alien' during the First World War. He was arrested and interned at various places from 7 August 1914 until March 1919. In September 1914, he was held at York Castle, living in a tent on Castle Yard.

Fig. 3.2: Postcard of Clifford's Tower in York with Bechtel's caption: 'In the foreground the prison yard surrounded by high walls as one can see. Here stood our tents.' (Bechtel Family Archive).

On 21 November 1914, Richard was moved to Leeman Road in York, a hastily erected camp using, among others, disused railroad sheds for accommodation. One of his *Stallkameraden* ('stable buddies') was a Pastor Herzog, who, as a member of the clergy, was released and repatriated to Germany. In early December 1914, Richard Bechtel was sent to the former mail ship *HMT Royal Edward* (until 1910: *RMS Cairo*), which now served internment purposes and was moored about a mile from the pier at Southend-on-Sea.

Fig. 3.3: The drawing by Otto Hahn shows crowded conditions at Leeman Road in York (Bechtel Family Archive).

Fig. 3.4: Civilians under guard arriving at Southend-on-Sea (Bechtel Family Archive).

Fig. 3.4 shows a photograph of civilians under guard in Southend-on-Sea. Richard Bechtel's ironic caption reads: 'As we were marched through, people shouted a good number of pleasantries after us' (translated from German). In contrast to the street scene, conditions aboard the *Royal Edward* evoke a more courteous climate, with permissions given to hold a Christmas concert in 1914. Among the committee members were Baron von Nettlebladt and Baron von Horst.[1] The two men would feature in two separate inquiries in connection to Lieutenant-Colonel Gregory Sinclair Haines, who was Commandant at Lofthouse Park between 1916 and 1918.[2] The Commandant on the *Royal Edward* in December 1914 was Lieutenant-Colonel Ernest de Cordes. There were about 1,400 internees on the ship.[3]

Accommodation on the *Royal Edward* was separated into three classes, which was dependent to a certain extent on social standing, but also on the ability to pay the additional expenses. Members in the first-class mess paid two shillings (10p) a day in advance. The first-class mess was in addition to the so-called 'club', whose members 'can more or less cater for themselves', according to a report which was published in 1915.[4] First-class cabins were available for a payment of between five shillings (25p) and two and six pence (12.5p), and payment was in advance. Regular steerage quarters were available to those unable to pay for first-class accommodation.[5] Eventually, the *Royal Edward* was requisitioned as a troopship and had to be vacated by the internees.[6] On 12 April 1915, Richard Bechtel arrived at Lofthouse Park Camp with a group of about 300 civilians from Southend-on-Sea, escorted by the Surrey National Reserve.[7]

A small booklet of sketches has survived in our family containing two accomplished watercolour drawings of Lofthouse Park Camp by the young artist Max Schnös

(Figs. 3.5 and 3.6).[8] They show basic wooden huts with a door at the gable-end or side elevation and six windows along the front of the huts, with a slightly inclined asphalt roof. The pictures suggest that furnishing consisted of rustic wooden beds, benches and tables on a wooden floor. Personal belongings were stored in trunks and suitcases on the floor. Other utilities shown in the drawing are coat hooks, wooden shelving and clothes lines; even a decorative map has found a place. A drape serves as a screen to create a sense of privacy. The scene is overlooked by a watchtower in the background. The outdoor area shows a vegetable plot and flower garden with sitting accommodations. A metal flue indicates stove heating.

Like other remaining civilians, Richard Bechtel would have had to leave Lofthouse Park and Yorkshire in October 1918 for Knockaloe on the Isle of Man to make space for incoming military prisoners. Oddly, however, there is no respective reference in his personal documents. After his release from internment in March 1919, Richard Bechtel went to Hamburg, Germany. On 18 October 1919, he started a new career with Illies & Co., a company that had established trade relations with East Asia in the nineteenth century and is still operating today. Bechtel was chief engineer in Japan for several years with a focus on marine and production machinery.

Between 27 January and 28 April 1927, Richard and his wife Auguste travelled back by ship from Japan to Hamburg. His well-preserved diary about their voyage provides interesting insights into travel conditions at the time. As a senior employee, Richard Bechtel had extended signatory powers (*Prokura*); when they expired after 1933, he retired at the age of 55. He died on 2 June 1954 in Hamburg and was buried in the Bechtel family plot on Riensberg Cemetery in Bremen. Auguste survived her husband by nearly four years and was interred beside him after her death on 20 March 1958. They had no children.

My maternal grandfather and Richard's younger brother, the merchant Leopold Clemens Bechtel (*1881 Baltimore, +1956 Bremen), had researched the family history and collected extensive data as well as documents, photographs and items from deceased family members. Among them were a few objects that belonged to his brother Richard, for instance the booklet on Lofthouse Park. Some years ago, I started to examine the documents and enter the information into a family history programme in order to complement them with the help of databases and online resources. Some ancestors ceased to be mere datasets; a few came to life more fully due to the number of available sources and existing documents – such as Richard Bechtel.

The Bechtel family in Bremen can be traced back to the wine grower Niklas Bechtel (1585-1639) from Eppstein near Frankenthal in the Palatinate. His great-grandson, the wine merchant Cornelius Bechtel (*1734 Frankenthal, +1801 Bremen), emigrated to Bremen in 1755; his son, the merchant Georg Jonas Bechtel (*1781 Bremen, +1854 Bremen), was the elected Eltermann, head of the Bremen merchants ('Olderlüde des Koopmanns'), for 25 years. He cultivated close business and personal links with Baltimore, where as early as 1821 the politically autonomous city of Bremen opened a consulate. Several children and grandchildren, most of them merchants too, spent their apprenticeship years in Baltimore, as did Richard's father. The family tradition of working in international trade as well as the resulting mobility and affluence made Richard Bechtel a typical representative of the multilingual and well-to-do 'gentlemen' who found themselves interned at Lofthouse Park during the First World War.

Figs. 3.5 and 3.6 on the following pages: Lofthouse Park watercolours by internee Max Schnös, 1915 (Bechtel Family Archive).

Lofthouse Park ~ Prisoner of War Camp ~ Wakefield ~ England. ~

Richard Oswald Siebenhüner:
Lofthouse Park and Knockaloe

Richard Oswald (Morley)

Richard Oswald Siebenhüner was my great grandfather. He was born on 7 November 1872 in the small village of Riestedt, near Sangerhausen, in Germany. He was a hairdresser by trade, and a very good one too: but the prospect of being called up to do compulsory military service in the German Army made him more determined to make a new life for himself, and he left Riestadt for London in 1893.

He later married Ottilia Rolfs, the daughter of German-born parents who were already naturalised. Richard Siebenhüner and Ottilia moved to Leeds from London in 1910. Sometime in the early 1920s, Oswald – as he was known to most people – changed his name to Richard Oswald, which is where my own name originates.

Oswald Siebenhüner became a well-known and respected hairdresser in Leeds, where he worked in a salon on The Headrow. Many of his customers were wealthy and some were quite famous. It came as a great shock to his family and friends when he was arrested without warning in 1915 and taken to Leeds Town Hall. After spending a night on the floor at the Town Hall, he was taken to Lofthouse Park internment camp between Leeds and Wakefield.

Ottilia went to see her husband regularly, catching the tram from Leeds City Square for the short visit. Oswald's first request was for his overcoat as it was getting cold in the camp and he expected to be there for a while. The visits also helped his morale. To his dismay, the authorities had taken his scissors and razors when he was arrested, and he was unable to practice his trade.

Life in the camp could be very monotonous. This prompted Oswald and some of the other internees to look for something to do to stop them getting bored or becoming idle. One of Oswald's friends in the camp was Moritz Heuer, who had overhead that a man he had seen walking around the camp was a Quaker from the Woodhouse Lane Meeting House in Leeds. The man had asked the authorities if he could visit the camp to see what could be done to raise the spirits of the prisoners, and it was decided to approach the man to see if he could help ease their sense of monotony. A few days later, books and magazines arrived, followed by tools and materials for making handicrafts. Materials, however, were limited and the men had to scrape around for whatever they could use.

Ottilia continued to visit Oswald at Lofthouse Park. She had also remarked that his usual immaculate appearance had slipped somewhat: his hair had grown, and his normally highly polished shoes had become dull and dirty. He had also grown a beard. He did not have the heart to tell her that the guards had taken all of his tools and personal equipment. All this changed for the better after the visit from the Quaker, and the rise in morale prompted Oswald to keep up with his appearance.

A short time later, Oswald and a group of fifty internees were told to pack their belongings because they were being transferred to Knockaloe Camp on the Isle of Man. Oswald had heard about the camp and was concerned about what they might face on arrival. Because of the short notice, Oswald had no way of letting his family know that he was being moved, and Ottilia unknowingly set off to visit Oswald at Lofthouse Park Camp the following day.

The long and bitterly cold train journey to Liverpool was made even more difficult when the men were taunted and spat on and called 'dirty Huns'. Oswald's thoughts were wandering during the journey and he exclaimed to Moritz that Henry, one of Ottilia's children to her first husband, would now be 24 years old and could be fighting for Germany in the war. It was a very daunting thought.

It did not take Oswald long to realise that conditions at Knockaloe were much worse than at Lofthouse Park. However, he soon put himself forward for work in the hospital wing, which he had been told about at Lofthouse by one of the men who had been interned on the Isle of Man.

Fig. 4.1: Richard Oswald Siebenhüner, Knockaloe Camp (Isle of Man). He was held in Camp 3, Compound 3, Hut 5a, while at Knockaloe.

Oswald had gained a lot of respect from the other internees and decided to enlist their help to make gifts for his wife and six children. Among the gifts were a pair of picture frames for his wife, a jewellery box for each of his five daughters and a ship in a bottle for his son George, who was my grandfather. The skill used and the quality of these items is second to none. I know this as I am fortunate enough to own three of the jewellery boxes and the two picture frames which were given to Ottilia. Unfortunately, the ship in the bottle was lost many years ago, and one of the jewellery boxes was destroyed by Oswald's daughter Clara, who hated anything German or connected to Germans.

Oswald remained at Knockaloe until he was discharged and went home in October 1919. During that time, Ottilia was helped financially and socially by the Quakers' Special Committee, which was set up to assist with the care of interned civilians and their wives and dependents.

Oswald lost contact with his friend Moritz Heuer on the first day at Knockaloe. The two friends were reunited four years later when Moritz visited the barber shop which Oswald had set up in his front room at 6 Winfield Mount, Woodhouse, Leeds.

Richard Oswald Siebenhüner died on 13 August 1960 at St. James's Hospital, Leeds. He was 87.

This chapter is dedicated to the life and memory of John Oswald Walling, who was my father's cousin, and the only son of Edith Florence Siebenhüner, daughter of Oswald Siebenhüner. John Walling spent much of his life re-searching and writing about the Oswald family history and died on 17 July 2016, aged 88.[1] I also dedicate the text to my father, Edward Oswald, who sadly passed away while I wrote this chapter.

John Henry Brickmann:
A Forgotten Victim of the Great War

Alan Muddiman (Middlesbrough)

My father had often said that we had a German relative in
our family, so when I began to research my family history
several years ago, I was puzzled by the lack of any German
element being uncovered. It was only when I decided to
broaden my research to include my grandparents' siblings
that I solved the mystery. My relative – John Henry
Brickmann – was interned as an enemy alien in the First
World War. This is his story and the connections I made
during my research.

My paternal grandparents both originated from
Northamptonshire. My great grandfather was James
Moore. He was a steelworker who had moved north with
his family in search of work. The family had lived in
Sheffield for a brief time, before moving to Middlesbrough
and settling in Cook Street. James and Mary Ann Moore
had seven children: five girls and two boys. Annie
Elizabeth was the eldest of the five girls. My grandmother
was the youngest.

In the 1901 Census, Annie Elizabeth is named as the
wife of John Henry Brickmann. Two children are also
mentioned: James and Annie. John Brickmann was working as a millwright in an ironworks at this time. His birth
place is given as Germany.[1] Further research shows that he
was born in Memel, East Prussia, which is now known as
Klaipeda, in present-day Lithuania.[2]

Previous research had indicated that John Henry
Brickmann was a seaman, who had arrived in England
sometime after 1891. I am assuming he moved into the
Moore household as a lodger, based on the fact that his

address on his marriage certificate is given as that of the Moore family. A romance obviously blossomed between John Henry and James Moore's daughter, as three years later John Henry Brickmann and Annie Elizabeth Moore were married at the Primitive Methodist Chapel in Gilkes Street, Middlesbrough.

Fig. 5.1: The wedding of John Henry Brickmann and Annie Elizabeth Moore, 8 February 1894, at the Primitive Methodist Chapel, Gilkes Street, Middlesbrough (Muddiman Family Archive).

It seems John was welcomed into the family. He remained a seaman for several years, until the birth and death of one of his children, whom he had never seen. It was possibly the death of his child which persuaded Brickmann to give up the sea and to seek employment in the local ironworks. John and Annie's family grew, and they moved into a small terraced house in Adam Street, Middlesbrough.

However, tragedy struck the Moore family in 1899, when my great grandmother, Mary Ann Moore, died suddenly whilst visiting her sister in Northampton. Despite having his own wife and three children, John Henry Brickmann brought his father-in-law James Moore into the family home, and three of his wife's siblings: James, Edith, and my grandmother, Maria. Further evidence of John Henry's role in the family can be found on the marriage certificate of Charlotte Moore, when he stood in for her father who had died in 1907. Charlotte had married Charles Wilkins on 30 July 1908. Charles Wilkins was a publican and ran the Marquis of Granby in Hill Street, Middlesbrough. John Henry Brickmann can also be seen in a photograph taken in 1912 of the annual pub outing which was run by his brother-in-law. Two years later, all this was about to change.

Fig. 5.2: John Henry Brickmann, pictured outside the Marquis of Granby pub in 1912. John appears to be well integrated into the local community (Muddiman Family Archive).

The outbreak of war in August 1914 meant that all 'aliens' were required to report to the authorities, which John Henry Brickmann duly did. He registered at the Alien Registry Office, Middlesbrough, on 8 August 1914, and was given the serial number 129. Many aliens, however, chose not to register, and local newspapers over the following months carried stories of the courts handing out fines for those not complying with the authorities. The *North Eastern Gazette* carried a report on 4 September 1914 of a German seaman who had been seen loitering around the dock. This man was said to have spoken several languages. He was sentenced to six months of hard labour.[3]

There had been some instances of shops and properties belonging to foreigners being targeted by what the press called 'hotheads'. This relates to events in which a butcher's shop and a local off-licence were attacked. The German butcher had lived in Middlesbrough for forty years. The off-licence was vandalised because the owner's daughter had married a German. The ringleader of the mob was fined forty shillings (£2) and ordered to pay damages of £4. He was also warned that if he defaulted on the fine he would be sent to prison.[4] Attitudes in general, however, seem to have been fairly tolerant towards some of the local people considered 'alien' in the first few weeks of the war.

John and his son James Henry worked in the local industry during the first months of the war. John Henry had worked as a rope splicer at Dorman Long and Co. in Middlesbrough for twenty years. It is possible he learned his splicing skills as a seaman. I have often wondered how my grandmother and her sisters viewed John Brickmann. On the one hand he was their brother-in-law who had helped them when their need was greatest. On the other, their husbands were in France and Flanders, fighting his countrymen. It seems that the family remained close – although everything changed on 16 December 1914 when German warships bombarded Hartlepool, Whitby and Scarborough, causing many civilian casualties.

The public were outraged, and feelings ran high. Within days the authorities acted, and on Christmas Eve 1914,

John was arrested and sent to the internment camp at
Lofthouse near Wakefield. Whether this was to appease
public opinion or for the protection of the aliens is unclear.
He would never see his family again, and no letters from
John Brickmann to his family have been found.

John Henry Brickmann died on 21 September 1916, in
the 2nd Northern General Hospital, Leeds, of a cerebral
haemorrhage. His death certificate records him as a general
labourer, of 51 Albany Street, Middlesbrough. The certificate was sent to the registrar by the Leeds coroner. No
mention is made of his wife on the certificate, although the
coroner knew his address in Middlesbrough, which was
possibly supplied by the Lofthouse Park Camp administration.

I travelled to Wakefield in the course of my research,
and was told that older locals had said that the non-military
prisoners (civilian internees) were marched round the
outside of the camp for their daily exercise and that local
youngsters would congregate knowing the prisoners would
throw them coins.

However, it is also a fact that the camp was situated in
an area from which many local battalions were drawn, and
these suffered high losses on the first day of the Battle of
the Somme in 1916. One story was that a local man, who
had recently lost a relative, drove his van into the column
of walkers, killing or injuring several internees during their
exercise. I was also told that this was never reported in the
press, the authorities having suppressed the story.

A gentleman named John Walling had published a book
entitled *The Internment and Treatment of German Nationals
during the 1st World War* (2005) and also a novel called
Coming Home (2008). This dealt with a family who moved
to Leeds from London and the German-born father who
was interned in Lofthouse before being transferred to
Knockaloe Camp on the Isle of Man. John Walling sent
me an email regarding this:

I mention some of the things about the camp in there including the story about the lorry. The story of the man who drove the lorry is in a small paperback book 'Going Back a Bit' (Book 2) by R.P. Rhodes and it is in Wakefield Library – don't remember it mentioning the date.[5]

Whether this incident ever took place, we will probably never know, but John Henry Brickmann's death was reported in the Teesside press on 22 and 23 September 1916. His obituary read:

Brickman – On the 21st September, Harry, dearly-beloved husband of Elizabeth Brickman, cortege leaves 51, Albany-street, Monday, 3 p.m. Friends and work-mates kindly invited.[6]

John Brickmann was buried in Linthorpe Cemetery on 25 September 1916. John's widow Annie then had to reapply for British citizenship as she was regarded as German on her marriage to John. I obtained copies of the forms and letters sent by Annie to the authorities to this end. Local dignitaries on Teesside spoke up for her, and eventually she regained her British citizenship, having paid the appropriate fee of five shillings.

The documents also show that James Henry Brickmann had been helping his mother financially since his father's arrest in December 1914. He was working at the Dorman Long Britannia Works as a munitions worker, according to correspondence between the Middlesbrough Constabulary and the Home Office in 1916.[7]

Little else is known about Annie Brickmann's later life. She never remarried and remained in the house she had shared with John in Albany Street until her death some twenty years after her husband's. She was buried in the same grave as John in January 1937.

Perhaps the fact that Annie's family still called her 'Beloved wife of the late John Henry Brickman' after twenty years a widow tells us something not only about their relationship, but also how other people regarded John

Henry Brickmann. Another sister-in-law, for example, named one of her sons John Henry.

John Brickmann was just one more death amongst the millions who died in the Great War, one more person whose only crime was to be in the wrong place at the wrong time.

Case Studies I

David Stowe (Leeds)

Dr Gerhard Bartram: *S.M.S. Kronprinz Wilhelm* and *S.S. Hellig Olav*
H. Brammer: The *Eleonore Woermann* and 'Neutral' Territory
Professor Gustav Adolf Bredow: Sculptor
P.W. Brünger: Director of Niger-Berne Transport, Warri, Nigeria
Ludwig Lichtenstadter

1. Dr Gerhard Bartram: *S.M.S. Kronprinz Wilhelm* and *S.S. Hellig Olav*

Gerhard Bartram had served as a medical officer on the German auxiliary *Kronprinz Wilhelm* when the former liner was involved in the Atlantic raids between August 1914 and April 1915. The *Kronprinz* had spent over eight months at sea without anchoring and captured over 60,000 gross tons as prizes in that time. Heavily dependent on coal and in urgent need of other provisions and repairs, the decision was taken to make for a neutral port: she was held at the Hampton Roads on the Virginian coast on 11 April 1915. Some of the crew had been suffering beri-beri due to poor diet and the length of time at sea.[1]

Bartram was released by US authorities in October 1915 and took passage on the *S.S. Hellig Olav* which was bound for Denmark. The *Hellig Olav* was stopped by British authorities at Kirkwall on the Orkney Islands, where Gerhard Bartram and a number of German nationals were removed from the ship. Bartram's claim was that he was entitled to repatriation as a medical officer who had been released from internment by the Americans and was still under orders as a military medical officer as such. Although captured in civilian clothes, Bartram further claimed that he was still on active duty under the protection of the Hague Convention, and that his papers held by the British at Kirkwall proved this.[2]

Bartram's petitions were also about payments due to him as a reserve officer, as in the application he made at the end of February 1916:

> Sir – I was during the war on board S.M.S. Kronprinz Wilhelm on duty as a Marine-Assistenzarzt der Reserve and was captured by the British Authorities at Kirkwall on 25 October 1915 when I was on journey to Germany for doing further medical service there. I naturally expect to receive the pay due to me as Marine-Assistenzarzt der Reserve. Before the outbreak of war I was registered at the Bezirkskommando Kiel. I shall be very grateful if you will kindly arrange the needful. I appeal to you in this matter without prejudice as to my previous protest against my imprisonment, which protest I still hold. Signed: I am, your obedient servant. Dr Gerhard Bartram.[3]

Bartram had been one of ten signatories on a petition which was submitted at Stratford Camp in January 1916 concerning their release or transfer to an officers or privileged camp. The reply in this case was that none of the physicians were entitled to repatriation, having been arrested on board ships and by naval authorities on a date subsequent to the conclusion of the agreement between Britain and Germany for the release of civilian doctors. The question of transfer to another camp was being considered.[4]

In respect of Bartram's request to be recognised as a serving medical officer, it was said in a letter from the British Secretary of State to the US Ambassador in April 1916 that Bartram did not come within 'Article X of the Convention if only for the reason that the Kronprinz Wilhelm was never captured by His Majesty's Fleet.'[5]

Some of the other names mentioned in connection with Gerhard Bartram include doctors Berthold Baneth, Casimir Caspar, Martin Ficker, Fritz Goldberg, Karl Hoch, Georg Richter, Dr Siebert, Franz Thalwizer and Ed. Gimper.[6] All but two were transferred to Lofthouse Park from Stratford East Camp in February and March 1916.[7] Casimir Caspar had also served as a medical officer on the *S.M.S. Kronprinz Wilhelm* and was interned with Bartram when the *S.S. Hellig Olav* was taken into Kirkwall.[8] Dr Gerhard Bartram and Dr Casimir Caspar were held in the West Camp while at Lofthouse Park.[9] Bartram was repatriated to Holland via Spalding Camp in January 1918. Casimir Caspar was repatriated at the same time.[10]

2. 1st Officer H. Brammer: *Eleonore Woermann* and 'Neutral' Territory

Brammer had been 1st Officer on the German steamer *Eleonore Woermann* when she was captured by *HMAS Australia* off the coast of Brazil in January 1915. The vessel had initially been part of the Woermann Line, which provided passenger and cargo services between Germany and African ports, but was in operation as a naval supply ship since 1914. The *Eleonore Woermann* had docked at Albrahos to take on coal and was later intercepted by *HMAS Australia* and ordered to surrender. The crew were taken off the steamer and put aboard the *Australia*, and the steamer was then sunk. The captain of the *Eleonore Woermann* had requested that his crew be released or that any further transportation should take place on a trade ship. Both requests were refused, according to Brammer. Brammer's protest against the circumstances surrounding his arrest were based on the following premise, namely that his arrest was:

a) In contravention of international law in transporting civilian prisoners on a warship.

b) In contravention of a law in holding prisoners in a neutral port.

Brammer had claimed that his ship was in Portuguese territory when he was taken prisoner. He had also requested his immediate release to Germany or a neutral port. His request for repatriation was denied, with the explanation

> that even had Portugal been a neutral country, prisoners of war would not have been entitled to release on entering a Portuguese port on board a warship, which, in such circumstances continues to enjoy extraterritorial rights.[11]

Brammer was writing from the South Camp in January 1916.

3. Professor Gustav Adolf Bredow: Sculptor

Professor Gustav Adolf Bredow was a renowned sculptor who was arrested *en route* to Spain from Argentina and interned at Gibraltar. He had left Buenos Aires on 29 May 1915 on the *Tomaso de Savoya* and was interned just over a week later. He submitted two known appeals to the Foreign Office requesting his release and guaranteeing his neutrality if permission was granted. His original application was sent in October 1915. He re-applied in January 1916. Bredow's second application was sent from Douglas Camp, on the Isle of Man.

> Sir, May I be permitted to draw your attention once more to my case, having received no answer to my application of 23 October 1915. My hopes that you will consider my case favourably are augmented by the fact that the Foreign Office in Germany have taken the matter in hand, and I have been given to understand that negotiations on my behalf are actually taking place. I respectfully beg to give you herewith once more a brief outline of my case, viz:
>
> Being a sculptor of renown I was commissioned by the Argentine Government in 1910 to execute a monument for the Centenary Festivities at Buenos Aires. This

monument is not yet completed, and utilising the postponement of the unveiling ceremony it was my intention to visit Spain in order to pursue special studies in Art enabling me to carry out further commissions already received in the Argentine.

I was arrested on board the Neutral steamer 'Tomaso de Savoya' and interned at Gibraltar on 7 June 1915. The date of my departure from Buenos Aires was 20 May 1915.

In support of the above statements I also beg to refer to His Excellency Dr Murrature, the Argentine Minister for Foreign Affairs at Buenos Aires and his Minister, Dr Marcos Avellaneda at Madrid, who will corroborate my claims.

In conclusion I beg to add that I am able and willing to give you on parole an undertaking of Neutrality on the understanding that I shall be allowed to return to Germany. Signed Prof. G.A. Bredow.[12]

Professor Gustav Adolf Bredow was transferred to Holland via Spalding Camp in March 1918.[13]

4. P.W. Brünger: Director of Niger-Berne Transport, Warri, Nigeria

Paul Wilhelm Brünger was the Director of Niger-Berne Transport in Nigeria. He was arrested and interned along with fifty members of his staff in 1914 before being transported to Britain and interned at Lofthouse Park Camp in late 1915.[14] In a series of letters between January 1916 and July 1917, Brünger petitioned the Foreign Office for the release of his staff and himself on the grounds of wrongful arrest, and that the arrests were in breach of international law. He cites the terms of the Berlin Conference Act of 1885 and the violation of the Niger-Shipping Act (1885) and also claims that when war broke out, Niger-Berne Transport was engaged in commerce and navigation in the areas affected by the Niger Act of Navigation. Additionally, Brünger expresses concern over the health of some of the men interned at Lofthouse Park due to malaria and liver problems, and the concerns of all on reading in the newspapers that their 'houses and ground properties, as well as other possessions, have been sold at auction by the Nigerian Government.'[15]

A transcript of Brünger's petition from January 1916 may be found below. This was signed on behalf of ten men. A translated copy of further correspondence in July 1917 lists fifty names, of whom twenty-two were interned at Lofthouse Park Camp and the remainder on the Isle of Man.[16]

> Sir – The undersigned German Subjects beg to submit to Your Excellency that they are wrongfully kept as Prisoners of War and beg you to intercede with the British Authorities for their release on the following grounds:
>
> 1. They were occupied, when the war broke out, in peaceful navigation on the River Niger and its tributaries and issues.
>
> 2. According to the International Treaty of Berlin of 1885, commonly called the Congo Act, which was signed inter alia by Germany, Great Britain, France and the United States of America, it was agreed, that the navigation on the River Niger, its Tributaries, Issues and the territorial waters stretching along the issues should be open to the subjects of all nations under the same conditions as the subjects of Great Britain and France, and it was particularly stipulated, that this should extend to times of war.
>
> 3. It was therefore illegal, when the British Colonial Authorities arrested us as Prisoners of War, deprived us of our property and transported us to England in November/December 1915, keeping us Prisoners of War until now.
>
> Signed P.W. Brünger, and 10 others. Director of Niger-Berne Transport Ges. B.H. Warri Niger.[17]

Named in correspondence: G.W. Bernhardt (1067), Carl Bock, Mart Bruhns (641), J. Cheim (706), H. Friedrichsen (2122), E. Gorlandt (704), Carl Hinst (770), Carl Kirsch (1591), Gust Laackmann, F.H. Michaelson (696), A. Morawski (699), Erwin Moller (1378), W. Nagel (777), P.A. Obst (704), Louis Pagenstecher, E. Prager (2124), John Ravens (711), Rene Rohwer (720), R. Schleutker (729), Alb. Schlue, A. Stoltenberg (787), Hugo Winkler (2127).[18] Paul Brünger (629) was writing from the South Camp in January 1916.

5. Ludwig Lichtenstadter

Ludwig Lichtenstadter (1335) was born in Germany and had declared his intention to become an American citizen when he was interned in 1914. He had also planned to marry Miss Edith Cohen, his future wife acting as guarantor that Lichtenstadter would return to the United States if released from internment to get married. A promise was also made that he would not engage in war against the British Government or its allies. The request was put forward by the Department of State in Washington under instructions from Lichtenstadter. The request was rejected.[19]

Case Studies II

David Stowe (Leeds)

Otto Froitzheim: Tennis Player
Guido von Georgevits: Aviator
Count Eginhard Beissel von Gymnich: *S.S. Caserta* and Gibraltar
Dr Karl Hoch: *S.S. Hellig Olav* and Report from Boarding Officer
Frederick Wiener and Alfred Klapproth: Escapees

1. Otto Froitzheim: Tennis Player

In a letter from Lofthouse internee and German tennis champion Otto Froitzheim to Miss Cassell in the United States, dated 17 December 1915, the author refers to F.B. Alexander and S. Wallace Merrihew. The first is a former national doubles tennis champion; S. Wallace Merrihew was editor of the magazine *American Lawn Tennis*. The newspaper article in which the letter was published also mentions Brookes and Wilding, who had played opposite Otto Froitzheim and his playing partner Oscar Kreuzer. Captain Anthony Wilding was killed in action on 9 May 1915 near Neuve-Chapelle, aged 31. He was serving with the Royal Marines Armoured Car Division at the time of his death.[1]

> My dear Miss Cassell: Your communication from Pittsburg and Haverford received. I see by these that you are happy and contented. I cannot say the same of myself. The long detention is becoming more and more depressing, especially now, just before the holiday season. Weather conditions thereabouts are not the best and the only meadow at our disposal, has been a swamp for months. The roads are very bad, being swampy and

seemingly bottomless, thus preventing us from getting needed exercise or participating in sports. I am getting sick and I am putting on weight on account of it.

Have been here since last May, interned in a detention camp with my teammate Kreuzer. We have everything democratic ourselves. On account of the weather conditions, we have put up partitions in the barracks to keep from freezing. Mine is about large enough for a bed and a chair. Nothing rosy, you can bet, although we can buy almost everything we can wish for except alcoholic beverages.

Money has risen to almost ten-fold its worth. My former English friends do not seem to care and probably do not know of my being here. Oh, if this war would only end. A person becomes imbued with the idea that he is entirely superfluous here, being inactive, and from sheer desperation, I have taken up the Turkish language. Although I am not thinking of going that way, you can't tell what the future might bring.

Give my best to F.B. Alexander and S. Wallace Merrihew. Tell them all of me. Write me sometime and let that be soon. Yours truly (Signed) Otto Froitzheim. Interne Number: 1198.[2]

The editor of the *Pittsburg* [sic] *Press* urged local friends to write to Froitzheim at Lofthouse Park Camp and gave his address so they could do so.[3]

2. Guido von Georgevits: Aviator

Guido von Georgevits (Georgevitz) was an Austro-Hungarian subject, arrested at Kirkwall on the *S.S. United States* in October 1915. He was briefly interned at Edinburgh Castle before moving to Lofthouse Park and Douglas Camp on the Isle of Man. He had also received treatment at the German Hospital at Dalston for his foot, which had been amputated, and mentions his prosthesis being heavy and uncomfortable. Previously declared as unfit for any military service by the Austro-Hungarian Legation in Peking, he was discharged and allowed to return home by the Chinese Government. Von Georgevits was also described as an 'aviator', although he claimed in an appeal for release in November 1916 to have been a cavalry officer who had only flown twice as an observation officer.

His appeal for repatriation covers more than a dozen files and almost fifty pages in the documents held at The National Archives in Kew, and concerns issues of fitness for internment and military service as both civilian and officer. These include claims by von Georgevits that he was entitled to repatriation as a civilian unfit for military service, and as an officer entitled to transfer to a neutral country. He also questions why he was not being paid as a military officer if treated as a military prisoner. Proposals to secure the release of Guido von Georgevits were put forward by the Austro-Hungarian Government in 1916, which included the exchange of Ian Fraser Ross and Captain (Arthur) Stanley Wilson, M.P.

Despite the amputation of his foot and claims that his eyesight had deteriorated since his internment, Guido von Georgevits was still considered a threat. He was found not to be suitable for repatriation on further examination for release in December 1916.[4]

3. Count Eginhard Beissel von Gymnich: *S.S. Caserta* and Gibraltar

Count Eginhard Beissel von Gymnich was captured on the *S.S. Caserta* in August 1914 and interned at Gibraltar before being transferred to Lofthouse Park. The following extract is from his third appeal requesting his release on the grounds of being unfit for military service due to ill-health. The letter was dated 24 January 1916:

> I have seen the Medical Officer of the Camp as my health has become very much worse and has affected my eyes. I

may say in this connection that I have what is termed 'Aegyptian eye disease' which has now broken out afresh as my health is completely deranged. According to the opinion of one of the medical officers a fresh operation will have to be performed. In view of this, and I believe my health generally, my name has been included in the list of invalids to be repatriated. It appears to me that early repatriation is most essential and I would request you to be good enough to lay my case before the British government with a view to procure speedy repatriation as my condition is solely due to the conditions of imprisonment.

Count Eginhard Beissel von Gymnich was repatriated in February 1918.[6]

4. Dr Karl Hoch: *S.S. Hellig Olav* and Report from Boarding Officer

The following study relates to documents taken from Dr Karl Hoch when he was removed from the *S.S. Hellig Olav* in October 1915. The request by the Foreign Office for his status was forwarded to the Admiralty in January 1916. Casimir Caspar and Gerhard Bartram are also mentioned in the original request, with questions being raised regarding the documents stated to have been in the possession of these men who were arrested at the same time as Karl Hoch. The reply from the Boarding Officer to the Admiralty Port Officer at Kirkwall is transcribed as found.

> From Boarding Officer to Admiralty Port Officer, Kirkwall. Dated 25 October 1915.
>
> Dr Karl Hoch was landed this afternoon from the Danish Steamer 'Hellig Olaf' and handed over to the Military. He produced a letter dated Washington, 12th February addressed to Count Bernstorff, signed W.J. Bryan, Secretary of State, signed by Sir Cecil Spring Rice. In both these letters it is presumed he is not liable to arrest unless circumstances of a suspicious character arise, and provided he gives his parole not to take part in hostilities

against the Allies, not to serve in his capacity as a Physician.

At the first interrogation on the point of his being liable to military service, he replied, if compelled to serve, he would only do so in the capacity as a Doctor.

When questioned today as to why he did not produce these papers when interrogated at the previous interrogation, he replied he could not find them. The above papers are attached.

(Signed) F. Murduson Jones, Lieutenant R.N.V.R.

Admiral Commanding Orkneys and Shetlands, Longhope. Submitted. Report from Boarding Officer F. Buckeridge, Lieutenant-Commander, R.N.V.R., For Admiralty Port Officer.[7]

5. Frederick Wiener and Alfred Klapproth: Escapees

Frederick Wiener was described in the press as an Austrian officer who had settled in America and was on his way to Austria when captured at Kirkwall, Orkney Islands. He was interned briefly at Edinburgh Castle before being transferred to Lofthouse Park. He was said to have spoken fluent English with an American accent. Alfred Klapproth was a former officer on the Hamburg-Amerika Line (HAPAG) and a German naval reservist. Wiener's story was reported in the Swedish and German press, with Wiener giving a very lengthy account of their escape from Lofthouse in May 1915. After abandoning plans to dig a tunnel because it took too much time, Wiener and Klapproth decided to order 'sporting costumes' from the camp tailor. The idea was to look as British as possible. They were also able to buy gold to the value of £30. In planning their escape, they then asked to see the Censor, knowing that he would not be in his house at the time. As the story goes:

> From the censor's office we went to the guard-room, and I was able, thanks to my perfect command of English, to

give the impression that we were British officers. A few generalities about military matters to the men on duty completely dispelled any lingering suspicion they may have had, and we succeeded in escaping without any molestation, after climbing a park wall about eight [*sic*] metres high. Our first objective was Leeds, the nearest biggest town. There we bought two first-class tickets to Manchester, without, however, making use of them, but travelled instead third-class to Liverpool. Of course, we were industriously searched for in Manchester and thus gained valuable time.

We went to London from Liverpool, but did not venture to stay at an hotel, fearing discovery. We spent a week living over nights in restaurants, night cafes, and dance saloons. Meanwhile we read, with much satisfaction reports of our escape in the papers. As my description in these reports stated that I spoke English with an American accent, we now spoke only French, and gave ourselves out to be Frenchmen. Incidentally, we dropped the commander of the camp a post-card stating that we were no longer speaking 'American,' but French.

After various vain attempts to secure passage on a cargo boat, we were finally able to steal on board the Danish steamer Tomsk, where we hid in one of the holds. Crushed between bales and boxes, without food or drink, we spent four dreadful days and nights until we reached Copenhagen, where we again made passing acquaintance with a prison.

My companion has already gone to Germany, and I propose going on to Austria as soon as I am able to complete personal affairs.[8]

This story does not end here. Frederick Wiener was interned at Berne, Switzerland, having later deserted his unit in November 1915, and making his way to Switzerland on a false passport. In an official letter sent through the Swiss authorities in Berne, Frederick Wiener asked for the immediate chance to return to Lofthouse Park, as found in the following extract from a document held in The National Archives, Kew.

> My name is Frederick N. Wiener [...] having been doing my military service at Austria, but deserted in November last, entering Switzerland with a false passport. On account of this fact I have difficulties with the Swiss Authorities and am interned here at Berne at the Military Prison. I could gain my liberty by leaving Swiss territory and beg to ask you to give me the immediate chance to return to the Concentration Camp at Wakefield. Prompt attention to this matter will be very much appreciated. (Signed) Frederick N. Wiener. Address. Territorial-kommando 111, Berne.[9]

The unofficial response was that his 'unsolicited testimony to the advantage of internment in the U.K. is very gratifying, but M. Wiener has made his bed and must now lie in it.'[10] The official response was that the British authorities were not prepared to take any steps on his re-admission.[11]

Max Schnös:
Artist and Illustrator

Franz Götz (Baunach)

Michael Max Schnös was born on 20 September 1889 as one of four children in Baunach, a small community near Bamberg in Upper Franconia, a region in Northern Bavaria. His father operated a hand weaving business and also engaged in wood carving and gardening. Inspired by his family's creative practices and his own childhood experiments with clay and pastel chalks, Max Schnös chose an artistic path and attended the lithographic printing school Fruhauf in Bamberg. After three years of training, he worked in Nuremberg as a porcelain painter and gained further experiences at the print and graphic arts school Schneller. He specialised in printing, lithography and graphic design. In 1910, Schnös moved to Dresden where he earned a living with commercial design while attending arts classes in the evening and associating with the art salon Emil Richter.

Max Schnös wanted to expand his horizon further. From Dresden he made trips to Bohemia, then he relocated to Bremen and finally the young artist decided to go abroad. He advertised his skills to various studios in London and arranged a formal professional visit. He stayed at a hotel in the city centre and quickly got a first commission from a British professor who asked him to create botanical illustrations for a scientific publication. These were followed by Chinese drawings and lithographs. Schnös visited London's many galleries and art collections in the afternoons and continued to take art classes in the evening. He came into contact with British people and also began to appreciate the purity and clarity of English water-colour paintings, which he attributed to the high quality of paints and artist papers.

Caught out by the beginning of the First World War, Max Schnös, like many others, tried to return to Germany with the help of the German consulate, but leaving Britain proved to be impossible. As he states in his recollections, 'one day I received a very polite visit from Scotland Yard and was primed to prepare for my life in a camp for civilians' (translated from German).[1] Schnös was initially held at the Olympia show centre in London and then on the internment ship *Royal Edward*. In the same period, his brother Josef was killed at Verdun.

Fig. 8.1: Etching by Max Schnös of internees at London Olympia (Heimatmuseum Baunach).

In 1915, Max Schnös was moved to Lofthouse Park in Wakefield. Here too he was quickly recognised for his skills by fellow internees and camp authorities. His portraits were very popular and, according to the artist's own account, he was given permission to set up a studio space at Lofthouse, a privilege he had already enjoyed on the *Royal Edward*.

At Wakefield, Schnös ran an art school with courses for beginners and more advanced learners. The local Quakers supplied him and his pupils with the necessary equipment and materials. In his own work, the artist favoured topographical representations and employed a romantic-realist style. He was skilled in the use of different art media and printing techniques, and it can be assumed that he taught his methods and style to his Lofthouse Park students.

Max Schnös was transferred to the Isle of Man in 1918 and eventually returned to Germany via Scotland, England and the Netherlands in 1919. As an artist who tended to engage directly with his environment, he had painted and drawn a good number of portraits, internment scenes and camp views during his years of detention abroad. Some of these had travelled with Schnös, and he presented his British works in a temporary exhibition at the *Kunstverein* in Bamberg upon his return.

In the post-war period, Schnös continued to combine commercial design with his artistic interests, working and exhibiting mainly in Bamberg and vicinity. Always eager to develop his practice, he took time out to study at the Dresden Art Academy and various painting studios in Munich. In 1925 he went on a trip to Italy and, back in Bavaria, he became a co-founder of the group *Fränkische Künstler* (Artists in Franconia) and was involved in a number of exhibitions.

In 1928, Schnös moved with his wife and daughter to Lichtenfels where he converted a barn into a studio in 1933. From the 1930s onwards, Schnös extended his practice even further, and his frescoes can be found on buildings, cemeteries and churches. During the Second World War and the post-war years under American occupation, he stood in as a temporary art teacher. His design for a 1939/45 war memorial won a competition, and the work was realised by the town of Lichtenfels. Schnös continued to work and exhibit until the 1950s and acted as a nature conservation volunteer. He died after a long illness in 1964.

Fig. 8.2: Pencil sketch by Max Schnös of Lofthouse Park with the Pavilion in the background (Heimatmuseum Baunach).

Translated from German by Claudia Sternberg

Hermann Carl August Dahms

My grandfather, Hermann Dahms, was born on 22 May 1869 in the village of Pritter on the Island of Wollin, which is now in north-west Poland.

When he was a child, both of his parents died in a smallpox or flu epidemic. He went to live with his uncle, a farmer who was also a local *Bürger-meister* (mayor). His uncle treated him very badly, so he ran away to sea. He travelled widely on the merchant ships, eventually landing in Middlesbrough, where he married my Irish grandmother. He started a big family, of which my mother Mary 'Minna' Dahms was the youngest.

In 1914 he was taken into custody and interned at Alexandra Palace (No. 22689) and Lofthouse Park (No. 23956). He was an amateur artist, and my late mother told me he painted and drew as a hobby whilst in internment. He was released in April 1919 and, as far as I know, went back to work in the steelworks on Teesside. Hermann Dahms died in 1956.

See also index card for Dahms, Hermann. Source: ICRC Database (Geneva). Photograph and information courtesy of Chris Arundel (York).

Gustav Wiesener, No. 1639:
A Victim of Circumstances

Corinna Meiß (Goslar)

It is one of many German stories that unfolded in Britain and the British Empire during World War One: a German merchant living in London had to report to the nearest police station, was interned in a camp, was repatriated to Germany and had to live apart from his wife and children for many years. His company was liquidated; a life's work created in almost 20 years was destroyed and irrecoverably lost. It is the story of Gustav Georg Wiesener, who emigrated to Britain in 1888, where he lived for more than 40 years and where he died peacefully in the presence of his loved ones shortly before the beginning of the Second World War.

Gustav Georg Wiesener was born on 15 July 1870 as the third son of the master shoemaker Louis Wiesener (1837-1919) and his wife Johanna née Henno in Goslar. The Wieseners were part of Goslar's 'establishment'. The family had lived in Goslar since the 16th century.[1] Initially they made money as miners in Goslar's Rammelsberg ore mine (which is today a UNESCO world heritage site) and later as master shoemakers and leather traders, non-executive directors and managing directors of the Goslarian branch of Credit Reform Association,[2] which was established to protect its members against bad debts.

Gustav's uncle, Theodor Friedrich Wiesener (1845-97), emigrated to Sydney shortly after his nephew's birth. In Australia he made a name for himself as a watchmaker and inventor of optical instruments. In 1887 his eldest son, Frederick Abbey Wiesener (1877-1951), was sent to Goslar to stay with his uncle's family and attend (like all male

Wieseners at that time) the local grammar school, the *Rats-gymnasium*. After a year, Freddy returned to Australia accompanied by his older cousin Gustav Georg, who stayed in Sydney until the early 1890s.

By then Gustav's older brother Heinrich August (1865-1929) was a member of the joint board of the *Verband der Vereine Creditreform e.V.* and also in charge of its international expansion, for example in the United Kingdom. In 1898, his two younger brothers Otto (1868-1903) and Gustav Georg became the managing directors of the Credit Reform offices in Belfast and Glasgow, respectively.

As soon as he arrived in Glasgow, Gustav became a member of the German Lutheran Church community and of the honourable German Club, and was temporarily elected as their treasurer. He married a German pastor's daughter, Anny Rabe, in Wiesbaden in 1903. The couple had three children – one son and two daughters. In 1908, the family moved from Glasgow to Richmond.

Fig. 9.1: Gustav from Rotterdam to his future wife Anna, 2 November 1902 (Meiß Family Archive).

In 1903, The Credit Index and The Credit Reform Association merged. Until 1909, Gustav Georg was the Governing Director and principal shareholder of The Credit Index Ltd. offices in London, Birmingham, Manchester and Leeds. The company flourished, and Wiesener had more than 40 local employees. Just before World War One, he bought a house for himself and his family at Grange Road in Chiswick.

In April 1915, Gustav Georg was arrested and taken to Stratford, East London, in June of that year, where he remained for three months before being transferred to Lofthouse Park Camp. His company was taken over by the Public Trustee under the Trading with the Enemy Act of 1914. Because he suffered from locomotor ataxia, which affects the control over bodily movement, and needed special treatment, his wife wrote numerous letters to the Home Office to ask for his release. Preserved records reveal that her requests were noted, but the turmoil of war prevented his departure to Germany before December 1917. The following excerpts from Wiesener's extensive file held at The National Archives in Kew give an impression of the internee's and his family's ordeal during the First World War.[3]

28 October 1915. Letter of Gustav's wife Anny to the Under Secretary of State, Home Office, Whitehall, London:

Sir, I most respectfully appeal if you would possibly make inquiry into the case of my husband, Gustav George Wiesener. He is interned at Lofthouse Park Wakefield and has been for many weeks in the Hospital. About 3 or 4 weeks ago, I went to see him at W. I was quite alarmed at the bad state of his health. Since he got worse, I am dreadfully worried & very anxious to know if you perhaps might hasten his release. Yours respectfully (Mrs) Anny Wiesener

7. December 1915. Anny writes again to the Under Secretary of State at the Home Office:

Sir, I respectfully appeal to you to make a fresh inquiry about the case of my husband G.G. Wiesener 1639 interned at Lofthouse Park, Wakefield. Since your last reply the Health Commission has been to Wakefield & strongly recommended my husband for release, so has the Dr. of the Camp for the last 2 months. The illness of my husband requires special treatment, which he constantly had to undergo for the last 6 years. Of course in the Camp he cannot have the medical care he needs & in the consequence his already bad state of health has become worse. I most sincerely beg you, either to release him or at least remove him to Dalston Hospital, where he could have the necessary treatment for his illness, further delay might be serious. A gentleman, who went to Wakefield, to confer business matters with Mr Wiesener hardly recognized him as he seemed physically and mentally a wreck. After this visit he wrote to the medical officer & had a reply that my husband was on the list for discharge. Is it not possible for you to hasten his release or removal to Dalston? I am most respectfully (Mrs) A. Wiesener[4]

11 December 1915. M.L. Waller to the Commandant Lofthouse Park, Wakefield:

Medical Report on a case that is not of great urgency
To the Commandant, Lofthouse Park Camp Wakefield
Sir, I shall be obliged if your Medical Officer will kindly furnish a brief report on the following person in the space opposite the name. It is especially desired to know whether continued detention in the Camp will seriously affect his health, and if so, in what way. I am, Sir, your obedient Servant, M.L. Waller

18 December 1915. Letter to Anny Wiesener:

Madam, In reply to your letter of the 7th instant, I beg to inform you that a medical report as to your husband's health has been obtained, from which it appears that his health is not suffering from detention in the camp at Wakefield. Yours faithfully [unsigned copy]

5 January 1916. W.S. Gordon, Military Hospital, Lofthouse Park, Wakefield:

George Gustav Wiesener 1639 is suffering from Locomotor Ataxy. I recommend his repatriation and this was supported by Dr. Treadwell 'Home Office'. Between the dates of his recommendation and the order for repatriation coming through the prisoner has become worse and in my opinion was unable to undertake the journey to Dartford. He is confined to bed and feeble. He is wishful to go into a nursing home for a few weeks and would pay all expenses. I recommend this. He is quite unable to escape. (Signed) W.S. Gordon, Capt. R.A.M.C.

8 January 1916. War Office to M.L. Waller:

Dear Waller, I send you herewith a copy of a medical certificate received from Wakefield in regard to G.G. Wiesener. Is it correct that the order for his repatriation has been made and if so, what action should be taken in this case? Your sincerely [unsigned copy]

10 January 1916. Letter to Captain C.G. Huggins, D.P.W., War Office, Whitehall:

Dear Captain Huggins, Waller has handed to me your letter of the 8th inst., with reference to the prisoner of war George Gustav Wiesener. This man has been passed for repatriation, by the medical referee, and was included in the list of prisoners who were transferred from Wakefield to Stratford on the 31st ult., and registered on the 5th inst. He did not however turn up at Stratford with the rest of the party and we have no information from the Commandant as to why he was not sent. From the enclosure to your letter however it would appear that he was too ill to travel. There seems no reason, so far as we are concerned, why he should not enter a Nursing Home temporarily, assuming that he is too ill to undertake the journey to the German Hospital at Dalston. It would be convenient if the Commandant would let us know as soon as he is sufficiently recovered to be repatriated. Yours very truly [unsigned copy]

13 January 1916. War Office to M.L. Waller, Home Office:

Dear Waller, Thanks for yours of the 10th, P.W. 2508; with regard to Gustav Wiesener. This man has been removed from the Nursing Home at Wakefield for treatment at his own expense as his condition is rapidly deteriorating and he is now unfit to look after himself. Yours [unsigned copy]

7 March 1916. The Commandant, Place of Detention for Prisoners of War, Wakefield:

Sir, I am directed by the Secretary of State to refer to the case of prisoner of war Gustav Wiesener (No. 1639, Wakefield) who has been passed by the Medical Referee for repatriation, and was to have left this country early in January, and to enquire whether, in the opinion of your Medical Officer, he is now in a fit condition to undertake the journey to Germany. I am, Sir, Your obedient Servant

8 March 1916. Dr. Hime to the Commandant of Lofthouse Camp:

In reply to the enquiry of the Home Office, P.W. 2508, of 7/3/XVI as to whether the P.W. Gustav Wiesener (No. 1639, Wakefield) is in a fit condition to undertake the journey to Germany, I have the honour to report that: Wiesener is quite fit to undertake the journey.

9 March 1916. From the Commandant to the Under Secretary of State, Home Office:

Sir. In reply to your letters P.W. 7319 of the 4th March P.W. 17136 of the 6th March, and P.W. 2508 pf the 7th March I beg to attach reports of Dr. Hime, Medical Officer doing duty at the camp. I am, Sir, your obedient Servant.

Gustav Georg Wiesener was then transferred to the German Hospital at Dalston. From there, on 18 March 1916, the following letter by Hospital's Secretary Cochrane was sent to the Home Office in Whitehall:

Dear Mr Adams, I am in receipt of your yesterday's letter, and note therefrom that Prisoner of War GUSTAV GEORGE WIESENER, who was admitted into this Hospital on the 16th instant, has been passed for repatriation, and I shall not fail to let you know, if it is proposed to discharge WIESENER, before I hear further from you on the matter.

Gustav Wiesener stayed at Dalston Hospital until January 1917, and from there he was transferred to Alexandra Palace. Due to the ever-changing war situation, however, he was not repatriated to Germany until mid-December 1917.[5]

Fig. 9.2: Gustav Georg Wiesener with his children Gustav and Gertie.

Gustav Georg Wiesener's German wife and British-born children stayed in their home in Chiswick during the war, and only in 1923 was the family reunited there. Gustav never became a British citizen and, during World War I, he lost his German citizenship and became stateless. He had to apply for visas until the end of his life, for example for travels by him and his wife to health resorts in the warmer south of Europe.

Gustav Georg died on 28 September 1938 in Chiswick. His internment and that of his cousin-in-law George Kuttner (Knockaloe POW No. 88224) remained a taboo subject in their families. It is only in the last five years that the grandchildren have learned of their grandfathers' detention and repatriation. For questions about the experience and its impact it is unfortunately too late.

German Pork Butcher Migrants and the First World War

Karl-Heinz Wüstner (Ilshofen)

It is well known that throughout the nineteenth century, many Germans left their homes to seek their fortunes in the New World. Less well known, however, is the fact that many emigrants chose the new world of Great Britain and not North America as their land of opportunity.

At home, prospective migrants had faced serious social, political and economic hardship. Difficult conditions primarily affected people at the lower end of the income scale in rural society, especially in Southern Germany. They included a rapid growth in population and poor crop yields. Plant diseases like the potato and wine blights led to high food prices and had other adverse effect on the local economy. The political unrest of 1848 had made its presence felt too.[1] At the end of the 19th century, young men also chose emigration to avoid compulsory military service.[2]

At that time, the immense industrial boom in Britain offered these German emigrants encouraging prospects, and they were able to find their place in different economic sectors such as sugar refining, confectionery and general service.[3] Others, especially from Northern Germany, were involved in the textile and steel industries and dealt with cloth and machinery. In this way, German communities evolved in a number of British towns and cities; among them was, for example, 'Little Germany' in Bradford.[4]

Alongside the work and industries mentioned, many German migrants gained a foothold in one key trade. As pork butchers they achieved a high level of success using their considerable home-grown expertise.[5] Business opportunities had become apparent at the end of the 18th century when a number of young butchers from Hohenlohe, an agricultural area located in what is now north-eastern Baden-Württemberg, made their way across the Channel and settled in London and a few other big cities. They quickly realised a gap in the market: the slaughtering and processing of pigs into tasty meat products such as sausages, ham and other delicacies.

Fig. 10.1: The pork butcher shop of George William Schneider at Harpurhey (Image courtesy of Richard Ford, Netherton, England).

The young butchers were perfectly placed in terms of skill and customer experience. Their families back home not only owned shops, but many ran country inns and served meals based on all kinds of meat. Once settled in Britain, the newcomers created what might be regarded as the first take-away shops in which they also offered full, hot meals.[6] With their reasonably priced specialities and ready meals they met the demand of the time. As many British women were employed in mills and factories, they had little time to cook at home.[7] Soon they figured out that German pork butchers could provide a wholesome and satisfactory meal with little or no preparation.

The German butchers quickly became innovators in the market. Their acceptance and success was communicated to friends and relatives in their native country, thus fostering chain migration. Numerous girls and young women were part of the tide of emigration and supported the men as shop assistants, nursemaids and domestic servants. Not infrequently, these women were also solicited as prospective wives. Intermarriage between the different migrant families and the inclusion of relatives, neighbours and friends in their niche business led to the emergence of a tight network of transnational dimension. Family tracing shows that the majority of the German pork butchers in Britain originated from the Hohenlohe area, the small town of Künzelsau being at its centre. This town can be regarded as the main starting point of the pork butcher emigration movement.[8]

A second phase of butcher migration soon followed. These migrants were the sons of local farmers. Many had attended courses with the nearest butcher during the quiet winter period, and when the slaughtering took place at home, 'their mothers [...] would have salted, smoked and pickled some of the meat for the winter months'.[9] Skilled and well-equipped with the knowledge of the trade, this group of migrants entered the market in Britain from about the middle of the 19th century, and the young men were often followed by their sisters or other farmers' daughters. These, too, brought with them a wide range of food preparation, cooking and baking abilities as well as a rich fund of delightful and secret family recipes.

In order to satisfy the ever growing demand for cheap, basic food, even more butchers were needed. Via their strong family connections, the German migrants summoned more personnel from their home country. Thus, a third wave of those willing to migrate left Germany from about the 1870s onwards. This time the Hohenlohe families sent their youngest to Britain. Adolescents who had just left school went on their way at the age of fourteen or fifteen to be apprenticed by a German butcher in Britain or, in the case of the girls, to serve in a German family's home.[10] For over a hundred years, these Hohenlohe migrants managed to create a close knit family and business network that enabled them to occupy most positions in the trade with fellow countrymen.

Fig. 10.2: A juvenile immigrant to be apprenticed at a German pork butcher (Image courtesy of Manfred Kümmerer, Jungholz-hausen, Germany).

Apart from building and maintaining their own networks, many of the settled Germans played an active part in the areas where they lived. Such endeavours gave the

Hohenlohe butchers ample opportunity to integrate and play a bigger part in their wider communities. For instance, a member of the Schonhut family was elected to Rotherham Borough Council in 1898. Another member of the family became a choral conductor and was the headmaster of a school in the town.[11] Other examples include a man who joined a rifle club, and another who bred dogs and became a member of a dog breeders' society.[12] Many more were active in the church or in choirs, while others were credited for their commitment in the meat trades' union and charitable institutions.[13]

The outbreak of the First World War, however, was to become a major turning point for the German butchers. Growing suspicion turned into rejection, and many of the butchers and their families found themselves confronted with hostility and resentment, especially after the sinking of the Lusitania in May 1915, with attacks on shops taking place in towns and cities where there was a German presence.

Georg Friedrich Ziegler had two butcher shops in Wakefield. His shop at Northgate was attacked late one Sunday evening and his shop window broken. A bricklayer's labourer was later charged with wilful damage to the premises. Ziegler had been naturalised, but his public appeal in the *Wakefield Express* to be treated as a loyal citizen in 1914 had not been heard by all.[14]

Carl and Paul Andrassy were also prominent butchers in the area. Their status in 1914 was that of 'enemy aliens' and both men were interned at Lofthouse Park Camp.[15] Some of the other butchers interned at Lofthouse were Georg Kuch of Frizinghall, Bradford,[16] Karl Rohn from Rothwell[17] and Johann Friedrich Leonhard Waldmann of Chesterfield. The three men were later transferred to Knockaloe Camp on the Isle of Man. Johann Waldmann is also known as Fredrick Waldman or Leonhard Wald-

mann in some accounts.[18] Waldmann was born at Künzelsau on 30 January 1871.[19] His application for emigration
was approved by the authorities on 16 December 1887,
when he was only 16 years old.[20] Thus he belonged to the
group previously described as the third wave of migrants
from Hohenlohe.

Entries in the Künzelsau registers, held at the local
archives, show that the emigrants had to give up their
Württemberg nationality when they wanted to leave.
Waldmann's entry states, in translation: 'in consequence of
the decree of the regal government of the Jagst district on
15th December 1887 for the purpose of emigration to
North America No. 7675, released from Württemberg
citizenship.' This means that the former citizens of
Württemberg became stateless subjects. They no longer
possessed a German nationality and had no legal
protection or back-up. Once in Britain, it took them
several years before they were able to apply for
naturalisation in their chosen country of residence.

Fig. 10.3: Civil registry entry for Johann Friedrich Leonhard
Waldmann, 1871-1918 (Stadtarchiv Künzelsau).

Interestingly, Leonhard Waldmann had originally applied
to emigrate to North America. Like many others, he first
went to England, probably in order to earn and save some
money before starting the second part of his journey.
Waldmann died in Knockaloe Camp on 15 July 1918 at the
age of 47.[21] He had suffered chest and lung problems. His
official cause of death is recorded as 'Mediastinal tumour
and bronchiectasis'.[22]

Karl Rohn worked for a pork butcher named Frederick
Keitel at his shop in Rothwell, near Leeds. His sister Louisa

was employed as a domestic servant. Patricia Richardson, a descendant of Louisa Rohn, has explored the family story:

> Karl Rohn, known as Charlie, came over to England as a 17-year-old boy in 1907. He worked for Keitels until the First World War. He was not naturalised so he was sent to a prison in Lofthouse, a small town near Rothwell. He was classed as a risk to national security. At the end of each day Fred Keitel would take to the prison any leftover produce, pork pies etc. that had not been sold in the shop that day for the inmates. Karl was later sent to Knockaloe prisoner of war camp in the Isle of Man. After the war he never forgave the British for not trusting him so he emigrated to America.[23]

Patricia Richardson adds:

> There was no trouble with the Keitels during the First World War. Apparently the coal miners liked Keitel's pork pies very much, saying they were the best they had ever tasted. They liked to have them for their 'snap' – this is the local slang word for their meal break – and took them down the pit to eat. Therefore Keitels had no trouble as it was a mining community.[24]

Finally, I return to Georg Friedrich Ziegler who had come to England in 1899 with only ten shillings in his pocket. In April 1905, he asked his father to send him 3,000 Marks because he wanted to buy his own shop in Wakefield.[25] Ziegler obtained British citizenship in 1911 and during the First World War served in the British Army as a sergeant cook. He later joined the West Riding Special Constabulary, attaining the rank of Assistant Commander with twenty years of service. In 1965, George Ziegler was honoured as one of Wakefield's 'most successful businessmen.'[26] By then Ziegler was senior chairman of Associated Dairies & Farm Stores Ltd. The business had 59 retail pork shops in many towns between Sheffield and Newcastle, 28 confectionery shops and cafés in Leeds and Bradford, plus a bakery in Leeds and cheese factories at Birstwith, near Harrogate, and Sowerby Bridge. The firm also had a bacon factory near Lofthouse and became one of the predecessors of today's ASDA supermarket chain. George Frederick Ziegler surely was an outstanding and splendid example of the energetic and industrious, but always humble Hohenlohe immigrant.

Fig. 10.4: George Frederick Ziegler giving soup to school children in the interwar years (image courtesy of Family Gerhard Leidig, Hörlebach, Germany).

Author's note: I would like to thank David Stowe for assistance with source material and information in the ICRC Database and Ruth Allison and Claudia Sternberg for their comments on the text.

Time Stands Still in Yorkshire: Paul Cohen-Portheim at Lofthouse Park

Claudia Sternberg (Leeds)

> My flat and my belongings were in France, my relations in Austria and Germany, I myself with summer clothes, painting materials, and £10 in an England one could not leave.
>
> Paul Cohen-Portheim (1931)[1]

The cosmopolitan painter and writer Paul Cohen-Portheim is the most widely known chronicler of life at Lofthouse Park Camp. His English-language memoir, *Time Stood Still: My Internment in England 1914-1918*, was published in London in 1931 and relates the author's experiences as an 'enemy alien' after the start of the First World War. In his detailed and considered account, Cohen-Portheim describes the time between his registration and arrest, his internment at Knockaloe on the Isle of Man and at Lofthouse Park, and his release to the Netherlands in February 1918. The book closes with his return to Berlin after the Armistice, a city he finds full of half-starved people, invalids and beggars as well as sailors and agitators embroiled in revolutionary upheaval.

Paul Heinrich Cohen-Portheim was born on 22 March 1879 in Berlin as one of three children to Ernst Cohen and Jenny Cohen, née von Portheim. His Jewish middle-class background provided him with a good education, proficiency in multiple languages and the freedom to engage in artistic and intellectual pursuits at home and abroad. In the 1910s he lived in Paris, but regularly travelled to the

South of England to paint. He was well connected to higher circles of British society and had links with the international opera scene in London.

Like many Anglophiles, Paul Cohen (as he would then probably have been known) was caught unawares by the downturn in British German relations and the loss of free movement across Europe which he and others had enjoyed before the war. The changed circumstances not only imposed restrictions, but increasingly affected social interactions:

> Once more registration, and now one was definitely treated as a suspect, humiliating questions were put, references demanded, statements doubted. I had ceased to see people, my friends were in the army, some families already in mourning; they could not really want to see me even if they were polite enough to say so.[2]

In May 1915, Cohen-Portheim was finally arrested and joined other men on their journey from Stratford in East London to the Isle of Man. The trip was full of contradictions:

> We were marched through the streets to the station, flanked by soldiers with drawn bayonets. The population must have known this was due, for in spite of the early hour the streets were full of a hostile crowd. The memory of a recent Zeppelin raid was fresh with them; this must have appeared to them as a sort of revenge. They spat, they insulted, they jeered, they threw things. I had been so utterly unprepared for this that I could hardly believe it was happening.[3]

> [...] a train composed of very comfortable corridor-carriages drew up, with plenty of room for everyone, and a very good lunch served by quite civilian and civil waiters (there is a connection between these adjectives). Man is a strange and illogical animal at any time, but this quick change was enough to make one feel slightly hysterical.[4]

Left without alternatives, Cohen-Portheim adjusted to camp life at Knockaloe and began to appreciate the social mix of internees and their diverse background. But early on he had been urged to request a transfer to another, 'better' camp:

> What would this new place be like? Discussions had begun again, some of the men knew all about it. It would be a marvellous place. Lofthouse Park was its name, not Wakefield, that was only the nearest city, but Lofthouse Park was a large estate with a mansion on it. Would we live in real rooms? Not only that, but everyone had a room to himself, there were gardens and a park, there was – one had read in the papers – a golf course. A gentlemen's camp, you understand, they said.[5]

When the small group of men arrived in Yorkshire, however, their expectations were not met:

> We got out of the train, walked through steep streets. There was a large church – I thought of the Vicar of Wakefield. More steep streets, workmen's cottages in serried rows, a smoky sky, a stiff climb, and then – barbed wire once more. Another gate, another camp.[6]

Apart from charging internees ten shillings a week 'for the privilege of being there',[7] Lofthouse Park did offer some gentlemanly amenities, at least in the earlier years:

> At that time, in 1915, prisoners were allowed to buy most things they could pay for, and the tradesmen of the neighbouring town of Leeds did not scruple to take advantage of that fact. When a new batch of prisoners arrived, a Leeds firm sent up a cart full of the furnishings that might be required, and thus I became possessed of a camp bed, stuff for curtains, and even a tin jug and basin. [...] Once a week a firm of Leeds hosiers displayed their goods in the camp and they must have made a lot of money, for here in Wakefield everyone was decently and conventionally clad, as gentlemen should be.[8]

Time Stood Still provides insight into the life and make-up of Lofthouse Park, which brought together about 1,500 clerks, colonial administrators, academics, businessmen, sportsmen, musicians, actors, aristocrats and the odd adventurer. Cohen-Portheim observed his fellow internees mostly from a distance and exercised his own mind through reading and writing. He also contributed to the theatrical life in the camp by putting up a few shows and designing the costumes and scenery.

As was the case in many all-male WWI camps, female stage roles had to be filled with male performers. Cohen-Portheim, who also includes a chapter on sexuality in his book, reflects on questions of gender within and without the camp:

> [...] our greatest actress, really remarkable in tragic parts, was originally very much of an athlete. He [...] looked bursting with health, and was very good at and enthusiastic about all games. I don't know how he ever came to be cast for a female part, but he was a success from the start and later on really powerful. [....] 'Es ist der Geist, der sich den Körper baut' (It is the spirit which builds itself its body) is a famous saying of Schiller's, the truth of which impressed me then; for as that youth became more and more of what I do not hesitate to call a great actress of the stage, he also became more and more feminine off the stage [...]. [...] This was a case of quite exceptional futility of effort. For what could all this mean for [him and some of the others] in later life? [...] I have often wondered how they fared when they returned to normal life, to their offices or studies?[9]

Unlike other internees who enjoyed the occasional guarded walks outside the perimeters of the camp, Cohen-Portheim refrained from exposing himself to the outside world. He turned to introspection and spiritual experiments, which were aided, paradoxically, by worsening conditions in the camp caused by war-time shortages, dried up means and new restrictions on parcels and visitors:

The years of internment, the physical privations were
having their effect on me as on everybody. I felt rather
weak, I had got very thin, I had to rest a good deal if I
wanted to get any work done. But there were compen-
sations, for one's sensibility seemed to increase with the
decrease of one's physical strength.[10]

In an autobiographical sketch which predates *Time Stood
Still*, Cohen-Portheim states that he, as a writer, 'was born
in the prisoners' camp of Wakefield Jorkshire [*sic*], England, roughly in the year 1917' (translated from German).[11]
He continues:

Wakefield was a peculiar cradle, and I would write a book
about it if I assumed that the world, or a part thereof,
were interested. I do not believe this is the case, however,
because all the people I met after leaving this penal institution showed not the slightest wish to find out more
about it; instead, they eagerly related their own –
undoubtedly much more important – experiences in great
detail. (translated from German)[12]

Despite his own misgivings, Cohen-Portheim realised this
project, but notably *Time Stood Still* became the author's
only book written in English and not initially in German,
as had been the case with his other works.

Until today, Cohen-Portheim remains a central voice
for our understanding of Lofthouse Park. But the author
also stands out as an important commentator on civilian
internment more generally. *Time Stood Still* makes tangible
the psychological and physical impact of alienism, encampment and the loss of freedom, means and autonomy. It
shows how personal and political uncertainty, a permanent
lack of privacy, imposed idleness, the threat of reprisals
and eventually 'hunger and the fear of hunger'[13] affected
individual and group behaviour. It also provides examples
of the ways in which self-initiated work, creativity and
education alleviated and counteracted a sense of 'helpless
interdependency'[14] and '*complete futility*'.[15]

Fig. 11.1: Paul Cohen-Portheim's interwar books were popular in German and in translation (photograph: Claudia Sternberg).

After the war, Cohen-Portheim resumed his itinerant life-style and worked across countries and languages as a foreign correspondent, translator and author of short and long non-fiction. His monographs about France, England and London as well as about Europe before and after the First World War are informed and opinion-rich analyses of the complexities of transnational connections and national differences. Cohen-Portheim's prose can be Eurocentric, metropolitan and even imperial – in line with his time, class and upbringing; on other occasions, however, the writing reflects the discerning mindset of the cosmopolitan and even a planetary consciousness. From the vantage point of the 1920s, the author also presciently muses about the relationship between England and Europe:

> Since the War England has been going her own way more than ever, and that way has been taking her far from the Continent: she has become almost a stranger to Europe, while Europe has almost dropped out of her field of view. […] In spite of all the hatred and all the quarrels between the continental nations the War and its aftermath have drawn them together and made them much more like each other; they have a common destiny but England has

its own, and that is the deep ground of their mutual estrangement.[16]

After becoming seriously ill during his travels to Spain and Portugal, Paul Cohen-Portheim died in France on 6 October 1932. Only a few months later, National Socialism took firm hold in Germany and eventually Austria, leading to the Second World War and the Holocaust. Had he lived to an older age, Cohen-Portheim might have shared the fate of his brother-in-law Siegbert Lachmann, born in 1865, and his cousin Paula Mühsam, née Guttentag, born in 1876, who were deported from Berlin to Theresienstadt where they died in 1943. Paula Mühsam's son Heinrich, born in 1900, survived the ghetto and was murdered in Auschwitz in 1944.[17]

Civilian internment at Lofthouse Park Camp compared favourably with experiences at other First World War camps. Neither its conditions nor purpose bore any resemblance to the system of concentration and extermination camps established by Nazi Germany during the Second World War. These important differences notwithstanding, Paul Cohen-Portheim captured two core principles of any form of encampment: to strip people of their individuality and construct a collective of undesirables.

> What was horrible was that one had ceased to be an individual and had become a number. One ceased to be oneself, an individual free to act and responsible for his actions and for his actions alone. What I mean when I say 'I suddenly realized what had happened,' is that I realized that I was no longer I, an entity, but a small particle of a whole, of an undesired community, called The Camp.[18]

Author's note: I thank Corinna Meiß, Beth Arscott and Alix Nicolas for their support with Cohen-Portheim's family history and Frank Schütz at the Berlinische Galerie for access to his autobiographical sketch.

Lager-Bote:
The Camp Magazine
of Lofthouse Park

Emily Bagshaw (Leeds)[1]

For the several hundred thousands of internees across the world, internment was a time that had to be filled.[2] As the men gradually began to establish routines for their everyday life, other opportunities began to present themselves and made the monotony of camp life more bearable. One common activity in prisoner-of-war and internment camps alike was to produce a magazine, written and published within the camp by the inmates. Large internment camps like Knockaloe and Douglas on the Isle of Man had more than one magazine in circulation; smaller camps had just one. The name of Lofthouse Park's camp magazine was *Lager-Bote* (Camp Messenger).

For the internees, the camp magazine provided a platform to share views and experiences with each other. It was also an outlet for the men to express themselves creatively by writing poems and stories. Furthermore, it was a useful source of information. The internees were able to advertise their professional skills through dedicated advertisement pages. Examples of this are to be seen on the back pages, with tailors, masseurs, hairdressers, dentists and language tutors offering their services. Hut numbers and working hours were published in order for other internees to find them. The table on the following page shows a sample list of some of the names and services on offer.

Name	Services	Camp
F.M. Bajohr	Dentist	North
Arnold Fuchs	Tailor	North
W. C. Hiene	Sculptor	North
R. Hoffmann	Shaving Salon	North
Walter Mann	Dentist	West
L. Patigler	Masseur	-
P. Schwarzlose	English Lessons	South
Emil Dauber	Tailor	North
FW Herbert	Turkish Lessons	North
I. Hieringer	Carpenter	North
Adolf Lindner	Portrait Painter	South
W. G. Mollman	Tailor	South
G. Schab	French Lessons	South
G. Selber	Watchmaker	South

Source: *Lage-Bote*, February and March 1916.

Two editions of *Lager-Bote* still exist today. They were published half a month apart, on 15 February and 1 March 1916. Both editions contain articles which provide insights into the life in the camp and how the men coped with it. One article is entitled 'Stacheldrahtkrankheit' (Barbed Wire Disease) and describes how being imprisoned can lead to mental deterioration, which can manifest in an decreasing ability to concentrate when reading.[3] It is poignant to read that the men were aware of their own struggle to remain sane.

A two-part article by Dr. B. relays the supervised walks that the men took outside of the camp, and refers to them as a *Scheinfreiheit*, which can be translated as 'sham freedom' or 'pretend freedom'.[4] The walks are described as liberating on the one hand, because they gave the men a sense of normality and the prospect of their future freedom, but as 'sham' on the other, because they only gave an illusion of the freedom that the men were longing for as they remained trapped in the camp for an uncertain length of time. The author of the article explains that people were constantly dreaming of freedom, and of the train that would eventually take them away from the camp, Wakefield and Yorkshire, never to return again.

Fig. 12.1: Title page of the first issue of *Lager-Bote*, 15 February 1916 (Staats- und Universitätsbibliothek Bremen).

Articles like that by Dr. B. give an indication of the frustration that the men felt at being imprisoned and brings their
thoughts to life through their own words, written and published at the time of internment. In terms of immediacy
these texts differ from the reflective and perhaps more
objective accounts written in retrospect, such as Paul
Cohen-Portheim's memoir *Time Stood Still*, published in
1931.

The magazines also demonstrate the range of pursuits
that the men established during their internment. The first
page of the first edition of *Lager-Bote* provides a 'programme of the week', with details of theatre productions
and concerts. The advertisements at the back of both
editions display activities the men could get involved in, as
well as the different services that were available and the
number of professions – medical, artisanal or educational
– that some of the men were still able to practise during
their internment. The magazines are therefore a vital
demonstration of how the men proactively filled their time
in the camp.

One of the major undertakings of camp life was the
theatre, which Lofthouse chronicler Cohen-Portheim was
also involved in, directing and producing several of the
plays which were staged in Lofthouse Park. In his book, he
recalls his first theatrical venture in the camp, for which
the costumes were ordered from Poiret in Paris, highlighting the importance of the theatre to the internees.[5]
Both *Lager-Bote* issues give insights into the camp theatre,
with several reviews being published as well as advertisements for future productions. These announcements show
that the plays were performed separately in the South,
North and West Camp, and that each compound had its
own theatre company, which is also reviewed alongside the
plays.

Fig. 12.2: A South Camp comedy production 'on tour' in Lofthouse Park. *Lager-Bote*, Issue 1, 15 February 1916, p. 2 (Staats- und Universitätsbibliothek Bremen).

The plays discussed in the magazine are mainly comedies, suggesting that a central aim was to provide light relief and amusement. The number of pages dedicated to the theatre shows that it was highly valued and of great interest to the internees; the focus also demonstrates that the men managed to provide their own entertainment throughout their internment.

A compelling article written by Fritz Draeger details how a lack of physical exercise leads to mental deterioration. The author advocates that physical activity and movement are essential to keep fit and healthy.[6] His article comes across as a lecture to his readers, prompting them to engage in sports and gymnastics in particular to combat low moods and other mental health issues.

Apart from the walks, physical activity and sport is not covered in the camp magazine, although tennis courts and other fitness opportunities were available. According to Cohen-Portheim, no sports took place in the 'colonial' South Camp, but a great deal of drinking did.[7] In the advertisement section of the magazine, however, reference is made to two 'English Billards' (billiard tables) located in what is referred to as the *Turnhalle* (gymnasium) of the

South Camp. It appears that much of the physical activity which took place in the camp was through manual labour, and that a lot of the activities that were introduced to tackle boredom were intellectual rather than physical. For those like Fritz Draeger, however, who recognised the benefits of sport and exercise for mental wellbeing, exercising was of great importance. A similar spirit is also evident in the articles about the guarded walks outside the camp and L. Patigler's advertisement for baths, massages and *Koerperausbildung* (physical education).

Fig. 12.3: L. Patigler's health and wellbeing offer. *Lager-Bote*, Issue 1, 15 February 1916, p. 11 (Staats- und Universitätsbibliothek Bremen).

Another significant aspect of the magazine is the openness with which the experiences were presented. Given that all of the internees' correspondence with family members, acquaintances and business relations was filtered by censors, it is interesting to note that *Lager-Bote* shows no obvious signs of external editorship. As Rainer Pöppinghege has suggested, censors may have found it harder to understand the literary language of edited publications than the more familiar colloquialisms used in letters, and therefore the censorship of camp magazines was not too strong.[8]

We do not know if *Lager-Bote* was censored, but upon reading the magazines, it is unlikely that much robust censorship had been applied or was considered necessary. Frustration with camp life is openly addressed; the introductory editorial of the first issue talks about the 'painful fact [...] that so many precious years of our lives, and who knows how many, are filled with such trivial outer experience, that they're of no more value to us than a few weeks in freedom are' (translated from German).[9] The next article, written by North Camp internee Fritz Grah, entitled 'Probleme' (Problems), lists some of the struggles of camp life, including anxiety and seclusion.[10]

Sandwiched between the two editorial contributions is a poem credited to H.T. In contrast to the wordiness of the prose articles, 'Huetten' (Huts) uses the economy of poetic language to relate the bleakness of the uniform barracks to a life that is perceived as empty and without purpose.[11]

Huetten

Ihr Huetten kahl, ein nuechtern Dorf der Not
Zu duestrem Zweck von fremder Hand erbaut,
Wie's euch ein totes Ebenmass gebot,
Von froher Himmel Weite selten ueberblaut.

Ihr herbergt teilnamslos [*sic*] – auf welche Zeit?
Ein Menschenknaeul, von Willkuers Narrenspiel
Aus tausend Erdenwinkeln hergeschneit
Zu einem Leben, leer und ohne Ziel.

Hat euch des Nebels gierer Schlund verschluckt
Mit all' dem Tatentraum, der drinnen lacht,
So steht ihr wie von bleicher Angst geduckt,
Als ob ein hartes Schicksal euren First bewacht.

The camp magazines also display a sense of hope and pragmatism. In the second issue of *Lager-Bote*, Dr Busse reminds the internees of the importance of work as a means to distract themselves and counter despair.[12] Writing articles and preparing the magazine for printing constituted the kind of work that was possible within the confines of an internment camp. A humorous poem in Issue 1 of *Lager-Bote* states as the magazine's objective – for producers and readers alike: 'if it brings us happy hours through word and image [...] then its purpose is fulfilled' (translated from German).[13]

It is important to acknowledge, however, that only two issues of *Lager-Bote* have survived in public archives, and in the absence of others, it cannot be determined to what extent this medium became popular in Lofthouse Park. If only two magazines were ever published, the question remains as to why such a helpful means of communication was discontinued while camp magazines flourished elsewhere. This open question notwithstanding, the two existing issues still contain sufficient material to illustrate how camp life was structured and organised, and how the men found ways to express themselves during their internment. In this respect, *Lager-Bote* provides a useful snapshot of Lofthouse Park in 1916, including the hopes and concerns of the men interned there.

Hermann J. Held and Lofthouse Park Camp University

Henning Ibs (Meldorf)[1]

Mobility, exchanges and transnational appointments have long characterised European university education and research culture. They were also common in the decades before 1914. It is hardly surprising, therefore, that a good number of professors, lecturers and students were among the civilian internees at Lofthouse Park and other camps. One of them was Hermann J. Held, whose later career as a legal scholar at Kiel University in Northern Germany spanned more than forty years. He and other academics were instrumental in offering educational opportunities to fellow internees during the time of detention. Learning enriched the men personally and intellectually, but it also helped, like musical and theatrical activities, to ward off boredom and reduce anxiety.

Hermann Held was born in 1890 in Freiburg, Southern Germany, where he grew up with his three sisters in a well-to-do middle class family. During his childhood and adolescence, he experienced the liberal climate of the Baden region and the artistically minded Catholic environment provided by his parents. It was by no means clear that Held would turn to jurisprudence after his *Abitur* (A-levels); he also considered a career as a singer, but did not pursue this option because his parents insisted on a respectable education.

From autumn 1910, Held read law at Albert-Ludwigs-University in his home town Freiburg and also spent one semester at Ruprecht-Karls-University in Heidelberg. He was a good and diligent student who was keen to reach beyond the narrow confines of his field. While still a taught student, Held already occupied himself with a potential doctoral project on 'International Law in the Russo-Japanese War'. To study this topic further and round out his knowledge in the area of international law, Held went on a research trip to the University of Cambridge in 1912. Upon his return, he became private assistant to Professor Dr. Woldemar von Rohland (1850-1936) and Kustos (custodian) of the School of Law library in Freiburg.

In the summer of 1914, Held wanted to complete his doctoral thesis. For this purpose, he needed specialist literature, mainly written in English, which he could access at the Squire Library in Cambridge and the British Museum Foreign Office Library in London. He was also hoping to get support from Professor Dr. Lassa Oppenheim (1858-1919), a German expert on international law who taught at Cambridge and had been contacted by another researcher at Freiburg on Held's behalf. Driven by his desire to do research abroad, Held took a period of leave and travelled to England in July 1914. He did so despite mounting tensions between the European powers that followed on from the assassination of Archduke Franz Ferdinand in Sarajevo on 28 June 1914.

Alongside working on his thesis, Hermann Held had intended to attend lectures in Cambridge during the Michaelmas term that would start on 15 October 1914, but this plan did not come to fruition. After the outbreak of war between Britain and Germany on 4 August, Held's attempt to return home failed. It had been practice at the time to grant 'enemy' nationals a short time to leave the country. The Aliens Restriction Order of 5 August 1914 permitted Germans in Britain to depart via specified ports by 10 August. As Held wrote in a legal reference work published in 1929, this caused

> thousands and particularly the best among the *Auslands-deutschen* [German expatriates] to rely on the official

permission to leave and proceed hurriedly and un-
suspectingly to the designated ports for embarkation,
without special preparation and precautions. (translated
from German)[2]

According to Held's publication, however, a Secret Notice
had been issued to 'Shipping Companies, Masters of Ships,
and all other whom it may concern' that restricted the
Order to a considerable degree. Held wrote that the Notice
stipulated that, from 6 August onwards, no person,
irrespective of nationality, could enter or leave the country
without the permission of a *Fremdenaufsichtsbeamten* (civil
servant for aliens affairs). Enemy aliens in particular were
only allowed to leave with the written consent of a
Staatssekretär (senior official/undersecretary). No one was
in the possession of such permission, nor – had the content of the Notice been widely known – would there have
been sufficient time to obtain one. Thus the enemy
civilians, in the majority Germans, were 'an easy prey for
the English authorities' (translated from German)[3] and
arrested in large numbers in the ports. Held was among
those, but because there were not yet enough camps for
internment, he was released to continue his studies, albeit
as a registered alien and thus under police surveillance.

After three months, on 21 October 1914, Held was interned at Lofthouse Park and his belongings were confiscated, including his nearly completed doctoral thesis. He
was to remain in internment for four and a half years until
March 1919, affording some of the modest amenities the
gentlemen's camp near Wakefield offered.

Life in the camp was monotonous; one day was like any
other. The internees were able to occupy themselves with
sport, crafts, games, gymnastics, gardening and walks
around the camp, but in the longer term these activities did
not provide sufficient challenges for the mind. Interned
university professors, lecturers and other academics began
to organise a diverse programme of talks and lectures.[4]

Fig. 13.1: Hermann J. Held (third from the right) and fellow internees at Lofthouse Park, summer 1915 or 1916.

Held contributed enthusiastically to the educational programme. One the one hand, he too wanted to escape the intellectual isolation of the camp, on the other hand teaching others came naturally to him. At the beginning of 1915, he started his comprehensive teaching activity covering almost all areas of legal studies. He advertised his sessions with handwritten notices, for example for a lecture entitled 'Outline of the English Constitution of the Courts and Criminal Proceedings' (Fig. 13.2).

Held started out with an introduction to legal studies, followed by series of lectures on the British courts system, German merchant shipping law, international law and insurance law. In response to his lectures on British criminal law and proceedings, Held received the following note of thanks from his students:

> We feel the need to express our sincere gratitude for your constructive undertaking. We found the way in which you combined purely theoretical considerations with the discussion of practical examples particularly instructive and beneficial.[5]

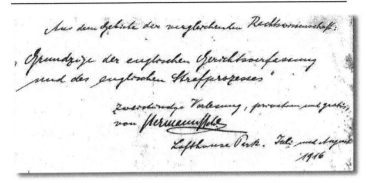

Fig. 13.2: Invitation to attend Hermann Held's 'private and free' two-hour law lectures, July and August 1916.

In the summer of 1917, the educational activities at Lofthouse Park were formalised as 'advanced academic training courses', offered within the framework of an organised *Lagerhochschule* or camp university. The historian Professor Dr. Hermann Waetjen (1876-1944) from Karlsruhe acted as *Rektor* (vice-chancellor). The first semester began on 1 October 1917 with an opening ceremony; teaching commenced on the following day. Courses ran from Mondays to Saturdays with five sessions of 45 minutes per day. Lessons started at 10.30am and finished, after an extended lunch break, at 4.45pm. Of roughly 1,500 internees in the camp, 651 had enrolled as students. 67 lecturers read 140 hours a week.

Almost all courses were well attended until Christmas 1917. When activities resumed two weeks after the Christmas holidays, external circumstances had changed. The lengthy and often interrupted negotiations between Germany and Britain about the exchange of civilians seemed to have achieved a tangible result at last. The following comment was included in the Lofthouse Park *Vorlesungsverzeichnis* (course programme):

The renewed hope for a general or at least extensive exchange brought to our lives and work a restlessness which adversely affected the concentration of most; it even robbed some of their ability to focus altogether. Even after the final lists had been published, a nervousness persisted – among those who were preoccupied with their imminent departure and no less among those who had to stay and were bitterly disappointed. (translated from German)[6]

Due to the exchange of internees, the camp university had lost its *Rektor* and 33 of its lecturers, but academic activities continued. Wherever possible, courses were taken over and completed by someone else. The first semester officially ended, without any special ceremonies, on 30 March 1918. Quite a few courses carried on until May because the instructors had not finished delivering their material.

During the summer of 1918, no courses were on offer at Lofthouse. Internees occupied themselves with vegetable gardening, which had become more indispensable each year as an additional food source. Those who did not want to interrupt their studies were able to use a small library of about 600 scholarly books for a modest fee. The library's collection was compiled from privately owned volumes and accessible in a reading room.

The second four-month-long semester began on 16 September 1918. Not only had the number of lecturers and students decreased after the releases, but the choice of courses had also become smaller. Since a good sum had been accumulated through fees in the previous semester, the courses were now offered for free. It was still required, however, to sign up in the office.

Lectures and seminars at the camp university covered the following subject areas: Business and Law, Modern Languages (eleven languages ranging from English and French to Arabic and Ukrainian), Technology (e.g. ferroconcrete construction or the use of geometry in surveying),

Science (e.g. chemical processes in everyday life or animal breeding), Humanities (e.g. Eastern Religions, English Prose Fiction since Dickens or Modern German Literature). Hermann Held taught on 'Selected Topics of British and American Law' and 'Problems of International Law' and also offered tutorials on civil and criminal court procedure.

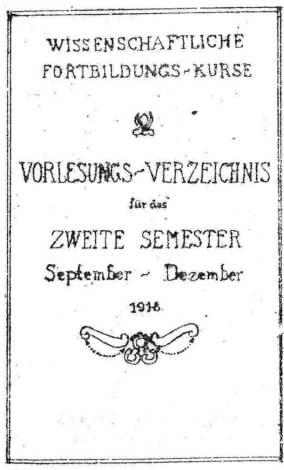

Fig. 13.3: Title page of the course offer for Semester Two, September-December 1918.

Lofthouse Park students were able to obtain written confirmation for their attendance and participation. This was meant to give attendees, especially those who had been in education when the war broke out, the chance to present certificates for credit when they resumed their studies in Germany and compensate them for the time lost. It appears, however, that the hopes attached to these certificates remained largely unfulfilled. Nonetheless, Held and his students accomplished quite a lot under the circumstances, and even when a third semester, planned for January to April 1919, did not materialise, he continued to hold private sessions. One of his small-group tutees was Herr Casparius from Berlin, who wrote to Held on 12 January 1920:

> Your private lessons were of utmost importance to me. From February 1918 to March 1919 you taught me and three other gentlemen on a daily basis in the following subjects: applied civil law (with eleven written assignments), applied criminal law (with eight assignments), merchant shipping law, exchange and cheque law and private insurance law.[7]

Apparently, Held had set Casparius up well for his law studies after the war.

The German government had already put a ceasefire request to US-President Woodrow Wilson on 4 October 1918, but hostilities did not end until 11 November 1918. As late as October 1918, Held and the other remaining internees had been moved to Knockaloe on the Isle of Man while Lofthouse Park was converted to a military prisoners-of-war camp for officers. It remains unclear whether any of the teaching planned for the third semester took place on the Isle of Man. In light of the circumstances, which were known to the internees, and an impending armistice, agitation and excitement might have been too great to return to business as usual. Held continued to teach privately, however, and kept himself and his students occupied at a time of guarded anticipation. Finally, on 28 March 1919, Held and many others were released from British internment and he travelled to Freiburg by way of Rotterdam.

Hermann Held returned home physically and mentally exhausted. After a short period of recovery, he began to write a new doctoral thesis in which he integrated his experiences of wartime internment as civilian. In October 1920 he received his doctorate. Despite having achieved a highly regarded scholarly qualification, he did not have the two state examinations and three years of practical training required to become a solicitor, attorney or judge in the German legal system. Nearly thirty years of age, Held chose to embark on an academic career instead and took up a position in the Institute for International Law and later in the Institute for the World Economy at Kiel University. He completed his *Habilitation* (postdoctoral thesis) and received his university teaching qualification in May 1927 for the Law of Nations and International Law.

Fig. 13.4: Held at his desk in the Institute for International Law at Kiel University.

Despite his qualifications, publications and teaching experience, Held was not appointed to a chair during the years of the Weimar Republic. When the National Socialists came to power, Held prospects declined further. While he had published on the Treaty of Versailles and thus shown a 'national' position, he was automatically suspect as a practicing Catholic. In a newspaper advertisement, Held had publicly supported Paul von Hindenburg's candidacy for the German presidential elections in 1932. Through this he had *de facto* spoken out against Hitler, and he was not a member of the NSDAP. The situation was compounded by the fact that universities no longer appointed their staff independently, but acted upon directives received from Berlin.

For a while employment chances looked precarious for Held, who by then was looking after a family of five, but in 1942 his teaching remit was extended to include administrative law and he was made professor *extraordinarius*. This was a response to a lack of senior staff during wartime rather than a change of heart among the Nazi-synchronised collegiate or the Berlin-based authorities. In 1945, after the end of Nazism, Held saw his chance to be appointed full professor, but he remained unsuccessful until his retirement in 1956.

Despite the fact that Held never held a chair, he had a substantial publication record that covered a wide range of areas, even though he did not become well-known for a specific work. Where he excelled above his colleagues, however, was in teaching: at the lectern, Held performed with aplomb, speaking without notes, rich in gesture and with clarity of language and diction. According to a former student, his lectures were inspiring and full of wit. He was exceptionally popular not only as a teacher but also as a supervisor for doctoral work. The foundations for Held's success as an academic educator were laid during his involuntary stay at Lofthouse Park so that this time, in the end, had not been without benefits for himself and his students.

Fig. 13.5: Held at Kiel University in 1948 (Christian-Albrechts-Universität zu Kiel).

Translated from German by Claudia Sternberg

Lofthouse Lifelines:
An Illustrated Postal History

Postal Historian (West Yorkshire)

The post was a lifeline for many at Lofthouse Park. It was an important link to the outside world and for some it was the only means of contact with friends and relatives in Germany, Britain and other countries.[1] A collection of surviving correspondences, which was built up over time entirely through philatelic circuits, shows that outgoing mail was sent to German cities such as Berlin, Hamburg, Hanover and Cologne as well as to British ones including London, Brighton, Glasgow and nearby Leeds. One letter in the collection was sent to an address in Budapest, highlighting the internment of Austro-Hungarian nationals at Lofthouse Park. Indeed, there is much insight to be gained into the inmates and their links to the wider world and social relations – not only through envelopes but complete letters. Before going into further detail, however, some basic understanding of postal conventions is necessary and the system that was put into place to deal with prisoners of war and civilian internment.

The first provisions were laid down under the terms of the Hague Convention (1907) in which it was agreed that there should be free postal facilities for military prisoners of war and civilian internees.[2] In 1914, this typically meant one 'postage-free' letter per week, allowing for two letters in 1918. This was not without restrictions. Prisoners were only permitted to write a maximum of twenty-three lines per letter, and each letter had to be written in plain language on official paper which had been specially designed. In order to aid delivery, correspondents refrained from using the German *Kurrentschrift* with its many lines and sharp angles and opted for Latin script instead, which was commonly used and easier to read.

It was also stipulated that letters had to be about private and family affairs only, although business letters were permitted, providing that they did not infringe on any law or regulations.[3] One item in the collection was addressed to the *Reichskolonialamt* (Imperial Colonial Office) in Berlin, Wilhelmstr. 62, which suggests that interned colonial administrators maintained some form of contact with their government agency. Personal letters were postage free up to a weight of 2 ounce (56g). Some concessions were made. For instance, Christmas and Easter cards were allowed,[4] but, on the whole, stringent controls were applied, and all correspondence was subject to scrutiny and censorship.

The mechanisms in place for postal censorship involved several government bodies and underwent a number of changes in the period between 1914 and 1919. For instance, the Hostile Countries Branch of the Postal Censorship became the Prisoners of War Branch in December 1914. Similarly, M.O.5 (H) in 1914, which was designated M.O.9. in April 1915 and M.I.9 from January 1916 onwards, was a division of military intelligence which dealt with postal censorship. The responsibilities of the Prisoner of War Branch included, amongst other duties, the censoring of registered mail, parcels and all outward mail.[5] A good example of the postal censor's mark can be found in Fig. 14.10 and correspondence received at Lofthouse Park from the Prisoners of War Information Bureau in London.

The main censor's office at Lofthouse Park was in the North compound. It features quite prominently in the escape narrative of Frederick Wiener, where he and Alfred Klapproth had asked to see the Censor, knowing that he would not be in his office. The original plan had been to dig a tunnel, but the idea was abandoned because it would take too long. Instead, they decided to order some 'sporting costumes' from one of the camp tailors. The idea was to look as British as possible. According to Wiener: 'From the censor's office we went to the guard-room, and I was able, thanks to my perfect of command of English, to give the impression that we were British officers'.[6] To what extent the story about the censor's office is true is open to speculation. Nonetheless, the escape was successful, and security was tightened up shortly after the two men escaped in June 1915.

The population of Lofthouse Park at the time of Wiener's and Klapproth's escape was almost at full capacity, with more than 1,400 civilians held in three compounds, so that thousands of mail items had to be processed.[7] The Table below shows a sample list of senders for 1915-18.

Outgoing Letters: Sample List of Senders[8]

Name	No.	Name	No.
H. Aderholdt	1957	Leidharz	976
Hugo Coln	1609	W. Riessuer	2143
Ernst Firle	N/K	Hr. Rosenfiel	1739
H. Heckmann	1609	G. Schick	574
Max Fiegel	936	Solbisky	N/K
Franz Lehmann	1280	Blu. V. Wirlkintz	---
Francis Revesz	2669	G.F.K. Bauer	1916
Rosemeyer	1637	T. Fechirm	866
F. Shersman	1733	Max Gelberg	N/K
Willie Schlundt	894	Arnold Katsenstein	2103
A. Willieloir	872	W. Laszazyh	688
C.D. Bastie	N/K	H. Ostheide	821
Hr. Dickl	2206	Walther Rohde	2509
A. Fot	N/K	W. Schirmmer	N/K
Otto R. Heyn	905	G.Schimmelpfennig	552
E.W. Knoth	961	F. Steinhorst	13
F. Rowland	974	Arnold Wittenstein	1608

In looking at some of the sample material offered at the end of this chapter, it can be seen that the envelope or standard field post card yields much more information than simply name and address or sender. Additional data can be identified such as date, size and colour of cachet, and whether struck in red, purple or the more commonly used black. The cost of the postage where paid for, or the use of registered post, might tell us something about the weight and possible contents of the package or envelope, or the nature of business and transaction. The censor's mark also reveals a great deal about the process, with most correspondence passing through the Prisoners of War Information Bureau in London for screening before being forwarded to Lofthouse Park and further scrutiny.

Much sending and receiving of parcels and money was going on for the fee paying internees. This does decline in later years due to diminishing funds, new restrictions and general shortages, but the evidence is quite clear from some of the envelopes and correspondences. Registered letters were often used to send monies or remittances from family members and friends, with the contents or amount noted in some cases on the envelope.

While addresses, stamps and marks help to reconstruct names, connections and postal routes, surviving letters give at least a partial impression of personalities and preoccupations in the camp. In light of wartime restrictions, writing conventions and a lack of contextual information, however, any reading of the documents remains speculative to some degree.

Outgoing mail frequently contained confirmation that letters and parcels had been received together with expressions of gratitude. Letters and cards were also used to arrange visits where this was at all possible. The official card from the camp administration (Fig. 14.8) announced an appointment time for a visit for H. Ostheide. The reverse of a postcard (Fig. 14.12) included the request of

Will Schlundt (POW 894) for a few items to be brought along by Max Gutbrod, a friend from Bradford. In an English language letter of 28 December 1917, addressed to Mr C.F. Bruch in Shipley (Fig. 14.13), West Camp resident Siegfried Zobel (POW 1692) conveyed how welcome and exciting a recent visit had been for the internees, especially because it involved a female visitor:

> Dear Mr Bruch, First of all please accept my most cordial thanks as well as those of Mr. Koye for your visit and transmit these thanks also to Miss Daws. Both Mr. K. and myself are agreed that it was the most pleasant hour we have spent in these last two years of our captivity. I only hope you landed [...] home safely and that the strain of talking we subjected you to did not cause you any troubles.

The letters differed in tone, depending on the occasion and context. Max Fiegel's (POW 936) birthday greetings of 16 January 1917 to Käthe Seegall in Berlin were light-hearted, giving the letter an air of banter and normality. In Georg Schimmelpfennig's more serious letter of 20 October 1917 to Mrs Davies in Ashton-under-Lyne, the writer expressed his hope that an operation would improve the addressee's health. Schimmelpfennig's lines made explicit his frustration about the inability to offer any tangible support:

> Many thanks for the contents of your letter of the 13rd last and I tell you in reply how much I would like to help you and to be of assistance to you in the adversities of life's battle. However take courage and do your best to get better, I shall not fail you when the time comes for me to act.

In a French language postcard, dated 21 July 1915 and addressed to Monsieur Laigle in Germany (Fig. 14.16), Lofthouse Park internee C.D. Bastie included the saying: 'L'espoir fait vivre' (Hope is what makes us live). A glimpse of hope was also communicated by Walther Rohde (POW

2509) in his letter to Bruno von Koch in Hamburg, dated 20 September 1917:

> Today I can inform you that I am in good hope that after all I will be able to get away from here before the end of the war. We were informed a few days ago that we, as officers of the reserve, are included in the Hague Convention among the class of officers captured in the field and thus would be transferred to a neutral country, provided we have been interned for more than 18 months. This is the case for all of us. (translated from German)

In one of the few surviving incoming letters (Fig. 14.14), sent from Dresden on 4 July 1915 and received by Lofthouse Park internee Hans Seibt (POW 3919), the sender wondered: 'Wie mag es Dir ergehen?' (How may you be faring?) The writer also planned to pray over a grave for peace and for 'Euch alle' (you all) so that everybody could be united again soon.

Internment was particularly difficult for families. Often, the main breadwinner was detained, regular income had stopped and other war-related events impacted on parents, siblings, wives, children and in-laws. Military service led to further male absences and also brought with it injury and bereavement in both countries. A good number of interned men had British wives who were considered German or Austrian according to nationality laws at the time. Travel and mobility were limited and regulated. All of this and the drawn-out war resulted in significant anxiety which can be detected in some of the letters to family members.

On 7 February 1917, F. Bauer wrote to his son Fred in Kidderminster. While insufficient information makes it impossible to reconstruct the circumstances that led to the son's telegram referred to in the letter, the father's repeated appeals and assurances in the response convey a strong sense of urgency. Linguistic errors and idiosyncracies add to this impression of agitation. The latter also reveal, however, that the interned father communicated with his children, children-in-law and grandchildren in English, which was not his own native language:

> My dear Son, Lizzi & my little grandson! I received your telegram also letter, but you need not send telegrams when you can send a letter over nigth, because I canot reply tu it unless it where very urgent, well my dear lad, I know it is very hard whate you state in your telegram & letter but Fred you must take things calm and not get in a temper. My dear lad, I dont only want your Wife to be at the Factory untill the war is over, but I hope and trust for yourself and Wife will be at the Factory many years after the war, you know yourself as no one will ever trouble you as long as I am a live, they is no one else in power as can du you any wrong you must du what I told you in my last letter and then you will be quite shure as things be kept for you untill your return [...] I shall put everything in Order for you so dont trouble your mind about silly things, just for the sake of your Father [...].

Two letters by Ernst Firle (POW 2388) to his mother-in-law, Mrs Henderson in Glasgow, are included in the collection. Parents and parents-in-law were often the first port of call for wives whose husbands had been interned. On 9 March 1917, Firle showed his appreciation for the support his wife and daughter received from his mother-in-law: 'it has made my mind and daily thoughts ever so much happier now that I know that my dear Margaret and little Erna will not be in want of anything.' In the same letter, he also acknowledged his wife's courage and resilience and was hopeful that there would be years to come in which 'I can make up to her for all that she has missed'. Ernst Firle was also imagining a post-war future and wrote:

> should I take [Margaret] to Germany after the war you may be sure that there are only too many of my people who are anxiously waiting to show her in deeds the

esteem they hold her in as recognition for all she has been to me in these sad times of my separation […].

Over a year later, Firle was still interned and his feelings of gratitude towards his wife and mother-in-law had intensified further. His letter of 2 June 1918 was written after his family had visited him at Lofthouse Park in late May 1918. Firle described to his mother-in-law his delight in seeing his daughter, but he also recognised that his long absence had taken its toll on the child's familiarity with her father:

> I must honestly say I cannot give you all and in particular dear Margaret […] enough credit for the way she has brought her up, such a sturdy & strong & healthy child, & yet with all so very daintily made, of course as a hard fate would have it, she is as yet a living little stranger for me, although the 2nd day she felt already more at home with me, but of course that will be allright the moment we are all 3 together again.

Once again, Ernst Firle made plans for the future. He emphasised that 'a man has to keep his family', but also that anything ought to be done to avoid any further separation from his wife and daughter once the war ended. Possibly in light of occasional releases and repatriations, Firle expected, quite rightly, that 'there is only the chance for me on the other side, at least as far as one can judge to-day.' He asked for his mother-in-law's understanding and promised again that Margaret and their daughter would be warmly welcome by his own family once a reunion would become possible. Whether Ernst, Margaret and Erna Firle did indeed relocate to Germany together cannot be determined from the letters.

Compared to field correspondence, internment mail is a minor area of the postal history of the First World War in terms of scale and scope. But like letters and cards of prisoners of war, it has its own specificity. The diversity of destinations reflects the often transnational social, business, diplomatic, colonial and artisanal circles from which the internees came. Add to this the multiplicity of languages in the correspondence (English, German, Hungarian and French in the case of this Lofthouse Park collection), and the contents provide a potentially rich and fascinating source of study.

Fig. 14.1: Under international convention, prisoner-of-war correspondence was issued 'postage free'. Business letters had to be pre-paid at the appropriate rate. Such letters were probably allowed as extra to the number of free letters, which, in Great Britain at this time, was usually one per week.

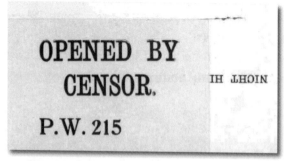

Fig. 14.2: The official censor label is applied to the reverse of the envelopes.

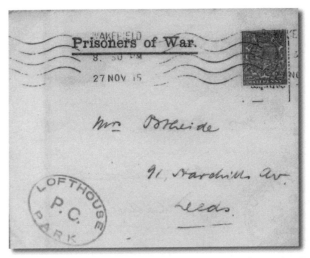

Fig. 14.3: 27 November 1915: Official envelope from the Camp with the special oval censor mark struck in red and a 'Krag' machine cancellation of ½d stamp. A number of cachets and labels were used to confirm censorship.

Fig. 14.4: Censor marks. An example of a square cachet struck in red. Note the address for 'Harrods Ltd'.

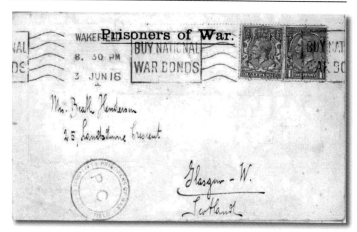

Fig. 14.5: The envelope shows a small double circle cachet struck in violet. It was posted on 3 June 1918, the day on which the letter rate was increased by 50 per cent to 1½ d. Note the postal slogan for 'National War Bonds', which was the first postal slogan to be used at Wakefield.

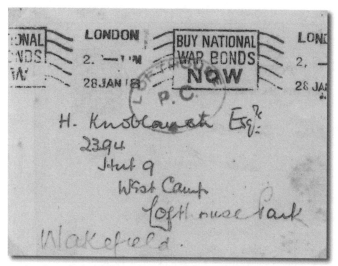

Fig. 14.6: Surviving incoming mail which was also censored. The example shows an envelope from London, addressed to H. Knoblauch, Hut 9, West Camp, dated 28 January 1918.

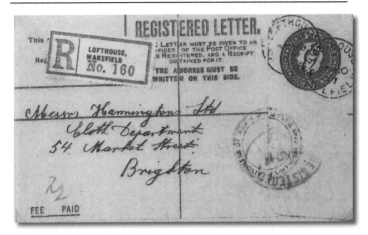

Fig. 14.7: The amount of business mail sent from the camp was considerable. Note the 'Lofthouse' registration labels and date stamps. Postage at this time was 1d and registration 2d.

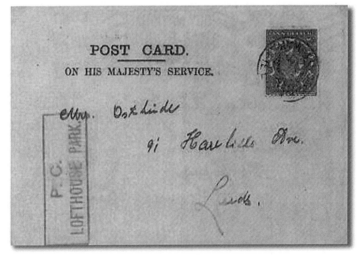

Fig. 14.8: Official Postcard, July 1915. The message on the back reads: 'I have to inform you that you have permission to see P.O.W. Osthinde [Ostheide] 821 on Wednesday, 14 July at Lofthouse Park at 2.30 p.m.'

Fig. 14.9: Christmas post card sent from Lofthouse Park. Similar cards were also printed in German.

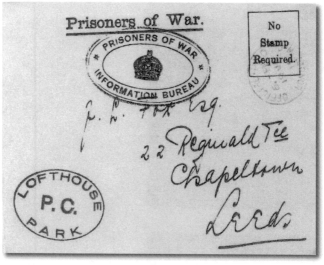

Fig. 14.10: Censor Marks. Although sent to Leeds, the letter had travelled to the Prisoner of War Information Bureau in London. Note the oval cachet struck in purple. The initials 'P.C.' stand for 'Postal Censor.'

Fig. 14.11: A postcard sent by Willy Schlundt, No. 894, to Max Gutbrod in Bradford on 30 August 1915.

Fig. 14.12: The message on the back of Schlundt's card is written in anticipation of a visit: 'Dear friend: Please bring along: 3 two pound jars of a good marmelade (James Keller & Sons, Dundee marmelade), two ordinary face towels and 1750 square cards, cheap visiting card style, size as per illustration, colors: 1000 white, 250 dark gray, 750 reds and 250 blue, or other colors easely distinguishable. Please note all your expenses so that I can settle, while you are here. Have you any good german books to spare (Kosmos, Hundezeitungen? Your sincerely, Schlundt'.

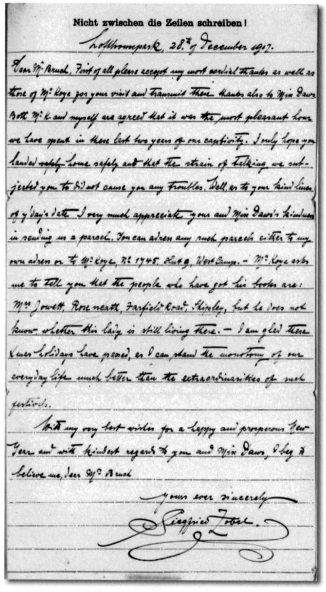

Fig. 14.13: English-language letter written on 28 December 1917 by internee Siegfried Zobel.

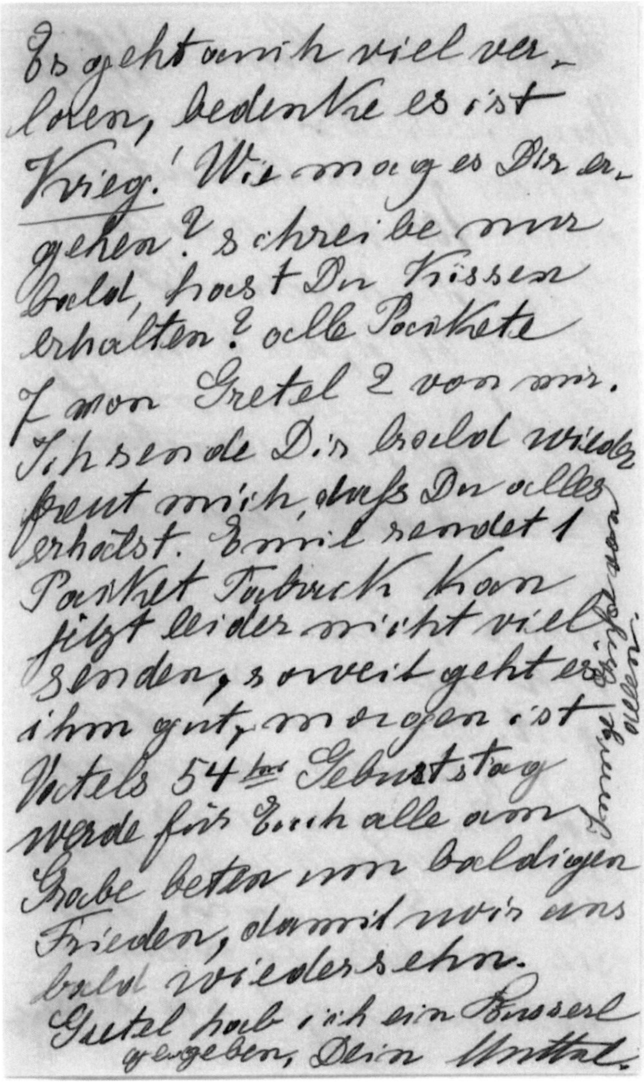
Es geht auch viel ver-
loren, bedenke es ist
Krieg.' Wie mag es Dir ergehen? schreibe mir
bald, hast Du Kissen
erhalten? alle Pakete
7 von Gretel 2 von mir.
Ich sende Dir bald wieder
freut mich, daß Du alles
erhalst. Emil sendet 1
Paket Tabak kan
jetzt leider nicht viel
senden, soweit geht es
ihm gut, morgen ist
Vaters 54ten Geburtstag
werde für Euch alle um
Gnade beten um baldigen
Frieden, damit wir uns
bald wiedersehn.
Gretel hab ich ein Busserl
gegeben, Dein Mutterl.

Fig. 14.14: Second page of a German-language letter sent to internee Hans Seibt on 4 July 1915. The writer states: 'Es geht auch viel verloren, bedenke es ist Krieg!' (Much also gets lost, pray consider there is a war on!')

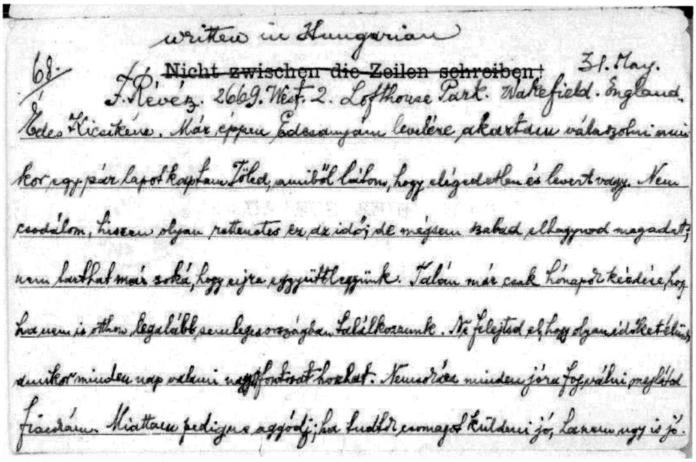
written in Hungarian

68. Nicht zwischen die Zeilen schreiben! 31. May.

J. Révész. 2669. West. 2. Lofthouse Park. Wakefield. England.

Édes Kicsikém. Már éppen Édesanyám levelére akartam válaszolni mikor egy pár lapot kaptam Tőled, amiből látom, hogy elégedetlen és levert vagy. Nem csodálom, hiszen olyan pettenetes ez, de idő; de mégsem szabad, elhagynod magadat; nem tarthat már soká, hogy újra együtt legyünk. Talán már csak hónapok kérdése, hogy ha nem is otthon legalább semleges országban találkozunk. Ne felejtsd el, hogy olyan időket élünk amikor minden nap valami nagy fontosat hozhat. Nemsokára minden jóra fog válni, meglátod fiacskám. Miattam pedig ne aggódj; ha tudtok csomagot küldeni jó, ha nem úgy is jó.

Fig. 14.15: Most of the correspondence was in English or German, but this letter is written in Hungarian.

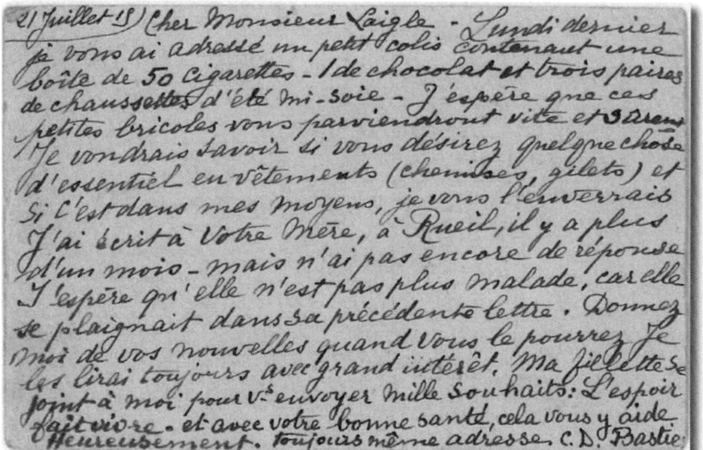
21 Juillet 18) Cher Monsieur Laigle - Lundi dernier je vous ai adressé un petit colis contenant une boîte de 50 cigarettes - 1 de chocolat et trois paires de chaussettes d'été mi-soie - J'espère que ces petites bricoles vous parviendront vite et bien. Je voudrais savoir si vous désirez quelque chose d'essentiel en vêtements (chemises, gilets) et si c'est dans mes moyens, je vous l'enverrais. J'ai écrit à Votre Mère, à Rueil, il y a plus d'un mois - mais n'ai pas encore de réponse. J'espère qu'elle n'est pas plus malade, car elle se plaignait dans sa précédente lettre. Donnez moi de vos nouvelles quand vous le pourrez. Je les lirai toujours avec grand intérêt. Ma fillette se joint à moi pour vs envoyer mille souhaits: L'espoir fait vivre. et avec votre bonne santé, cela vous y aidera heureusement. toujours même adresse. C.D. Bastie

Fig. 14.16: A French-language postcard addressed to Monsieur Laigle, *infirmier militaire*, in Gütersloh, Germany.

Religion and Faith at Lofthouse Park

David Stowe and Claudia Sternberg (Leeds)

The Reverend Pastor Martin was one of the first ministers to be arrested as an 'enemy alien' when war was declared in August 1914. He was interned at Lofthouse Park for a short time before being released in November. Martin was a Lutheran and pastor of the German Protestant Church near Manchester.[1] His experience is instructive for the following insight he offers into the various religious groups and denominations held captive at Lofthouse Park:

> There are about five hundred of us altogether representing all sections of society. Among them were Poles, Ruthenians, and Hungarians, as well as Germans and Austrians. We had concerts occasionally, and on Sundays we had religious services. Mass was celebrated by a Catholic priest, and I conducted the service for the Protestants. We had religious gatherings also in the course of each week. There was a Rabbi for the Jews.[2]

Provisions for the religious welfare of the internees had been put into place almost immediately, with lists of officiating clergy and laity drawn up in areas where representation was needed in the camps around Britain. The following list of names are among other members of the Lutheran Church who ministered to German civilian internees in the various camps across Britain: Pastor A. Scholten, Pastor A Maetzold, Pastor C. Waldenberg, Pastor O. Goehling, Pastor A.E. Rosenkranz, Pastor G. Abraham, Pastor Neitz.[3]

An appeal for the services of Jewish ministers to visit the various camps was also made. This involved the Chief Rabbi and the Secretary of the Board of Guardians making representations to the War Office on behalf of the internees and was especially important where the request for the provision of kosher food was made. Rabbi Moses Abrahams was appointed to take charge of Jewish interests at Lofthouse Park.[4] Appeals were also made to Leeds University and through the *Jewish Chronicle* for co-religionists willing to give their services as interpreters in Russian and German for the non-English speaking internees.[5] Rabbi Abrahams continued to minister at Lofthouse Park until his death in 1918.

The Leeds Quakers were also very much active at Lofthouse Park. The Society of Friends had been instrumental in securing additional books for the camp library through the help of Michael Sadler, the Vice-Chancellor at Leeds University, who had generously agreed to extend the Library's loan facilities.[6] Many non-conformist groups were active too, as was the Young Men's Christian Association (YMCA), which had helped in the building of two huts. The Reverend Donald Truss had conducted Sunday afternoon services at Lofthouse Park since the camp had opened in 1914. Truss was President of the Wakefield Free Church Council, and worked closely with other faith groups, including ministers of the Lutheran Church and Germans of the Roman Catholic faith.[7] The Roman Catholic internees were visited by their own clergy under the 'superintendence' of the Archbishop of Westminster.[8] The religious service which was conducted at Lofthouse Park in July 1917 under the Reverend Donald Truss and the Bishop of Wakefield was reported in the *Yorkshire Evening Post* at the time:

> Since the Autumn of 1914, the Rev. D.G Truss, President of the Wakefield Free Church Council, has conducted a Sunday afternoon service at Lofthouse Park for Prisoners of War, which has throughout been well attended and much valued. On Sunday last, the Bishop of Wakefield, to show his sympathy with the nonconformist minister's

work, attended and took a prominent part in the service. The Rev. D.G. Truss took the opening part of the service, and extended a warm welcome to the Bishop, who proceeded to preach the sermon and subsequently offered the closing prayer, and concluded by pronouncing the Benediction in German.

The Bishop, who wore his Episcopal robes, was received with great deference and cordiality by a large congregation which overflowed the spacious hall, joined in the service with heartiness, and followed his lordship's able and appropriate discourse (which was based on the text, "Jesus Christ, the same yesterday, today, and fore-ever") with manifest interest and appreciation. Before the congregation separated, Pastor Reiuke [sic], a Lutheran minister from German West Africa, thanked the Bishop on behalf of the congregation for his presence and helpful ministrations.[9]

One group not considered so far are the Muslim civilian internees who were held in British camps. This may be seen more specifically in connection to the Isle of Man where requests were made on behalf of the Turkish Government that internees be allowed to prepare their own food in accordance with national customs, and that separate arrangements be made allowing Turkish Muslims to worship.[10] The number of Turkish subjects interned in the United Kingdom in 1917 was 110. This included one naval prisoner of war.[11] The civilians were interned in the following camps: Alexandra Palace (8), Knockaloe (61), Dartford War Hospital (1), Dorchester (24), Douglas (10), Donington Hall (1), Pattishall, in Northamptonshire (1), and Wakefield. The number of Turkish civilians at Lofthouse Park is recorded as three.[12] This number had risen to five in February 1918, of whom the boxer Sabri Mahir was almost certainly one.[13] However, it is worth noting that not all of the men were of Muslim faith. Khedouri Shasha was a Sephardi Jew of Turkish birth, born in Baghdad.[14]

Fig. 15.1: Camp view showing Lofthouse Church in the background. Illustration by imprisoned theology student *Leutnant* Knoch, included in Hans Schmidt's published sermons from Lofthouse Park (*Aus der Gefangenschaft*, 1919, p. III).

The spiritual needs of the military prisoners-of-war, who remained at Lofthouse Park until December 1919, was also a consideration. Hans Schmidt (1877-1953) was professor *extraordinarius* of theology at the University of Tübingen in 1914 and a captain in the German Army during the First World War. As an ordained protestant pastor he conducted services at Lofthouse Park Camp after his capture in the field. After the war he went back to Tübingen (until 1921) and held further professorships at Gießen (from 1921) and Halle-Wittenberg (1928-45), having joined the NSDAP in 1933. Schmidt was dean of the Faculty of Theology in Halle from 1936 to 1945 and returned to military service during the Second World War. He retired in 1945, losing his pension as a denazification measure.[15]

Schmidt's sermons from Lofthouse Park reveal how the memory of combat and concurrent events like the Armistice, the defeat of Germany and the Versailles Peace Conference were integrated into camp services. The sermons were published with the help of Schmidt's wife before his release in 1919 and he continued to write about the war afterwards.[16]

In the preface, Schmidt gives an example of how he connected his sermons to the shared experience of the imprisoned officers. This is the opening to the discussion of the Parable of the Talents:

> When we were together in the hut yesterday, one of us said: 'Strange how one does no longer hear any artillery fire.' We all relate to this. When we wake up at night on our wooden bunk beds and become aware of where we are, then we feel the enormous change: only a while ago the roar and howling of battle, just recently the experience of hourly danger and the strain of responsibility, and now suddenly stillness, safety and idleness. For us the war is the past. The thought is paralysing somehow. We look around and stare into emptiness. – But slowly, one after the other, figures appear from the dark: Thoughts, images and experiences which concerned us before the war, are rekindled and fill the emptiness around us. Among them the One must not be missed, for whom at this hour the sparse ringing of the church bells at home is heard, Jesus Christ. On these Sundays, I would like to let his parables speak to us one after the other. (translated from German)[17]

The role of religion and faith in the everyday life of many of the civilians and military prisoners of war at Lofthouse Park would seem pretty much significant on the face of it. To ensure the religious provision, pastors from British and German churches visited the camps. Qualified inmates were also put in charge. The German YMCA and the *Evangelische Blättervereinigung für Soldaten und kriegsgefangene Deutsche* provided further support, as did faith leaders from other denominational groups such as Quakers, Roman Catholics and Jews. Not all men participated in services to the extent that was suggested in the article of July 1917 in the *Yorkshire Evening Post*. Celebrating festivals, however, especially Christmas or Passover, was a significant social activity in the camps and led to reflection not only about religious teaching, but also war and peace, national identities and personal circumstances.

Fig. 15.2: Military prisoners celebrating Christmas at Lofthouse Park in 1918 (illustration by *Leutnant* Knoch, published in Hans Schmidt, *Aus der Gefangenschaft*, 1919, p. 78).

Inside the Wire:
Music and Theatre at Lofthouse Park

Claudia Sternberg (Leeds)

Unlike the camp magazine *Lager-Bote*, which may have folded after only two published issues in 1916, Lofthouse Park's theatrical and musical scene thrived until the internees were removed to the Isle of Man in the autumn of 1918. Listings and reviews in the magazines, surviving programmes[1] as well as Paul Cohen-Portheim's chapter on 'The Stage' in his memoir *Time Stood Still* give an impression of this part of camp culture.[2]

Concerts and plays were produced by dedicated companies and groups of musicians in the three compounds. Issue II of *Lager-Bote* (March 1916) advertises regular concerts by the musicians Hofmann, Henschel, Walter and Ronis, which took place on Sunday afternoons between 3 and 5pm in the *Wintergarten* of the South Camp.[3] The venue reminds us that the buildings of the former amusement park were particularly suited for entertainment purposes. The *Wintergarten* might even have regained some of its previous atmosphere when taking into account that coffee and cake as well as snacks and wine were on offer.

As reviewer R. relates in his article 'Aus unserem Musikleben' (From our Musical Life) in the camp magazine, concerts began in the South Camp, the first compound to be opened in October 1914.[4] Initially Herr Ronis made use of a single piano that was already on site, another vestige of Lofthouse Park's earlier calling. As the camp expanded, professional and amateur musicians grew in number, and chamber music became a staple for an enthusiastic audience that would not be deterred by the 'Polarkuehle des ungeheizten Konzertraumes' (polar chill of the unheated concert room) in the North Camp.[5] One of the chamber concerts, that of 4 February 1916, was presented to a full house. The concert was conducted by Professor Feuerberg, who also played the violin. The performance comprised a trio in C minor for violin, cello and piano from the early works of Ludwig van Beethoven, a sonata in A major for violin and piano composed by the Belgian Cesar Frank and a sonata in C minor by the Norwegian Edvard Grieg.[6]

Fig. 16.1: Professor Feuerberg, conductor and violinist, at a dining room table in the 'Gerichtslaube', Wakefield (Imperial War Museum HU 58701).

Musicians and conductors were readily available among the internees; sheet music and instruments had been brought along, could be sent for or purchased. But the Lofthouse Park endeavours reached beyond chamber music. *Kapellmeister* P. Henschel was in charge of the *Grosse Orchester* (Great Orchestra) that performed, for example, in the South Camp in March 1917. Concerts were complemented by musical theatre and light opera, such as *Der*

Bergfex, oder Auf der Hohlnsteiner Alm, a Bavarian mountain farce by Aloys Dreyer with songs by Josef Bill, and *Guten Morgen, Herr Fischer!,* adapted by Wilhelm Friedrich from Lockroy, with music by Eduard Stiegmann.[7]

In addition to the various *Instrumentalvereinigungen* (musical societies) in the *Stacheldrahtidylle* (barbed wire idyll) Lofthouse Park, theatre companies were in charge of the drama provision. As in other wartime camps, the interned men build up an impressive dramatic infrastructure, drawing on those with professional skills and experience while also training up volunteers to a good standard. As R. notes in Issue I of *Lager-Bote,* the *Deutsche Theater-Verein* of the South Camp had come a long way from the crude theatricals of its first performance on 18 July 1915 to the refined stage craft of early 1916.[8] Paul Cohen-Portheim confirms this assessment:

> When I first came to Wakefield both the South Camp and the North already possessed 'companies,' but things were very badly done and most amateurish. They were, however, destined to develop to a most extraordinary degree, and some of the shows I saw there towards the end of my stay were as good as any you could see outside the wire.[9]

He interprets this progress as the consequence of a general propensity found among those involved in the theatre in combination with the more singular effects of encampment:

> In camp that natural indifference of the actor to all outside the theatre was intensified for the simple reason that everyone there tried hard, in self-defence, to persuade himself of the real importance of the work he had undertaken in order to forget its inherent futility, and so the actors found no work too much for them.[10]

Each of the three compounds had its own theatre company, but programmes reveal that camp authorities permitted for individual performances to be made accessible to the different sections. Most productions were of a light nature, ranging from farce, satire or dialect play to popular, romantic, satirical and drawing room comedies. Among the plays were Franz and Paul von Schönthan's *Raub der Sabinerinnen* (1884), *Die wilde Jagd* by Ludwig Fulda (1888), Gerhart Hauptmann's *Der Biberpelz* (1893), *Alt-Heidelberg* by Wilhelm Meyer-Förster (1901), *Im Klubsessel* by Karl Roessler and Ludwig Heller (1909), *Moral* by Ludwig Thoma (1909), and *Die Sorina* by Georg Kaiser (1917).[11] Some of the plays seen at Lofthouse Park would have been performed a decade earlier at the *Deutsches Theater in London* (German Theatre in London), a German language repertory theatre that catered to both German and British audiences from 1900 to 1908.[12]

Fig. 16.2: South Camp programme for Ludwig Fulda's *Die wilde Jagd*, February 1916 (State Library Berlin, PPN749375043).

Most plays performed at Lofthouse Park were written by German or Austrian playwrights, but the theatre companies also staged dramas by the Norwegian Henrik Ibsen, the Frenchmen Henry Bernstein, Paul Gavault and Robert Charvay, and the Irishman Oscar Wilde.[13] Leo Kunodi, an internee, had prepared a German translation of Wilde's *Der Fächer der Lady Windermere* (*Lady Windermere's Fan*), which was performed in March 1918. He had previously co-translated *Sei Ernst!* (*The Importance of Being Earnest*) with Dr. Straube, which was staged at the camp in April 1917.[14]

Historical drama was presented by the North Camp. Among the productions were Paul Heyse's *Colberg* (1865) and Ernst von Wildenbruch's *The Quitzows* (1888), as well as Friedrich Schiller's *Wallenstein's Camp* and *Wallenstein's Death*.[15] Schiller's plays about the Thirty Years' War and General Wallenstein had first been performed in Weimar in 1798/99 under the direction of Johann Wolfgang von Goethe and occupied the most serious and classical end of the theatrical spectrum at Lofthouse Park.

The West Camp was the last compound to set up a theatre company. A review in Issue II of *Lager-Bote* draws attention to the small size of its stage and auditorium. The request to refrain from smoking due to poor ventilation, which can be found in a programme of 1915, confirms the conditions of a confined space (Fig. 16.3). According to reviewer R., however, the intimate stage and a carefully designed single setting was put to excellent effect in the production of *Flachsmann als Erzieher* (*Flachsmann as Pedagogue*).[16] The latter was a popular Wilhelmine play of 1900, written by the teacher Otto Ernst, in which Flachsmann, a corrupt and authoritarian schoolmaster, is pitched against his younger colleague Flemming, who advocates a teaching style that liberates rather than subjugates the new generation of pupils.

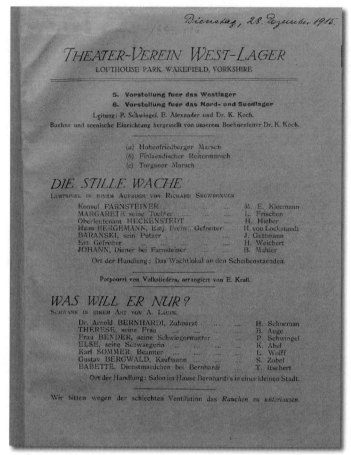

Fig. 16.3: West Camp programme of marches, folk songs and humorous short plays, 28 December 1915 (State Library Berlin, PPN750715081).

As a resident of the West Camp, Lofthouse chronicler Paul Cohen-Portheim produced a number of shows himself. Under the influence of his earlier behind-the-scenes work in the opera, he at first devised a cabaret show with music, dance, song and jokes. At that time, the West Camp did not yet have a stage, and Cohen-Portheim's production was performed in the North Camp, 'before a crowded hall and with the commandant and some officers in the first row.'[17] Two years later, he tried his hand again, using the West Camp studio stage for an evening of chamber music, followed by the one-act play *A Merry Death* (1908) by the Russian dramatist Nikolai Evreinof. A second production included a short play by the Swedish author August Strindberg; a third one was to combine a Japanese Nô-play and a piece by the Bengali Rabindranath Tagore, but it did not materialise due to Cohen-Portheim's release to the Netherlands.

As the theatre programmes of Lofthouse Park Camp show, acting companies were not deterred by plays with a good number of female characters. As elsewhere, men were cast in women's roles and, through practice, achieved a high degree of proficiency in representing comic and serious, young and old, formal and vernacular femininity. A *Lager-Bote* reviewer in Issue II acknowledges Karl Abel's performance as the painter Melanie Dalberg-Weiprecht in Fulda's *Die wilde Jagd*, praising his talent to impersonate a lady of society.[18] Abel's stage presence was made even more convincing by lavish costumes and an attractive stage set. As the reviewer notes, the paintings for Dalberg-Weiprecht's studio came from internee L. v.d. Decken,[19] who is also credited for the scenery on the programmes for *Die von Hochsattel*, a comedy by Leo Walther Stein and Ludwig Heller, and Melchior [Menyhért] Lengyl's Japanese-themed *Taifun*, which marked the 100th performance to be staged at Lofthouse Park's South Camp.[20]

While the West Camp occasionally offered songs in the intermission of their plays, the larger stages programmed short musical performances by the *Kleines Lofthouse Park Orchester* (Small Lofthouse Park Orchestra). Among the pieces played for the satyr play *Der Häuptling* by Paul Apel (1917), performed in August 1918, was Otto Nicolai's overture for his opera *Die lustigen Weiber von Windsor* (*The Merry Wives of Windsor*), based on the eponymous

Shakespearean comedy, and a potpourri from William S. Gilbert and Arthur Sullivan's comic opera *Der Mikado* (1885).[21] The latter, notably, had been staged in 1917 – in its entirety with a full cast and orchestra – by the British civilian internees held at Ruhleben Camp in Spandau and became one of this camp's most memorable productions.[22]

In August 1918, Alexander [Sándor] Reschofsky performed the interludes during the intermission for *Liebelei* (1895), a drama by the Austrian playwright Arthur Schnitzler. Reschofsky, a Hungarian composer and music pedagogue, had collaborated with Béla Bartók at the Academy of Music in Budapest on *Zongora Iskola*, a 'piano school' for musical instruction, in 1913, but happened to be in England in 1914, which led to his internment at Lofthouse Park.[23] The musical interludes by Joseph Haydn, Franz Liszt and Franz Schubert were dedicated to the Austro-Hungarian monarch Karl (Charles) I on the occasion of his birthday on 17 August.[24] Karl I had stepped up as Emperor of Austria after the assassination of Franz Ferdinand in 1914 and was also King of Hungary (as Karl IV) and Bohemia (as Karl III). This display of Austro-Hungarian devotion notwithstanding, a caption reveals that the respective theatre programme had been printed by (William Henry) Bean & (Charles Henry) Halliday, who were stationers, printers and booksellers with premises on Boar Lane in nearby Leeds.

Music also played a role in separate and stand-alone events. A strongly patriotic musical programme, involving the *Lager-Orchester*, musical societies and the audience, was put together for the celebration of the birthday of the German emperor Wilhelm II in January 1916. The programme was made up of speeches, prayers, marches, anthems and recitations. It had a focus on the allies Germany, Austria, Turkey and Bulgaria, but also included a nod towards the neutral Netherlands.[25] Less jingoistically charged were the seasonal concerts, especially at Christmas, when choir members and other internees sang Christmas songs together.

Fig. 16.4: Christmas concert programme of 1915, containing misspellings due to faulty typesetting (State Library Berlin, PPN74651660).

Musical and theatrical activities at Lofthouse Park were frequent and popular and continued at least until September 1918. As Christoph Jahr has argued,

> music, sport and education were important vehicles for the self-empowerment of inmates in all camps. The most freedom for the creative engagement with one's own situation was provided through dramatic play. On the stage, different roles could be tried out – also and in particular gender roles. (translated from German)[26]

Fig. 16.5: Programme cover for an evening of theatre and music in October 1915. (State Library Berlin, PPN746446969).

We can only speculate about the quality of the productions and to what extent the on-stage worlds and concerns generated discussion and reflection amongst the internees. Cohen-Portheim suggests that plays were mainly chosen to fit the players' limited range and possibilities,[27] but this did not rule out further considerations with regard to directing, dramaturgy and style. Cohen-Portheim's own productions give the impression of an aestheticism and cosmopolitan defiance that could well be seen as an indirect critique of nationalism and sectarianism, big and small.

Comedies and satirical plays provided distraction, but also enabled audiences to take a distanced look at human relations, aristocratic and bourgeois preoccupations and regional idiosyncracies. Furthermore, they offered opportunities to engage with ideas of German- or Austrianness from a point of view that was more informed and benevolent than the sentiments in circulation outside the camp at the time. Historical plays like the ones from Schiller's Wallenstein trilogy invited, at least in abstraction, a reflection on war, military logics, loyalties and the relationship between monarch, high command and soldiers.

And finally, contemporary works like *Liebe* by Anton Wildgans (1916), performed at Lofthouse Park in September 1918, were unsettling plays about sexuality, love and extramarital affairs. These must have had a particular poignancy in the homosocial environment in which younger and older, married and unmarried, hetero- and homosexual internees lived together without privacy and deprived of the contact with women – except for a few visitors. In the camp, therefore, female characters on the stage stood in for 'real' women in more than one respect, and male partnerships developed to fulfil the human need for close affective bonds. Paul Cohen-Portheim offers this summary in his chapter on 'Men without Women':

[Y]ou cannot deny that relationships among prisoners as among all men are predominantly of an emotional nature. Barbed wire was responsible for an all-pervading atmosphere of hate; it was also responsible for the birth of a great deal of love, and the manifestations of both hate and love were conditioned by it, were of a peculiar nature, were as far removed from the normal, conventional, and usual as was all that existence.[28]

Fig. 16.6: Theatre programme for *Liebe* by Anton Wildgans, Lofthouse Park's 145th performance in September 1918 (State Library Berlin, PPN750714093).

Studie in Grau:
Arts and Crafts at Lofthouse Park

Claudia Sternberg (Leeds)

The largest British camp for civilian internees during the
First World War was Knockaloe on the Isle of Man. A
diverse and sizeable selection of artworks and objects
made by internees can be found at the Manx Museum and
in the Manx National Heritage collections. By comparison,
the admittedly much smaller camp at Lofthouse Park is
characterised by an absence of such items, at least in
publicly accessible collections.

This lack of a material legacy is surprising because
activities of making and creating were also widespread at
Lofthouse Park Camp, as is evidenced in a surviving programme for the camp's second *Kunst und Handfertigkeits-
Austellung* (Arts and Crafts Show).[1] The showcase event incorporated work from all three compounds, made within
the previous year, and took place from 20-23 September
1917 in the tent of the West Camp. It was organised by a
committee and helpers under the leadership of E.W.
Mennecke. Entry to the display of works was free, but the
programme was sold for 6d (2.5p); the money would be
used to cover printing costs, and any surplus would be
donated to wounded military prisoners of war.

That Lofthouse Park was conceived, at least by some,
as a site for developing an artistic practice is suggested in
E.M. Koch's title page for the programme. It depicts an
unclothed sculptor or stonecutter working under the gaze
of a muse-like young woman against the backdrop of the
camp buildings (Fig. 17.1).

Fig. 17.1: Title page for the programme accompanying the second Arts and Crafts Show in 1917 (Berlin State Library, PPN746319851).

The pages of the programme for the *Kunst und Handfertig-keits-Austellung* mainly consisted of a numbered list with titles or short descriptions and the name of the respective craftsman or artist. 500 items were put on display in the West Camp and included oil paintings, sketches, water-colours, pastels, wood and metal works as well as sculptures and a set of architectural drawings of a stately house. Some objects were of utilitarian use, such as trays, boxes, notebooks, plates, wardrobes, picture frames, tables, chairs and even twelve pairs of socks. Others combined use value with decorative appeal, for example carvings or inlays. Painting and drawing genres ranged from (self)portraits, still lives and landscapes to pastoral or mythical scenes, memento mori, bookplates and images of plants and animals.

In the context of internment, some works appear to have been more responsive to their makers' environment and situation than others, but titles alone evoke rather than concretise the content and orientation of the representations. There is no doubt, however, that a central motif in the visual arts was Lofthouse Park itself. The list of items contains numerous studies of the camp in general and of individual scenes (e.g. view from the sports pitch, football match, private hut, view from the window, lecture in the tent, North Camp concert, the commandant's house, Huts 8 and 16 in the South Camp, the Y.M.C.A. tent, snow and ice in the North Camp, evening idyll and even a camp flower seller).

The choice of camp motifs reflects the limited opportunities to draw from life, but also the impulse to preserve and process everyday occurrences through artistic means and craft a sense of 'home' at a time of acute displacement. The image by an unidentified artist at the end of this chapter (Fig. 17.3) highlights the peculiar mix of the older buildings of the Lofthouse amusement park and the added-on camp architecture. Heavy clouds bear down on this wartime settlement in a claustrophobic way, but the buildings blend into the wider community beyond the fence. The image captures the ambivalence of confinement and safety which is typical for civilian internment during the years of active warfare.

Other camps feature too in the paintings and drawings of Lofthouse internees. Nos. 41 and 45 on the programme list by F.X. Woelfle were entitled 'Knockaloe Studie' (Knockaloe Study), O. Jera's No. 54 was called 'Alexandra Park, London', and A. Lindner's No. 108 depicted the 'Internirungsschiff [*sic*] Canada' (Internment Ship Canada). Theatrical scenery painter L. von der Decken[2] presented a series of works inspired, perhaps, by the changeable Yorkshire weather: 'Ruhiges Wetter' (Calm Weather), 'Sommersonne' (Summer Sun), 'Studie in Grau' (Study in Grey), 'Regen bei Nacht' (Rain at Night), 'Vorm Sturm' (Before the Storm) and 'Sturm' (Storm). Under his name, two further paintings are listed, entitled 'Das Opfer' (The Victim) and 'Hoffnung oder Tod' (Hope or Death). Two artists, F. Hestermann and E. Rauschning, made reference to a 'Friedensgarten' (Peace Garden, No. 68 and 284), but whether such a garden was part of the camp and what such name might have implied cannot be known.

It is notable that some sketches and portraits are of children and women, for which, if based on real people, there would not have been any live sitters. The ten sculptural works listed for O. Hiene contain a bust and head of a child alongside a bust and relief of Field Marshall Paul von Hindenburg and a military-themed 'Vorposten im Feindesland' (Vanguard in Enemy Territory). Among the few political drawings and paintings are V. Bender's 'Die glücklicheren Tage Karls I.' (The Happier Days of Charles I.) as well as O. Wuppermann's 'Sufla Bucht' (Suvla Bay), the place where British troops landed in the August Offensive during the Battle of Gallipoli. Three drawings without any further detail are attributed to P. Cohen, quite

possibly the painter Paul Cohen, who would later trans-
form into the writer Paul Cohen-Portheim, and whose
internment memoir *Time Stood Still* (1931) constitutes an
important point of reference throughout this book.[3]

M. SCHNOES MALSCHULE.		
250	Campstudie	Dr. Bromberg.
251	"	
252	Der Blumenhändler in Nordlager	I. Sedlmair.
253	Baumstudie im Südlager	"
254	Dorfstrasse „ „	"
255	Abendidyll „ Nordlager	"
256	Zelt im Südlager	"
257	Schnee ® Eis im Nordlager	.,
258	Fussballplatz Nord. I.	"
259	" „ II.	
260	Nordlager	F. Sedlmair.
261	Hamburger Kriegsschiff 16. Jahrh,	
	(Copie)	"
262	Ex libris Thöle	"
263	Affenkfiäg	"
264	Haus des Komandanten	"
265	Camp Motive	V. Bender

Fig. 17.2: Pupils of Max Schnös presented their work at the arts
and crafts show in 1917 (Berlin State Library, PPN746319851).

The Arts and Crafts Show programme also reveals that at
least two *Malschulen* (painting schools) were in operation at
Lofthouse Park, one run by E.M. Koch in the West and
the other by Max Schnoes (actually: Schnös) in the North
Camp. Both men were part of the show's organising
committee and put their own as well as their pupils' works
on display. E.M. Koch's drawings included 'Portrait eines
Unbeliebten' (Portrait of an Unpopular Person), 'Blick auf
ein Hüttenwerk' (Overlooking a Steel Mill), a camp view
and 'Kaiser Franz Josef Feier' (Emperor Franz Josef
Celebration) as well as a number of caricatures. Max
Schnös showed a number of his camp illustrations, which
might have looked similar to the ones that came into
possession of internee Richard Bechtel and are reproduced
on pages 46 and 47 of this book. Schnös was in his twenties
when he ran his art school at Lofthouse Park. He originally
came from Baunach in northern Bavaria, where his personal papers and some of his works are still held today.[4]

Fig. 17.3: Lofthouse Park camp view; artist unknown (Bechtel Family Archive).

'24 on/24 off':
The National Reserve and
Royal Defence Corps

David Stowe (Leeds)

The Royal Defence Corps was formed in March 1916. Its principal role was primarily home defence. It also provided men for guard duties and prisoner-of-war camps. These duties could be varied in some cases and might include guarding vulnerable points such as docks and wireless stations, or working in special military areas and for military intelligence.[1] The soldiers were often recruited from older men and those who were less fit, including men recovering from war injuries. Surviving service documents show that a number of guards at Lofthouse Park were drawn from the supernumerary companies of the West Riding Regiment and 5th West Yorks. The units raised were formed into protection companies and listed by command. There are strong connections to Protection Companies 151 to 155 where some of these men had enlisted from Leeds.[2] The terms under which the Royal Defence Corps was afforded recognition are outlined below.

> George R.I. Whereas we have deemed it expedient to authorise the formation of a corps to be entitled 'The Royal Defence Corps'; Our will and pleasure is that the Royal Defence Corps shall be deemed to be a corps for the purposes of the Army Act. Our further will and pleasure is that the rates of pay of the officers, warrant officers, non-commissioned officers and men of this corps shall be those laid down for our infantry of the line

in our warrant for the pay, appointment, promotion and non-effective pay of our army, dates 1st December 1914. Given at our Court at St James, this 17th day of March, 1916, in the sixth year of our reign. By His Majesty's command, Kitchener. [3]

The origins of the Royal Defence Corps can be found in the formation of the National Reserve and the Territorial County Association recruiting on behalf of the Territorial Force in towns and cities such as Barnsley, Bradford, Halifax and Leeds in the pre-war period. Local branches were formed and asked to help raise a National Reserve through the registering and enrolment of officers and men who had served in the various armed forces.[4] The principal regulations governing the National Reserve were given official approval by the War Office in November 1911. These included the terms and conditions under which members might apply.

The active recruitment of members may be seen also as a way of bringing the Territorial Force up to strength and increasing the military resources for national defence at a local and regional level in the pre-war period. It was estimated in February 1912 that some 500 men were needed in Leeds to bring the Territorial units up to war establishment strength, with between 12,000 and 15,000 National Reservists needed in other Yorkshire towns and cities.[5] It was hoped that the recruitment drive at York was able to raise 500 men, thereby forming an additional five companies needed in the event or threat of war.[6]

Colonel H. Ditmus was appointed Secretary in York, and an office opened at the new headquarters at Tower Street.[7] The strength of the West Riding National Reserve in April 1914 can be found on the following page.

The West Riding National Reserve
April 1914

Towns	No. Registered
Barnsley	324
Batley	133
Bradford	364
Dewsbury	519
Doncaster	242
Halifax	697
Harrogate	499
Huddersfield	769
Keighley	221
Leeds	1,280
Morley	104
Ossett	134
Pontefract	183
Pudsey	34
Rotherham	247
Settle	96
Sheffield	520
Skipton	144
Wakefield	496
York	641

The Yorkshire Post, 28 April 1914, p.10.

Recruiting for the Leeds National Reservists took place at No. 1 Queen's Square, under Lieutenant George Rayner, with applications being made to Acting/Sergeant Major Young. A further call was made at the beginning of the war for a large number of time-expired Territorials and old soldiers to serve at home and abroad, and further appeals were made in the local press asking for more men between the ages of 40 and 50 to act as guards for civilian and military prisoners of war. The appeal specifically requested

Class II men – the medical grade and classification re-
leasing men for other duties or active service.[8] The age
restrictions were later raised to include older men.

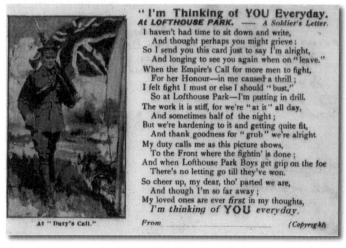

" I'm Thinking of YOU Everyday.
At *LOFTHOUSE PARK.* —— *A Soldier's Letter.*

I haven't had time to sit down and write,
  And thought perhaps you might grieve :
So I send you this card just to say I'm alright,
  And longing to see you again when on "leave."
When the Empire's Call for more men to fight,
  For her Honour—in me caused a thrill ;
I felt fight I must or else I should " bust,"
  So at Lofthouse Park—I'm putting in drill.
The work it is stiff, for we're "at it" all day,
  And sometimes half of the night ;
But we're hardening to it and getting quite fit,
  And thank goodness for " grub " we're alright.
My duty calls me as this picture shows,
  To the Front where the fightin' is done ;
And when Lofthouse Park Boys get grip on the foe
  There's no letting go till they've won.
So cheer up, my dear, tho' parted we are,
  And though I'm so far away ;
My loved ones are ever *first* in my thoughts,
  I'm thinking of **YOU** *everyday.*

At " Duty's Call."   *From* ....   *(Copyright)*

Fig. 18.1: Postcard of 'A Soldier's Letter' (Private Collection).

One of the men who served at Lofthouse Park was
Corporal Robert Brown. His hours of duty at the camp
consisted of 24 on and 24 off.[9] He had joined the Royal
Defence Corps in June 1916, aged 55.[10] He was a labourer
in his day job and also engaged as a caretaker at the All
Hallows' Church Institute, which was not far from his
home in the Hyde Park area of Leeds. In an interesting case
heard at Wakefield in December 1917, Robert Brown was
summoned to court by the Yorkshire (West Riding)
Electric Tramway Company for refusing to pay the full
tram fare from Leeds to Lofthouse in November. The
court heard that the West Riding Tramway Company had
offered concessionary fares up until recently, allowing
soldiers to travel for half fare. The concession had since
been withdrawn, owing to a number of factors, including
the gradually increasing number of soldiers that were

travelling. It was also stated that under the concessions the only people allowed to travel at half fare were artisans, mechanics or daily labourers. Corporal Brown had refused to pay the full 3½d, paying only 2d instead. He offered the following statement in his defence:

> I am representing the British Army [...] in this case. We take it as a direct insult to the King's uniform to make us pay full fare when men in exactly the same position, although they have not got khaki on, can go for working-men's fares. I not only ask you to dismiss this case, but ask for an apology from the Tramways Company.[11]

The case was adjourned for a week. A decision was later found in favour of Corporal Brown.

As mentioned previously, the duties of the guard could be varied. In a letter to the *Yorkshire Evening Post* in October 1939, one former member of the Royal Defence Corps recounts his experience of guarding a railway line near Goole in which the guardroom was an old railway coach. The writer also talks of his time at Spurn Point as part of the Humber Garrison. Finally, in what is a lengthy, but fascinating account about daily routine, censorship, black-outs, lighting and a Zeppelin raid, the writer shares some of his experiences at Lofthouse Park, where he spent eighteen months before being sent to Spurn Point. An extract of the account is reprinted below. It was modestly signed 'H.M.N':

> From Goole about thirty of us were sent to Lofthouse Park. I liked being there, because I could come into Leeds every other day. We were guarding German and Austrian prisoners, who were in compounds surrounded by barbed wire.

> Although the towns were blacked out, Lofthouse Park was always kept well lighted with big arc lamps all round each compound. Among the prisoners were some very clever artists, sculptors, woodworkers, and musicians. In one compound they got an orchestra together and gave

concerts. Some of the better-off prisoners had their own wooden bungalows with flower gardens in front. Parcels sent to the prisoners were placed in a hut behind a counter, and an officer, sergeant, and corporal had to open them and see that no letters or money were enclosed. They were then handed over.

The prisoners used to get dozens of boxes of cigars, and they always asked us to have a few.

I had been in Leeds one evening and caught the last car to Lofthouse, when about three-quarters of a mile from the Park our car stopped, and all the lights went out. This meant a Zeppelin raid. I walked onto the Park and went into the sergeants' and corporals' mess, and told them. They would not believe it at first, but later we heard explosions a few miles away [...].[12]

The Zeppelin raid referred to was probably the same raid which Matthew Marley records in his diary and the 'raid over Lofthouse Gate and district' on the night of 27 November 1916. Matthew Marley worked at the Lofthouse Colliery. His diaries, which cover several periods between 1907 and 1942, also mention the death of Sergeant Jack Newman in January 1915. Jack Newman was a National Reservist based at Lofthouse Park. He was buried in Outwood Cemetery with full military honours.[13]

Among some of the other soldiers who served at Lofthouse Park were Pte. Henry Braginton, James Patrick Gillen and Charles Dobson, who was a Warrant Officer. Charles Dobson had joined the Leeds Rifles as a Private at the outbreak of war and transferred to the National Reserve where he was promoted to Colour Sergeant in November the same year. He was later transferred to 154 Protection Company, shortly after the Royal Defence Corps was formed in 1916, finishing the war attached to the Military Police as an Acting/Regimental Sergeant Major. Charles Dobson was demobilised in December 1919. He had also seen service in the King's Own

Yorkshire Light Infantry during the Boer War, where he was wounded in the chest, and was later active in the Home Guard in the Second World War. His death, and that of his service in three wars, was reported in the *Yorkshire Evening Post* in September 1946. According to his sister, Charles Dobson had 'carried the bullet with him for over forty years.'[14] It had never been removed.

Henry Braginton was a bill poster in civilian life. Born in 1863, he was a supernumerary in the 2/5th West Yorkshire Regiment, having joined in 1915. He died shortly after being discharged from Lofthouse Park in January 1919.[15] Private James Patrick Gillen had collapsed and died at Lofthouse Park while mounting the guard on 25 October 1916. His cause of death was given as 'Heart Failure.'

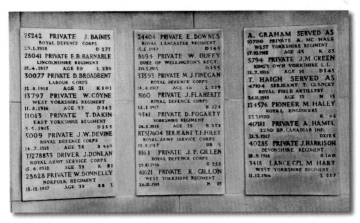

Fig. 18.2: Commemoration of Privates Baines, Devine, Finegan, Flaherty and Gillen of the Royal Defence Corps on memorial panels at Killingbeck Cemetery, Leeds (Photograph: David Stowe).

Aged 48, James Gillen had previously served with the 1st Leicestershire Regiment and had seen active service in the Burma Campaign in 1887-89 and the South African Campaign in 1900-1902. His funeral was held at the

Killingbeck Roman Catholic Cemetery in Leeds.[16] There is an entry in the *National Roll of the Great War* (Leeds) for James Gillen. It reads as follows:

> Gillen, J. Private, Royal Defence Corps. He volunteered in 1914, and after a period of training served at various stations on important duties with his unit, and rendered valuable services. He was taken ill, and died on 25th October 1916. 'Steals on the air the distant triumph-song.' 10, Burton Road, Hunslet, Leeds.[17]

Private Henry Braginton and James Patrick Gillen had served with 154 Protection Company, along with Pte. John Flaherty, Richard Lucas, Daniel Jobson, and Sergeant William Fiddes.[18]

The typical war establishment of one company consisted of six officers, including one major and one captain to command fifty per cent of the company, four subalterns, one company sergeant major, one company quartermaster sergeant, ten sergeants, sixteen corporals, and 216 privates. Two paid lance-sergeants and sixteen paid lance-corporals were also included in the total establishment of 250.[19] Northern Command had thirteen provisional and two reserve companies under its command. The companies were designated the numbers 151-157, 160-166 and 199-200.[20] The number of Commands in May 1918 included Eastern, Western, Northern, Scottish, London, Irish, Aldershot, Guernsey, with some companies held in reserve for Ireland.

This was also a period of reorganisation and change for the Royal Defence Corps, with figures showing a sharp decrease in numbers between January and July 1918, and a reduction in the same period of more than 7,500 men. In the same period, there had been a steep increase in the number of prisoners being taken, adding to the difficulties of guarding POWs in some of the scattered camps when brought from the battlefields. Other factors affecting the availability of manpower included the disbanding of a number of companies and battalions of the Royal Defence Corps.[21] It was estimated that the percentage of guards to prisoners was around 17 per cent in a camp of around 400-500 prisoners, whereas only 7 per cent were needed in the larger camps.[22] The total number of guards employed in guarding the prisoner of war camps in July 1918 was 14,950.[23]

The percentage of guards to civilian internees was approximately one guard to every four civilians at Lofthouse Park – based on a company strength of 250. Indeed, the camp had undergone significant internal changes where a large number of civilians had been repatriated, with the number of civilians standing at around the thousand mark in May 1918.[24] In terms of the Royal Defence Corps, changes had been made to the hours of duty too, with the practice of allowing every man the second day off abolished, and replaced by a system which operated over six days.[25] This was mainly about freeing up manpower for other duties. The mounting of the daily guard was not directly affected.

Further changes to the Royal Defence Corps took place in the post-Armistice period where several protection companies were disbanded. The changes are also noticeable in the strength of the officer cadre at Lofthouse Park and the steady decrease in numbers throughout 1919. Lieutenant George Cecil Hebden formally submitted his resignation in May 1919. A single man, Hebden was a farmer before the war. His family home was at Dacre House near Scarborough.[26] Second Lieutenant Thomas Gray was one of three interpreters at Lofthouse Park. He gave notice in December 1919, and was demobbed one month later. Gray had offered his services to Military Intelligence in 1917. His 'Terms of Service' as an interpreter are reprinted at the end of this chapter.[27] One of the last officers to leave Lofthouse Park was Major Harry

Stuart Hassall, who was discharged on 22 January 1920. He had previously served at Leigh Camp, Lancashire.[28]

In January 1920 the guard was divided between Lofthouse Park and the former munitions factory at Barnbow, near Leeds.[29] The Commandant was Lieutenant-Colonel Robert Ronaldson. He had remained at Lofthouse Park until March when the financial affairs were finally settled and the camp officially closed.[30] It may be assumed that a reduced guard had been in place for some of this time.

Fig. 18.3: Screen wall at Killingbeck (Roman Catholic) Cemetery, Leeds (Photograph: David Stowe).

Terms of Service of Interpreters
for Prisoners of War Camps, Depots or
Other Places of Internment

1. A temporary commission as 2nd Lieutenant in the Army will be granted to candidates who are accepted. They will be eligible for promotion to the rank of lieutenant (without increased pay as such) after 12 months' continuous commissioned service as interpreters for prisoners of war. No further promotion will be granted.

2. Interpreters will wear uniform and be eligible for outfit allowance of £20. When they are accommodated at the public expense in hutments or under canvas, and necessarily provide themselves with camp kit, they will be eligible for a grant of £7.10s. camp kit allowance.

These allowances will be drawn from the source from which pay is drawn, the charge for camp kit allowance being supported by A.F.O. 1678 duly vouched.

3. (a) Pay will be at the initial rate of £4 a week without other emoluments, with such quarters as are available in the camps. When no quarters are provided, an extra grant of 15s. a week will be made. Interpreters to whom this 15s. grant is made are not eligible for the £7.10s. camp kit allowance. Pay will be drawn locally through the commandant of the camp or other place of internment.

(b) An interpreter will be eligible when he has completed 12 months' service as such, and provided that the commandant is thoroughly satisfied with the manner in which he performs his duties, for pay at the increased rate of £5 a week instead of £4 a week.

4. Should an interpreter at any time cease to be employed as such, he will except under special circumstances, be required to relinquish his commission and, in addition, the Army Council have power under Article 527, Pay Warrant,

to call upon any officer to relinquish his commission at any time should they consider that circumstances require it. On ceasing to be employed, he will cease to be entitled to any emoluments from Army Funds.

5. Full pay will be admissible during absence from duty owing to duly certified illness up to a total of 42 days in any period of 12 months.

6. Interpreters having accepted a commission will be liable to employment at any prisoners of war camps, depots, hospitals, or other places of internment as deemed necessary.

19/6/17. 0103/2/196 (M.I.6.c)

I accept employment as Interpreter under the foregoing conditions.

Source: TNA, WO 374/28808. Lt. T.E. Gray.

Gregory Sinclair Haines: Prison Reformer and Commandant of Lofthouse Park

Ruth Allison (United Kingdom)

> As my active service draws to a close I can
> honestly say, and with pride, that I have always
> looked upon the 'human being' among whom
> my lines so far have been cast, as my friends,
> both when free and when undergoing so called
> 'Punishment.'[1]

Lieutenant-Colonel G.S. Haines, 1912

Lieutenant-Colonel Haines, once described as the father of
the Detention System in England, spent nearly eighteen
years working in the prison service. He was widely
experienced in dealing with both criminals and offenders
against discipline in the British army and navy, and was
instrumental in implementing prison reforms which
introduced 'a more rational treatment of offenders against
society.'[2]

Haines was born in India on 14 November 1858 and
like his father, Field Marshal Sir Frederick Paul Haines, he
set his sights on a military career. He joined the British
Army and rose through the ranks to captain whilst serving
with the Dorsetshire Regiment. In 1887 he married Maud
Crossman who had also been born in India. After his
marriage and in order to serve in that subcontinent, Haines
transferred to the Cheshire Regiment where he was selected as aide-de-camp to the Commander in Chief, East
Indies. Regimental loyalties could be strong, however, and
despite being eventually given the position of adjutant, he

realised he would not be promoted further within this regiment.[3]

This halt to his career put Haines in an awkward position. It was a condition of his transfer that Haines had to retire if not promoted to major on or before 19 October 1900. He had reasoned that this gave him thirteen years in which to obtain the promotion and had thus agreed to the terms. In 1896, faced with the unwelcome prospect of being forced to retire early from army service, he accepted the position of Governor of Brixton Military Prison.[4]

Haines joined the Prison Department at a key time of prison reform. In 1895, a government committee report had suggested a number of changes to prison law. The Military Prison Staff Corps (MPSC), formed in 1901, slowly started to replace the warders in military prisons worldwide. Although unpopular with many of the old civilian warders, Haines and his fellow governors appreciated the positive effect of the Corps on morale amongst the prisoners.[5]

Haines served as governor in four prisons – Brixton, Dublin, Gosport and Dover – before being appointed commandant of Aldershot Detention Barrack on 14 November 1903.[6] Brigadier-General Charles Heath, who was in charge of administration at Aldershot, described Haines three years later as

> a thoroughly conscientious hardworking officer with marked ability and in all respects an excellent Commandant [...]. I cannot speak too highly of the excellent manner in which the Detention Barrack here is conducted.[7]

Horace Smith-Dorrien was equally impressed with Haines as Commandant when he arrived as General Officer Commanding-in-Chief (G.O.C. in C.) in 1907. Haines held the local rank of lieutenant colonel at this time, but was unable to obtain substantive promotion beyond captain due to the intricacies of army regulations. Smith-Dorrien intervened and on 21 December 1908 wrote his second appeal to the War Office recommending Haines for a half pay lieutenant colonelcy. He hoped the Army Council would,

> on consideration of [Haines'] most successful work in carrying out the conversion of the old prison system to the present enlightened detention barrack system, take some special steps to reward his splendid service.[8]

Smith-Dorrien's intervention was initially unsuccessful. However, in January 1910 he received a letter informing him that Richard Haldane, Minister of War, recognised the unfairness of the promotion system for commandants of detention barracks, and would address this in the near future.

Fig. 19.1: Commandant and Subordinate Staff, Aldershot Detention Barracks c. 1911-12 (U.S. Naval Institute, Maryland).

In December 1909, Haines was selected for the task of inspecting the Military Prisons and Detention Barracks in India.[9] Further international respect for Haines came from the Inspector General of the US Army and Secretary of the US Navy who were impressed both by the commandant and the detention system when they visited Aldershot in

1911. Haines was asked to write an article for the United States Naval Institute.[10] Eventually, on 20 March 1912, the War Office awarded Haines his much deserved substantive rank of lieutenant colonel and, having reached the age of 55 years, Haines retired on 14 November 1913.[11]

The outbreak of World War One, however, prevented Haines from enjoying a peaceful retirement. Almost immediately he was re-employed as Commandant of Prisoners of War Camps.[12] He commenced work on 26 August 1914 at Newbury,[13] a racecourse hastily converted into a temporary internment camp for civilians, the prisoners being housed either in the stables or in wooden-floored tents. Here Haines set up a system where the prisoners governed themselves within the compounds. British soldiers who were unarmed entered the compounds only when the commandant required a prisoner to be brought to his office. Rumours circulating in Germany of ill-treatment were proved to be unfounded, and Haines was described by one Austrian internee as 'a soldier and a gentleman' who possessed wisdom in the way he ran the camp.[14] The camp closed at the end of 1914 because of an excessively wet winter.[15]

Haines' reputation suffered a dent when he and Jordan Adams, an inventor with whom he had a business connection, were accused of blackmail by Miss Lillian Scott Troy, an associate of entrepreneur, suspected spy and Newbury internee Baron Louis Anton von Horst.[16] The accusation was investigated, but there was no evidence to support the allegation against Haines. Major General Rochfort, who examined Haines' diary on behalf of the War Office wrote: 'I am strongly of opinion that Colonel Haines can have had no dealing such as are described by Miss Troy.'[17] At the end of November 1914 von Horst was moved to the *Royal Edward*, an internment ship anchored at Southend-on-Sea, where he suffered a nervous breakdown. The *Royal Edward* was a floating equivalent of

Lofthouse Park, boasting three areas of segregation based on class and ability to pay, with additional privileges available for those who could afford them. Von Horst was transferred to Lofthouse Park on 13 April 1915 for two days before being moved to the German Hospital in Dalston.[18] Von Horst and Troy had been under surveillance by Special Branch for their connection with labour unrest, the suffragette movement and Irish nationalism. Both were deported after the war.[19]

After Newbury Camp closed, Haines was sent to the purpose-built timber camp at Blanches Banques, Jersey, which started taking German military prisoners of war on 20 March 1915. Haines was the first of six commandants who served until the camp closed in October 1919. Major Theodore E. Naish, who was Commanding Royal Engineers in Jersey from 1914 to 1919, noted that the prisoners were 'better disciplined' on arrival, but after a while they were slower to come to attention when seeing a British officer. He put this down to 'over indulgent methods.'[20]

Haines took over Stratford Camp in East London around July 1916. Richard Noschke, who was a civilian internee at Stratford, observed how this new commandant made an effort to talk to the internees and ask how they felt about the camp, the diet and other matters of concern. Instructions had also been issued that the guards were no longer to carry their rifles or handcuffs. Haines was the third commandant Noschke had experienced at Stratford. His kindness left a favourable impression on Noschke and had a positive effect on the civilian prisoners, who were now able to enjoy various sports. Noschke described Haines as 'a perfect Gentleman.'[21]

It was not only the prisoners who benefitted from Haines' presence at the camps. Soon after their arrival at Lofthouse Park, Edith, his second wife whom he had married in 1890, made an appeal in the *Yorkshire Post* for

Balaclava helmets, mufflers and warm gloves for the 273
'old soldiers' who guarded the internment camp. She
pointed out that these guards were all Yorkshiremen who
would have been fighting at the front along with their sons
and sons-in-law, had they not been exempt by reason of
their age or physical infirmity.[22]

Fig. 19.2: Lofthouse House served as the Commandant's office
and residence; drawing by David Arnold (with thanks to Roger
and Joan Byard).

Lofthouse Park Camp would be Haines' last posting as
commandant, his career being brought to a sudden end by
a heated discussion in the mess which ended in a court
martial. However, it was not Haines who was the subject
of the proceedings, but one of the old soldiers, Lieutenant
Albert Canning, who was 'charged on four counts with
breaches of military discipline.'[23] The discussion in the
mess centred on visits made to Baron Leopold von Plessen
by Mrs Leverton Harris, wife of the Parliamentary
Secretary to the Ministry of Blockade. Lieutenant Canning
was reported as having said:

'You have only to be a Baron in this camp to get preferential treatment.' When Lieutenant-Colonel Haines asked, 'By whom?' Lieutenant Canning replied: 'By you; you are always breaking the regulations.'[24]

Canning had also brought up the attempted escape from the camp by prisoners who had dug a tunnel. Von Plessen was believed to be the ringleader and had been moved from the north part of the camp to the less desirable south part as a punishment. However, after visits from Mrs Harris he had been moved back to his previous accommodation. Mrs Harris had also been suspected of smuggling in contraband for von Plessen. The Home Office wrote to Haines requesting longer unsupervised visits for her, although this was against regulations. Haines had refused and informed the War Office about the request, but during the trial admitted he could not remember if she had been supervised on her first visit.[25] Mrs Harris, who was not present at the court martial, later stated in a letter to *The Times* that she had visited Lofthouse Park Camp on four occasions and had been supervised on all of them.[26]

Haines was questioned about his role in the discussion and also about the administration of the camp.[27] Lieutenant Canning was eventually acquitted,[28] but Haines was dismissed from Lofthouse Park and forced back into retirement. The Army Council was of the opinion that

Lieutenant-Colonel Haines failed to exercise proper authority as Senior Officer in the Mess [...] and that instead of placing Lieutenant Canning in arrest he adopted the lamentably weak course of inviting that officer to repeat his previous remarks in the presence of Major Porter, the Assistant Commandant of the Camp.

The Council was not impressed by Haines' explanation that he did not arrest Canning 'because of the friendly nature of their associations and of their combined length of service.'[29]

Haines requested that he be allowed to instead resign and wrote to the General Officer Commanding-in-Chief, Northern Command, asking for his support. In the letter to be forwarded to the War Office he asked for his long service and record to be taken into account, then defended his actions in the mess and his evidence in the court. He denied having been involved in the discussion in the mess except for doing his best to stop it. His lack of memory at the court-martial, he explained, was the result of not having been prepared for questions relating to his administration of the camp, nor the carefully prepared volley of questions that were fired at him. He further protested that at least one of his answers had been incorrectly recorded and he had only been sent a partial copy of the cross-examination. Frustrated, he argued 'if my action be considered lamentably weak, it was not sufficient to send me away practically in disgrace.'[30] The G.O.C. in C. Northern Command forwarded the letter without comment and Haines' request to be allowed to resign was refused.

After his involuntary retirement, Haines was re-commended for the award of Commander of the Order of the British Empire (CBE), but his name was removed from the Military Division List amid concerns that severe criticism would follow any recognition of service awarded to him at this point. Haines had been recommended for the award by the Director of Prisoners of War (DPW) for services as Commandant of a Prisoners of War Camp. The citation read:

> Lieutenant-Colonel Haines was the earliest of Commandants and served for 4 years as such. He had the hardest of tasks in that he always had civilians under his charge, but was always able to maintain proper discipline among them. His methods were original but the results

good. He did very good service. He left owing to an un-
fortunate dispute with his Quartermaster for which I do
not think he was blameworthy.[31]

Gregory Sinclair Haines died at Farnham, Surrey, in 1921
at the age of 62.

Lofthouse Park
Prisoner-of-War Camp, 1918-1919

Oliver Wilkinson (Wolverhampton)

On 11 October 1918 a notice was displayed in Lofthouse Park announcing the mass transfer of the interned civilians held there to the Isle of Man.[1] The 'Camp Captains' reacted quickly, telegraphing the War Office in the hope of negotiating a stay. Their request was refused and within three days all 1,025 civilian internees had been transferred to Knockaloe.[2] So ended the history of Lofthouse Park as a civilian internment camp.

The following week a new phase commenced as the camp welcomed its first military residents. The arrival of German prisoners of war (POWs) extended the lifespan of the camp for 15 months, with Lofthouse Park becoming one of the largest camps for officers in the country.[3] Many of the first military inmates were newly captured German officers, largely taken in early October 1918.[4] The population swelled with transfers from other camps in the United Kingdom. Holyport, near Maidenhead, initially sent a group of 49 officers to Wakefield on 29 October 1918.

According to one of these men, Lieutenant Heinz Heinrich Ernst Justus (Fig. 20.1), the officials at Holyport used this transfer as an opportunity to rid themselves of the camp's 'bad boys'. Indeed, as will be shown below, Justus himself was to prove troublesome almost immediately.[5] By the time Lofthouse Park was visited by neutral inspectors in March 1919, it housed 852 German officers and 242 orderlies,[6] the latter being drawn from the Other Rank cache of German POWs and provided, as a social privilege, to 'serve' the officers and undertake the chores in the camp.

The military prisoners were accommodated in the huts vacated by the civilian internees, although only the north and west compounds of the camp were used. The private huts of the south compound, which had been erected at the personal expense of wealthy civilian inmates, were not occupied by the German officers. Inspectors found the camp to their overall satisfaction, the only issues being some dampness (attributed to the Yorkshire weather), a lack of hot water in the west compound and intermittent problems with electric lighting.[7]

The new military POWs had also drawn some advantages from their predecessors. The War Office order to evacuate the camp had been accompanied by strict limits on 'baggage allowance', resulting in the civilians having to leave many items behind. Hence books, tables and chairs, tools and, significantly, '[a]ll the vegetables in the camp which had been raised at great expense – notably cabbages' were all unwillingly 'gifted' to the new residents.[8] This was the cause of vocal complaints from the departing civilians.

Another grievance during the civilian occupation had been the restriction on movement in the camp caused by the creation of separate compounds.[9] The military captives enjoyed a concession; the gates between the north and west compounds were removed and left permanently open to allow inmates the freedom of the camp.[10] Such controls were in the charge of the British commandant, Lieutenant-Colonel Rouse, while the senior German officers were Major Karl Graf von Büdingen (north compound) and Major Schultze (west compound). As 'past-times' it appears that the German officers initially had the use of a bowling alley, albeit permission was later given to dismantle this to use as fire wood.[11] The camp had two theatres: the stage of the north compound was directed by an inmate called Hagedorn, the west compound performed under Wittmann. Between November 1918 and December 1919 the prisoners put on 32 separate productions, ranging from William Shakespeare's *Twelfth Night* to Johann Wolfgang von Goethe's *Die Mitschuldigen*.[12]

A final group of captives arrived at Lofthouse Park in late June 1919, following the scuttling of the German High Seas Fleet at Scapa Flow.[13] Survivors, totalling 144 German officers and 1,600 ratings, were taken to Nigg Camp on the Cromarty Firth. The naval officers were then dispersed between Oswestry Camp in Shropshire and Lofthouse Park. Once the latter arrived, they made immediate protests about the way they had been mistreated. Lieutenant S.R. Junker was one such officer who reported his experience at station stops *en route* to Wakefield:

> We were guarded by a Scotch officer and two men who, whenever the officer was absent, behaved in the most unseemly manner [...]. Threatened with the bayonet, my laurel badge was taken from my cap, and the ribbon of an order from my coat. We were also forced to perform humiliating acts and the populace threatened us in an insulting manner.[14]

Thefts, rough treatment and ritual humiliations, as many First World War POWs would attest, were par for the course following capture.[15] However, these particular Germans were met within a unique post-war atmosphere of charged 'Germanophobia' exhibited amongst the victorious allied nations.[16] By contrast their own national defeat could not be pushed from their minds.

Indeed, such feelings, informed by the context of their ongoing post-war incarceration when German POWs in allied hands were essentially being used as negotiating chips, weighed heavily on the captives. This had various effects. One response it elicited was an increased inclination to attempt to escape. Lieutenant Justus, for example, had already been a prolific escaper prior to his arrival at Lofthouse Park. While on the way to his new camp, he took the opportunity to jump from the train at South Elmsall near Pontefract. He had intended to head for Cardiff via London where he hoped to smuggle aboard a Spanish ship. His attempt was frustrated when he caught the flu, forcing him to give himself up. Justus's first taste of Lofthouse Park was thus admittance to the camp infirmary where others were similarly suffering from influenza.[17] Once he recovered, he was sentenced to 56 days confinement in Chelmsford Detention Barracks for his escape attempt.[18]

HEINZ H. E. JUSTUS

Fig. 20.1: Heinz H.E. Justus (Joe R. Ackerley, ed,. *Escapers All*, London: John Lane, 1932).

Yet most of the escapes by German officers held at Lofthouse Park took place post-armistice, and as such must be seen as motivated as much by the context, as prisoners grew dejected from repeatedly frustrated official repatriation plans, combined with more traditional escape motivators such as duty, attempts to retain one's combative status, and therein the quest, as Brian K.

Feltman puts it, for 'redemption'.[19] Lieutenants Julius
Lassen and Gerhard Sternkopf made their attempts in
March 1919 along with a third, unidentified, officer who
tried to smuggle himself out in the camp's laundry van, but
attracted the suspicions of the driver in the process.[20]

In July, Lieutenant Hans Leroe broke out of the camp
and managed to walk to Hull where he hoped to board a
vessel, but was arrested as he slept in a warehouse doorway
near the docks.[21] Four more Lofthouse POWs, Lieutenants Hans Martin Leroc, Karl Ernst Schwerin, Heinrich
Ruhlwind and Karl Henz, made escapes in August. All
were recaptured.[22] Then, in November 1919, the camp
witnessed a mass escape attempt, a tunnel being discovered
through which it was reported twenty of the Scapa Flow
officers had tried to escape. 'Scuttling Scuttlers' was how
the incident was reported, the prisoners having apparently
miscalculated the tunnel's length, leaving a sentry amazed
to see the earth open at his feet.[23] Linking this attempt to
those naval POWs, however, seems to be a calculated
targeting of them in reflection of the accusatory mood in
Britain at the time. The origins of the tunnel can in fact be
questioned, the *Nottingham Evening Post* indicating it had
been in progress for over eight months, hence predating
the arrival of the Scapa Flow POWs.[24]

Repatriation, however, was the issue that preoccupied
German prisoners held in Britain throughout 1919.
Prisoners faced ongoing anxieties about their wartime
fate,[25] including concerns about how their capture would
be viewed by family, friends and officials in Germany. Yet
in this post-armistice limbo of ongoing incarceration they
were also affected by new anxieties regarding post-war
employment opportunities and uncertainties about their
usefulness within the new German state. What was more,
the longer they languished in the camps, the greater was
the feeling that they had been abandoned by their nation.
In response, as Feltman has shown, prisoners tried to

attract attention to their plight to expedite their release, making appeals to the British government, to the War Office, and even trying to directly influence the British public. Banners were displayed from POW camps while messages were attached to balloons and floated over the wire.[26] The 'Prisoners of War, Lofthouse Park Officers Camp' also made an appeal by letter to the editor of the *Manchester Guardian* in order to

> make it publicly known that it is not France alone who after more than one year's cessation of hostilities is keeping her prisoners of war back, but that there is a considerable number of these sufferers left in England too [...]. Now Christmas [1919] is at hand, and still there is no sign of our imminent repatriation, our dearly cherished hopes to be home by then being shattered. [...] This state of suspense is telling on our nerves.[27]

That final claim was endorsed by Dr A.L. Vischer who had warned during the war that a lack of information regarding repatriation had the potential to contribute significantly to 'barbed wire disease'. This adverse mental condition affecting civilian internees and POWs alike was attributable to the trials of captive life and became manifest in irritability, irrationality, depression, remoteness and even complete withdrawal.[28]

Evidence from Lofthouse Park camp in 1919 bears out that claim. Tellingly it comes from the cases of foiled escapers including Lieutenant Sternkopf and the apparently insatiable Lieutenant Justus, whose post-war escape stories mask the view of mental turmoil in favour of the image of the plucky, playful absconder who masqueraded as a woman to effect one of his getaways.[29] In fact following their failed attempts and ongoing incarceration, these men were to suffer mental breakdowns necessitating their transfer from Lofthouse Park to Nell Lane Hospital, West Didsbury. Justus was sent there on 6 May 1919 and recorded as a 'Mental Case'; Sternkopf was admitted on 22 July 1919 suffering from 'Acute Mania'.[30]

While it was the uncertainty regarding release that was one of the leading factors in such mental anxiety, repatriation itself was the 'most powerful of remedy'.[31] Yet inmates at Lofthouse Park were amongst the longest to suffer, it being one of the last camps in the UK to be emptied. Figures cited in the press indicate that 743 German officers and 248 orderlies, 'with ages from 20 to 47, several among them prisoners since 1914 and 1915', were still incarcerated there on 13 December 1919. One month later it was claimed that Lofthouse Park was empty, the recent departure of 1,800 German POWs from Hull leaving only the Scapa Flow POWs and a handful of men undergoing medical treatment still captive in the UK.[32] Instead of being sent home, the Scapa Flow naval officers held at Lofthouse Park had been transferred to Donnington Hall Camp where they were reunited with their comrades from Oswestry. These men were finally released on 29th January 1920, their departure marking the final batch of German POWs to leave British custody.[33]

Lofthouse Park Camp remained open for a further six weeks before officially closing on 13 March 1920.[34]

Author's note: I would like to thank Anne Buckley, Douglas Arthur Johnson and David Stowe for the assistance with source material used in this chapter.

Meine Flucht:
Albert H. Brugger's Escape Narrative

Claudia Sternberg (Leeds)

Escapes from British internment and prisoner-of-war camps were rare and often unsuccessful. Military prisoners had a stronger motivation than civilians to attempt a getaway because they felt under pressure to rejoin their units for active service and usually had no personal ties within Britain. Another motivating factor for absconding was prolonged imprisonment after hostilities had ended.[1]

A long wait and uncertainty about their release triggered the escape from Lofthouse Park by POW No. 685, Albert Hermann Brugger, and fellow prisoner Siegfried von Waldenburg in December 1919. The narrative of their flight, authored by Brugger and published in German as *Meine Flucht aus dem Kriegsgefangenen-Lager Lofthouse-Park near Wakefield*, is among the few longer accounts of experiences relating to Lofthouse Park Camp. The text, just under 80 pages, contains sufficient detail to be credible to some degree, but unlike the getaway of the civilians Wiener and Klapproth in 1915,[2] Brugger's and von Waldenburg's escape was not covered by the local press. As a World War story addressed at a German readership in 1937, *Meine Flucht* also has to be understood in the context of the time of its publication. This chapter therefore constitutes a reading of Brugger's tale and viewpoint rather than a reconstruction of a historical incident.

Lieutenant Albert Brugger had been captured by the British near Cheluwe in Flanders, with the larger part of his regiment, on 14 October 1918. His journey to Wakefield, a 'gloomy town in the mining district of the county York',[3] was a lengthy one. It started with a long march on foot via Ypres to Poperinghe. On 17 October, the prisoners were transported in cattle trains to Calais and then on to Abbéville. While the ordinary soldiers were moved to central France, the officers arrived in Le Havre on the following morning – hungry and cold, as Brugger recalls. After being deloused and staying in tents for a few days, the men eventually crossed the Channel. They disembarked in Southampton where they spent some comfortable days in an old castle before taking the train to London and further north.

By the second half of October 1918, Lofthouse Park Camp had been emptied of civilian internees to make place for the increasing number of military prisoners. According to Brugger's – possibly embellished – account, the camp was filled to capacity after a few weeks, with 40 officers sharing a hut, sleeping on the floor until field beds, tables and benches could be obtained. The author describes the lack of food and hunger that were experienced by prisoners and English soldiers alike.[4] He acknowledges the efforts of those POWs who managed to prepare a Christmas meal in 1918 with very little resources.[5] Over time, conditions improved and Brugger also managed to occupy a chalet, Hut No. 35.

Although captured shortly before the war ended, Brugger and his fellow officers found themselves imprisoned for an indefinite period. Like the civilian internees, the men engaged in sport and play as well as educational activities. Additionally, they 'annoyed, whenever possible, the *Engländer*,[6] but Brugger reports that the camp commandant maintained very strict discipline, which he attributes to his previous position as a prison director in India.[7]

A good year after the Armistice and still without information about a possible release, Brugger decided to flee from the camp, together with his friend Siegfried von

Waldenburg, lieutenant of the Kaiser-Alexander-Garde-Grenadier-Regiment.

Der Verfasser und Lt. v. Waldenburg vor der selbsterbauten Hütte

Fig. 21.1: Albert Brugger and Siegfried von Waldenburg in front of their Lofthouse Park 'chalet' (*Meine Flucht*; Berlin State Library).

In keeping with the escape adventure genre, Brugger relates in some detail how their plan took shape. The main difficulties apart from exiting the camp unnoticed were to obtain money and civilian clothing. The possession of either was prohibited and punishable with jail sentences. The camp operated with tokens as a means of payment, and the rate for clandestine conversion into pounds was very high, a pound being traded for an equivalent of 800 Reichsmark.[8] But even in the context of military prisoners, British German relations existed and were put to good use. A fellow inmate had received money from an English aunt and gave it to Brugger and von Waldenburg for 50 Reichsmark per pound. Civilian clothes were created by altering uniforms, tailoring missing pieces from blankets and using onion peel and tea leaves as dyes.

On 6 December 1919, Brugger and von Waldenburg set
out to make their escape from Lofthouse Park. For
heightened effect, Brugger describes how the camp was
secured: it had a web of barbed wire, three metres in depth
and two metres high. Armed guards were positioned 30
metres apart, and 50 metres behind the wire was a wooden
fence of three metre height. Electrical arc lamps illu-
minated the area at night.[9]

In order to stand a chance, the escapers needed the help
of accomplices. A group of officers and a batman,
Musketeer Himken, distracted the patrolling guards of the
North compound with temper tantrums, acrobatics and a
brawl. They also sent warning signals to Brugger who, lying
on his stomach, tackled the barbed wire with a wire cutter.
Brugger and von Waldenburg eventually crawled through
a hole in the wire, which was later concealed by Himken,
and then onto open land. The next challenge was the fence,
but trained as infantry soldiers, the two young men 'took
the obstacle like on the drill ground'.[10] A moment of
elation followed:

> Free! It was a marvellous feeling to move about at one's
> own discretion, to be able to do as one pleases after
> having been condemned to live a schematical life for five
> quarters of a year as a mere number! This impression, this
> sensation belongs to those which imprint themselves
> solidly and forever on one's soul.[11]

To give the escapers a head start, the accomplices had
agreed to call out for them during roll call. Nevertheless,
Brugger and von Waldenburg had to depart from the scene
as quickly and inconspicuously as possible:

> It must have been just after 7pm when we crossed fields
> and meadows to reach the main road between Wakefield
> and Leeds. We came among people. It was a Saturday and
> the street was busy. We had to be careful and blend in so
> as not draw attention to us. We hardly knew the customs
> and traditions of the country. Thus we had to keep our

eyes and ears open. At the nearest stop, we got on a tram
to Leeds where we arrived after a short journey. The city
made a splendid impression. Its cosmopolitan hustle and
bustle was a long missed sight for us. Not even in Berlin
had I seen such lively activity.[12]

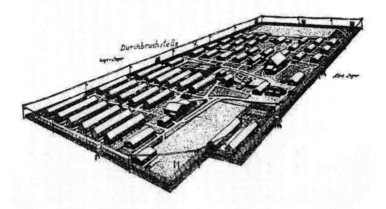

Fig. 21.2: Camp drawing indicating the *Durchbruchstelle* or exit
point (*Meine Flucht,* Berlin State Library).

Long deprived of civilian life but also avoiding hotel
controls under the Aliens Restriction Act, the men went to
the cinema. Brugger recalls that despite the continuing
aversion to anything German in Britain at the time, the
music during the screening consisted mainly of popular
German tunes. At the end of the programme, 'God Save
the King' was played to a standing audience:

> This mark of respect indeed gave me something to think
> about. In the Kaiser's Germany I had rarely experienced
> anything like it; the liberal Englishman did not seem to
> find that such an exercise was beneath him. As far as
> national consciousness is concerned, we can learn a lot
> from the Briton! But in this assessment one must not
> forget that England at the time experienced the highest
> stage of victory psychosis.[13]

The middle part of *Meine Flucht* recounts how the two escapers wriggled out of awkward situations, for example by pretending to be Frenchmen, and attempted to leave Britain by ship. Initially, they made their way to Hull, but were unable to convince the captain of a Swedish ship to take them to the Continent. While the merchant navy officer did not report the men to the authorities, he was not prepared to actively support the flight of German POWs.[14]

As remaining in Hull became too risky, Brugger and von Waldenburg decided to try their luck in Dover. By then, they were short of money and hoped to borrow some funds from the uncle of a fellow POW. To do so, they travelled to London where Brugger approached the unsuspecting Mr Salomony, a naturalised Jew from Frankfurt. To Brugger's dismay, Salomony was terrified when confronted with the men's predicament and request for money, fearing that his exchange of letters with the imprisoned nephew would come out. Salomony too declined to assist the men's escape.

Increasingly worried, Brugger and von Waldenburg followed up on an article from the *Daily Mail* which claimed that new and returning 'Huns', eager to resume business in Britain, were seen all over London, particularly in the City and the inns around Aldgate Pump. The men searched the local restaurants, but once again faced disappointment; no Germans could be found. Instead, they came across a shop selling German military memorabilia, which were displayed alongside anti-German labels.[15]

Finally, Brugger and von Waldenburg contacted the British politician and philanthropist Lord Parmoor, who presided over the Famine in Europe Council, to obtain the address of the Austrian representative Baron Ofenheim.[16] But before they could reach Ofenheim at the Cavendish Hotel on Jermyn Street on 10 December, they were arrested by plain clothes policemen and taken to Vine

Street Police Station. After it was known who the two men were, the authorities turned more hostile towards them. Brugger and von Waldenburg were put in separate dark cells until an escort arrived – comprised of one officer, a sergeant and six men – to return the men to Lofthouse.

> Throughout the transport, which was a period of recovery for us, we were treated correctly and even with a certain respect by the officer and the soldiers. The Englishman viewed the escape as a kind of sport and showed then as well as later great interest in us and our exploits.
>
> Towards midday, we arrived in Wakefield.
>
> News must have travelled that we were on our way back because we were expected by a large group of people outside the station, mainly miners who were changing shifts, and women. Contrary to our expectations, the attitude of the people was not in the least hostile. Quite the opposite was the case; we had the impression that we were held in esteem. Among the women, feelings of sympathy with our lot predominated. Here and there, people wanted to pass on cigarettes to us, and the soldiers had difficulties to keep people away. […] The friendly disposition of the population was not least a result of the systematic propaganda which had been distributed from the camp for months, and which had obviously impacted most on the neighbouring area.[17]

Back in Lofthouse Park Camp, Brugger and von Waldenburg were cheered by the other prisoners, but they were quickly removed to the nearby prison hut to await their court-martial. The ill-equipped gaol was mainly used for delinquent British soldiers and as a drunk tank. Brugger relates that some of the guards used the opportunity to harass the German prisoners, but the court-martial followed due procedure, with a hearing of evidence, witness testimony and translations. Fellow prisoner Hauptmann (Captain) von Zitzewitz acted as counsel for the defence, a role aided by the fact that he 'had worked for a German bank in London for a long time and spoke fluent English'.[18] Von Waldenburg's defence was led by sub-marine Kapitänleutnant (Lieutenant Commander) Sprenger. The two escapers were found guilty by three judges for absconding from the camp and wearing civilian clothes; they were sentenced to three months imprisonment.

Fig. 21.3: Illustration by Lofthouse POWs to draw attention to their prolonged imprisonment (*Meine Flucht*; Berlin State Library).

Brugger and von Waldenburg had expected to be transferred to a proper prison, but they remained in their separate cells at Lofthouse. Their request to spend some

time together on Christmas Eve was granted and they also
received food and drink from the camp. Soon thereafter
news reached them that Lofthouse Park would finally be
wound up. Happy for their fellow prisoners to be released,
the two men were concerned that they would have to stay
put for two further months. But in the early hours of 27
December 1919, Albert Brugger and Siegfried von
Waldenburg could go free with the others and travelled –
lawfully – from Hull to Germany.

Fig. 21.4: Book cover of Albert Brugger's *Meine Flucht*, published
in Nazi Germany in 1937 (*Meine Flucht*, Berlin State Library).

Brugger's narrative resembles other accounts of escapes that were already popular during the First World War and also published alongside wartime memoirs in the interwar years. It is important to note, however, that *Meine Flucht* is a late contribution to this kind of war literature. The book's preface by its Berlin-based publishing house reveals the motivation for printing this narrative at the height of the Nazi ascendancy:

> Particular attention should be paid to the attitude of the young officer who, amidst the great struggle, takes up a purely intuitive position against the Jews, without yet having a clear-cut explanation for his fundamental rejection of Jewishness. Thus it is understandable that the author, today SA-*Brigadeführer* and *Stabsführer* of the SA-Group North Sea, found his way to the [National Socialist] Movement early on.[19]

Born on 9 November 1895, World War One veteran Dr. A.H. Brugger was still in his prime in the 1930s and an active Nazi with SA leadership credentials. This fact is highlighted by the fascist publisher Hans Siep, who advertised a selection of other books from his ethno-nationalist programme at the end of *Meine Flucht*. Siep's allusion to Brugger's anti-Semitic "intuition" refers to a section in the text in which the narrator recounts how he had spoken out, in 1917, against the promotion of a Jewish sergeant to an officer's rank on the basis of principle, despite the man's suitability and general recommendation.[20]

Whether Albert Brugger had included this recollection of his anti-Jewish intervention from the outset or had been prompted by the publisher cannot be said. The episode nevertheless sheds light on the fact that, from September 1914 onwards, Jewish soldiers had been able to gain an officer's rank in the Prussian Army.[21] At the same time, persistent anti-Semitism, especially in the officers' corps, continued to discredit the achievements of Jewish servicemen and minimise their chances. Brugger embeds his reminiscence of the incident in the narration of his encounter with Mr Salomony. Brugger's description of Salomony, 'the cowardly Jew'[22] stricken by 'non-human fear',[23] contains numerous anti-Semitic stereotypes and the predictable conclusion that 'Mr Salomon has never been a German despite his German origins. The Jew has no fatherland and no national feelings.'[24]

Unlike in the case of the Swedish captain, Brugger shows no understanding for the fact that aiding escaped military prisoners would have been illegal and particularly risky for someone of German descent under pressure to ward off any suspicion of disloyalty towards Britain. It is not without irony that contemporary readers can find information about Lofthouse Park as a prisoners-of-war camp by turning to an obscure Nazi publication that has survived from 1937. It is even more poignant that Albert Brugger's *Meine Flucht aus dem Kriegsgefangenen-Lager Lofthouse-Park near Wakefield* based its initial appeal on the racist dismissal of a naturalised German Jew who would have been privy to the internment of German civilians during the First World War and who, according to the narrative, broke the rules by keeping in contact with a (Jewish) relative and POW at Lofthouse Park, but refused to support an anti-Semitic officer on the run in 1919.

Gentlemen's Internment Elsewhere: The Celler Schloss as Privilege Camp

Hilke Langhammer (Celle)[1]

British historians of the First World War are likely to be familiar with Ruhleben, the former horse-racing track to the west of Berlin which was used as a civilian internment camp for Britons from November 1914 to 1918. Although initially less prepared than Britain to deal with people of 'enemy' nationality, Germany had also developed the Holzminden internment camp for Belgian, French, Polish and Russian civilians at around the same time as the *Engländerlager* Ruhleben in Spandau. But as it was with the case at Lofthouse Park, nationality was not the only consideration when camps were established for foreigners in Germany.

In the village of Scheuen, about eight kilometres from the German town of Celle, in Lower Saxony, one of the largest prisoner-of-war camps in the province of Hanover was erected with a capacity to house 10,000 soldiers and officers. At the same time, the *Celler Schloss* (Celle Palace) was turned into a camp that had a very different character and was unique in Imperial Germany. It held 250 men who were referred to as 'Zivilpersonen höherer Lebensstellung' (civilians of higher standing in life).[2] One part of the prisoners was made up of the so-called *Feindstaatenausländer* (enemy aliens) who had been resident in Germany or had been travelling when the war broke out: businessmen and industrialists, musicians and students. The majority of these men were British and Russian. A second group consisted of hostages from France and Belgium; they were eminent figures of public life who had been arrested to exercise pressure on the population. The third group comprised about fifty French chaplains from the medical service.

Fig. 22.1: The Celler Schloss around 1914 (Bomann Museum Celle).

Depending on size, two to fourteen prisoners shared one room. The rooms were furnished with beds, tables and chairs. Further furniture could be bought or hired. One of the palace's larger halls was available for meals. It also served as a place for recreation, study, theatre performances and concerts. Additionally, there was a 'smoking hall', a billiard room and a library. While the sleeping quarters and common rooms for the prisoners were perceived as satisfactory and even comfortable, sanitary facilities were limited. The palace had previously not had running water. Water pipes, toilets, sinks and baths had to be installed. Sinks were placed in the corridors, but only two bathrooms were provided. Toilets were erected on the outside of the palace. Sports activities were possible in the courtyard, and prisoners were able to go on a walk within the perimeter fence of the palace. A football pitch or gymnastics equipment, which could be found in the larger barrack camps, were not available, so that a badminton club was founded instead. Like in other camps, inmates organised music, theatre and arts groups; they also offered language classes and lectures in a 'camp university.'

Fig. 22.2: A sample cell in the palace (Bomann Museum Celle).

On account of his uniform and the circumstances that led to his imprisonment, the Briton Duncan Heaton-Armstrong (1886-1969) was perhaps the most eye-catching inmate. In 1914, he had followed Prince Wilhelm zu Wied to Albania. Zu Wied had been appointed Duke of Albania by the Central Powers, and Heaton-Armstrong had taken up the position of private secretary.[3] When the situation in the Balkans became more unstable, the Duke of Albania instructed Heaton-Armstrong to escort his two children to Germany. At the end of August, they reached Munich. Although Heaton-Armstrong had been promised safe conduct, the German authorities did not allow him to leave the country and eventually interned him at the Veste Oberhaus in Passau. In November 1914, Heaton-Armstrong was brought to the Ruhleben Camp for British civilians. Shortly thereafter, he was moved to the Celler Schloss where he stayed until his exchange on 15 August 1916.

The most well-known among the Belgian hostages was Adolphe Max, the Burgomaster of Brussels. He had been arrested by the German occupiers in September 1914 because he continued to communicate with the population of Brussels through public notices without permission.[4] Max spent almost the entire war in different camps and prisons in the German Empire. He was an inmate of the Celler Schloss for nearly two years, where he was isolated from other Belgian hostages and had to live in solitary confinement.

Fig. 22.3: Adolphe Max, interned former mayor of Brussels (Bomann Museum Celle).

Well documented in the Celle police files is the escape
attempt of the Briton Gilbert McMicking (1894-1918),
who had been a student in Weimar before his internment.
Together with his countryman Robert A. Reddie, who
dressed up as a German non-commissioned officer, and a
Russian internee, he left the palace with a hand cart at the
end of February 1917 under the pretence to get the mail.
On account of bad weather and a cold, McMicking gave
himself up to the authorities, as did his comrades shortly
afterwards. Another attempted escape by McMicking also
failed, because the tunnel he had dug collapsed.[5]
McMicking did not recover from his illness. At the end of
1917, he was taken to the neutral Netherlands where he
died on 11 November 1918, the day the Armistice was
signed at Compiègne.

Fig. 22.4: British internees in the courtyard. Third from the left,
seated: Duncan Heaton-Armstrong; third from the right,
standing: Gilbert McMicking (Bomann Museum Celle).

In comparison to the larger internment camps Ruhleben and Holzminden, the Celler Schloss served those who could not reasonably be expected to endure mass detention. Behind such thinking lay traditional notions of societal status and class hierarchy. Yet the composition of the detainees leaves some questions unanswered. On the one hand, French clerics, as non-combatants, should have been on a par with prisoners-of-war according to the Hague Convention and transferred to a respective camp. On the other, there were many British students, professors, doctors, company owners, businessmen and engineers on the lists of Ruhleben internees – in addition to tradesmen, seamen and workers. It will probably remain unknown who determined whether an internee was deemed 'privileged' or if the decisions about 'higher standing' were mainly left to chance. However, it is less likely to have been chance where high-ranking prisoners were interned at the Celler Schloss, and some, such as Adolphe Max, were kept in isolation and not allowed to communicate with others. The decision in this respect seems as much political as anything else.

In terms of numbers, civilian internees played a minor role compared to military prisoners-of-war. The detention of 'enemy aliens', however, was contrary to international law and yet almost regarded as self-evident in Germany and other belligerent states, revealing the instability of the Hague Convention and attempts to restrict involvement to combatants. The practice is furthermore a clear indication of the totalising of war which began with the First World War.

Translated from German by Claudia Sternberg

Surplus to Requirements:
Dismantling Lofthouse Park Camp

David Stowe (Leeds)

The Disposal Board was set up under the auspices of the
Ministry of Munitions in January 1919. Its aim was simple:
to undertake the disposal of Government material that was
'Surplus to Government Requirements.'[1] One of the ways
this was effected was through auction and advertising the
lots for sale. There were some 552 lots advertised for the
sale of Lofthouse Park Camp in May 1920.[2] The auction
was carried out by Beaumont and Glover of King Street,
Wakefield, who were acting under the direction of the
Government Disposal Board and Ministry of Munitions.
Some of the contents which were marked for disposal can
be found in the table at the end of this chapter.

The disposal sale attracted between two and three
hundred people on the first day. The *Yorkshire Post* reported that 'the administrative block fetched £120, and
two buildings used for officers' quarters £80 apiece, while
the kit-house realized £73, and the reading room £95.'[3]
Amongst the other items which had been sold was a sentry
box which fetched £5 15 shillings, a telephone pole (15
shillings), a corrugated-iron kitchen (£6 10 shillings), a
bath-house (£9), and some small huts which had sold from
£40 to £70. The selling of the fixtures and fittings also
included the '41 bundles of very ancient barbed wire'
which had been bought for 17 shillings and sixpence on
the first day of the sale.[4]

The disposal of the fixtures and fittings offers some
insight into the material culture of camp life where these
items are found in newspapers and brochures such as the
Yorkshire Post or *Surplus*.

Fig. 23.1: Lofthouse Park Internment Camp, Leeds Road (Out-wood Community Video. Ref. L57).

Further insight may be found in the following list and table which was compiled from a notice in the *Yorkshire Post* advertising the three-day sale of furniture and fittings in June 1920.

Furniture Section: Sale 22-24 June 1920

1,575 Chairs	86 Bedside Tables
247 Table Tops	2,478 Turkish Towels
144 Folding Forms	52 fire extinguishers
60 Chests of drawers	2,850 Bolster/Pillow Cases
Desks and Roll-Tops	1,153 Paliasse Cases
Chatwood Safe	893 Hair Bolsters
67 three-gallon tea cans	99 Hair Pillows
1,292 Table and Bed Trestles	468 Glass Cloths
131 Folding Bedsteads	413 Table Cloths
352 White Counterpanes	265 iron fire buckets
89 Looking Glasses	

Source: *Yorkshire Post*, 22 May 1920, p. 3.

The sale of the huts followed a long and protracted competition between the authorities at Rothwell and Wakefield to secure the camp and turn it into houses. Although the

Wakefield Corporation had secured the provisional approval of the Housing Commissioner for a scheme to convert the huts into 139 houses, the project was abandoned when it was realised that there were two parties concerned in the ownership of the camp, and each was negotiating on its own accord without reference to the other. This was further complicated where it was found that the War Office had given pre-emption to the Wakefield Corporation, while the ground landlord had granted a pre-emption on the land to Rothwell Urban District Council. The result was deadlock, with neither party being able to proceed with the scheme. It was at this point that the Disposal Board put up the whole of the property on the site to auction.[5]

The sale of the site included its fixtures and fittings, including an assortment of items from the camp's kitchens and hospital block, such as chopping blocks, pastry and knife boards, rolling pins, potato masher, baking dishes, enamelled butter dishes, pudding dishes, flour dredgers, weighing machines and weights, mixing bowls, meat choppers, mincing machines, carving knives and forks, cork screws, egg slicers, ladles, spoons, trays, stone jars, glass water bottles, crockery, brush and knife boxes, scrubbing brushes, blocks and handles, mop handles, thirteen large cupboards, one dispensary dresser with drawers and cupboards, four cast-iron slipper baths and fittings, three large racks, earthenware bed pans, enamelled wash basins, quart jugs, foot warmers, bedside screens, ash-bins and coal boxes.[6]

To this may be added the sale and disposal of several thousand feet of electrical wiring which had been installed throughout Lofthouse Park Camp, including the poles, pole insulators, the switches and fuses, and the street lights and standard lamps which had been erected when the camp was built in October 1914.

The dismantling of Lofthouse Park was part of the Disposal Board's large-scale operation across the United Kingdom. The number of huts notified for disposal across the country stood at just under 90,000 in March 1920. The number of huts disposed of stood at 65,927. The total value of the sales effected by the disposal of the huts and building materials between January 1919 and 1 May 1920 can be found in the following figures: Huts, building materials (£4,060,929); Timber (£2,080,806); Furniture (£1,451,214). Total: £7,592,949.[7]

After the process was concluded for Lofthouse Park, all that remained on site were the former dance-hall and the Pavilion. The Pavilion was destroyed by fire on 22 April 1922. The *Yorkshire Evening Post* reported on the fire two days later:

> The caretaker, who lives in an old mansion overlooking the park, was spending the evening at a club, a short distance away, when the alarm of fire was raised. The fire was apparently seen from the electric power station of the West Riding Tramways Company, and the staff there immediately telephoned for the Wakefield Fire Brigade. The brigade, however, declined to attend, as the park is outside their area; and the fire had obtained a strong hold by the time the Stanley Brigade had arrived.
>
> Then the Stanley brigade had to contend with a water difficulty, the only available supply being from a beck two or three hundred yards away.
>
> The buildings were fitted with proper facilities for fire-fighting – including pipes, hydrants, etc., and a supply of water stored in two huge tanks at the tops of the towers. Had firemen been on the scene earlier these appliances and the water in the tanks might have saved the buildings, but the Stanley brigade arrived only to find themselves cut off from all the hydrants and the water tanks in the blazing towers. Nevertheless the brigade did excellent work in saving part of the skating rink.[7]

With the destruction of its iconic Pavilion building, what had been Lofthouse Park and Lofthouse Park Camp was no more.

Figs. 23.2 and 3: The final demise of Lofthouse Park after a fire destroyed the Pavilion on 22 April 1922 (Outwood Community Video. Ref. L18 and L19).

Fixtures and Fittings: Sale 25-28 May 1920

No.	Description	Fittings	Measurement
40	Wood & Corrugated Iron Buildings	Varied size	20 x 20 x 10ft to 140 x 21 x 10ft
26	Wood Living Huts	Wood and felt roofs	60 x 20 x 10ft
17	Corrugated Iron Living Huts	Wood floors	102 x 18 x 10ft
12	Corrugated Iron Buildings	Varied size	40 x 20 x 10ft to 102 x 13 x 10ft
12	Wood Huts: forming Guard House, Canteen, and NCOs Mess	Wood and felt roofs: wood floor, lined Asbestos	60 x 20 x 10ft
3	Sentry boxes		–
2	Brick-built Boiler Houses	R.E. Fixtures and Fittings	–
1	Corrugated Iron Building	Institute: wood floor	90 x 40 x 18ft
1	Corrugated Iron Building	Hospital: wood floor	70 x 28 x 10ft
1	Corrugated Iron Building	Cookhouse: lined asbestos	30 x 20 x 10ft
78	'Slogan' Stoves		–
19	Farm Boilers	20 & 30 Gallons	–
14	Ranges	48 and 72-inch	–
42	Glazed stoneware sinks	Includes Taps and Pipes	–
43	Sets of W.C. Fittings		–
1	Independent Boiler and Tank	–	–

Source: *Yorkshire Post*, 22 May 1920, p. 3.

Leeds and the Alien Register
1914-1920

David Stowe (Leeds)

The passing of the Aliens Restriction Act on 5 August 1914 lent itself to one of the most repressive measures imposed on a small section of the civilian population during the First World War. Far-reaching in scope, it covered such aspects as the right of residence, the prohibition of travel and movement, and greater powers of arrest. It also allowed for the mass internment of many who were considered a threat to a nation at war. Its impact was felt across the community. This chapter will look at this impact in the context of alien registration in Leeds between 1914 and 1920 and the classification of the domiciled 'other' as enemy alien in this period.[1]

The registration process took place at Leeds Town Hall almost immediately, where large numbers of men were arrested and kept under armed guard by soldiers of the Territorial Force. The authorities were mainly concerned with German-born men at this stage, and typically between 17 and 45 years of age or of previous military service and fighting age. The British declared war on Austria-Hungary a little over a week later, which was followed by more arrests. Many of those who had been detained during the initial arrests were later released, because the authorities were satisfied with their loyalty and good faith where naturalisation had taken place.[2]

The *Yorkshire Evening Post* reported at the time that there had been a rush from those anxious to become naturalised when war was declared, with up to 2,000 Russian and Polish Jews applying for naturalisation by 14 August 1914. The 'rush' reflected the demographics of Leeds where many Jews had settled after fleeing Russian persecution in the 1880s and the pogroms of the early part of the twentieth century. It was estimated that the staff at the registration bureau were dealing with about 400 applications a day during the first week of the war. Detective-Inspector Dalton of the Leeds City Police was in charge of questioning and cross-examination at Leeds Town Hall.[3]

The Leeds Jewish Naturalisation Society was very active here in offering help and assistance, as was the Jewish Board of Guardians and the many synagogues and their respective leaders in Leeds. The difficulties faced by some can be found in the following statement from Mr Barnet Manson who was the Honorary Secretary for the Leeds Jewish Naturalisation Society in August 1914. Not least of the difficulties were the written and oral tests where English was not the first language of many applying for naturalisation.

> Mr Manson declares that scores of Jews would have been registered in Leeds long ago but for the fact that the written and oral test are rather severe. Each applicant, for instance, is tested in diction, reading, and writing, and is then questioned as to his reasons for wishing to become an Englishman, and is asked pertinent queries respecting politics and current doings. It is hoped that the test will be rendered easier for the time being in order that many loyal Jews have their paths smoothed.[4]

The costs could be prohibitive too, with the Leeds Jewish Naturalisation Society charging the bare expenses (£3.50) for administration and the legal duties which needed to be carried out – especially where some charges could be as high as £4. 15 shillings (£4.75). Further applications were heard at the Jewish Institute in Leeds at the end of August 1914 with city magistrates and the commissioner for oaths in attendance. Each applicant had to bring five witnesses, with the testimonies forwarded to the Home Office for further investigation, according to reports.[5]

Elsewhere in Leeds, however, the arrest of suspected
enemy aliens was taking place across the city. It was much
the same in North and South Yorkshire and the wider
West Riding where a large number of German, Austrian
and Hungarian residents, who had been released on parole,
were re-arrested and taken under armed escort to York
Castle.[6] This coincided with the rise in the number of
prosecutions heard at the Leeds Police Courts at this time.

The first person to be prosecuted under the Aliens
Restriction Act was Julius Radl in September 1914. Radl
was charged with being in possession of a camera after
police had raided his home in the Harehills area of Leeds
and found a Busch camera in a drawer. A married man with
two young children, Radl was a head waiter at a Leeds hotel
at the time of his arrest and had been briefly detained as an
enemy alien at the outbreak of war. Giving evidence, the
police told magistrates that the military authorities would
take certain steps if Radl was discharged. The case was
dismissed and Radl found innocent. He was told to
surrender himself to the military authorities, which he did.[7]
Red Cross records show that Julius Radl was sent to Handforth Camp in Cheshire.[8]

Many of the cases which appeared before the Leeds
Police Court were brought for failing to register under the
Aliens Restriction Act with fines imposed in a number of
cases, such as the twenty-shillings (£1) imposed on 70-
year-old Henry Alfred Meyer. Henry Meyer had lived in
Britain for most of his life, and claimed he had no family
or friends in Germany. His story was accepted by
magistrates as a genuine one.[9] A similar charge of failing to
register was brought against Aaron Gross, aged 35, in
January 1915.[10]

Some charges were considered more serious. Albert
Katz, a German baker, aged 49, was sentenced to six
months hard labour in October 1914 after he was charged
with furnishing false information to a registration officer

at Leeds. He had also been charged with giving several false addresses and, when arrested, a number of letters were found addressed to him at the 'GPO, Leeds'. According to newspaper accounts each letter was enclosed with a registered envelope with the name 'Gustav Woolf, Berlin.' It was also stated that twenty marks were enclosed with each letter. Albert Katz pleaded guilty to giving false information, though claimed that the money had been sent by a relative. The court recommended that Albert Katz was deported after he had served his prison sentence.[11]

It is worth considering the way in which friendly, neutral and enemy aliens were classified in the police returns. For example, the police returns for the number of Friendly Aliens were broken down into male and female aliens, married or single, if under 18, between the ages of 18 to 41, or over 41 years of age. The returns for the period ending December 1916 show a total of 2,466 men and 2,510 women amongst the French, Italians, Romanians, Portuguese, Serbians and Russians registered in Leeds at this time. By far the largest group were Russian-born/Russian-descended men between 18 and 41 – of which there were almost 1,200, and a similar number of men over the age of 41 years of age.[12]

This is significant where it raises the question of men who might be liable for military service under the terms of compulsory conscription introduced earlier in the year. The question surrounding the position of male children of friendly, neutral and enemy aliens was raised in the local press at the time.[13] The view taken by legal advisors was that if fit and born in this country, then adult sons were eligible for military service. A similar view was taken of sons of neutral or friendly aliens where military service was also accepted under the Derby Scheme in 1915. The sons of enemy aliens would not be accepted under the scheme as it stood in February 1916.[14]

49

APPENDIX B.

Return of Alien Enemies registered in Leeds.

Nationality.	Males.	Fem.	Married.	Single.	Age. Under 18. M.	Age. Under 18. F.	Age. 18-45. M.	Age. 18-45. F.	Age. Over 45. M.	Age. Over 45. F.	Previous Military Training, etc.	Arrested.	Released and Exempted.	Transferred to Leeds on Release from Internment Camp.	Dead. M.	Dead. F.	Left the City. M.	Left the City. F.	Repatriated. M.	Repatriated. F.
GERMAN .. .. *128 German by Marriage, 3 of whom have since become re-naturalized.	217	*245	324	138	..	2	121	157	96	86	35	111	202	18	6	..	38	81	2	22
AUSTRIAN .. .. .. *57 Austrian by Marriage. †1 Since married to an Englishman.	137	*116	187	†66	1	2	104	91	32	23	18	40	145	28	1	2	30	31	2	2
HUNGARIAN .. .. .. *7 Hungarian by Marriage.	16	*11	19	8	..	..	9	5	7	6	1	6	17	5	..	..	2	1	..	1
OTTOMAN .. .. .. *2 Ottoman by Marriage.	21	*10	14	17	..	..	19	10	2	..	2	1	20	..	..	..	10	..	..	..
BULGARIAN	2	..	..	2	..	..	2	..	..	..	..	..	2	..	..	..	..	..	..	..
TOTALS	393	382	544	231	1	4	255	263	137	115	56	158	386	51	7	2	80	113	4	25

Fig. 24.1: Return of Alien Enemies Registered in Leeds 1915.

Further information on the classification system is found in documents held in the National Archives at Kew. Briefly summarised, the documents run to about five hundred pages and include a basic contents page, a preface and a list of alien cases which had been grouped according to country, and then sub-divided into counties and boroughs such as Barnsley, Bradford, Doncaster, Halifax and Leeds. An index is also given, and each case marked or ascribed a specific group or category according to 'alien' status, age or infirmity, length of residency, and whether married to a British-born wife or wife of foreign birth. Other groups include ministers of religion, if engaged in war work, and sons who had voluntary joined the armed forces.[15]

Some of the men listed in the returns for the Leeds Borough, for instance, included Leo Hompes, who was 68 years of age, and a journalist by profession. He had lived in Britain since the age of ten and had a son serving in the British Army. Carl Franz Hartman was a clerk. He was married with three children. Two of his sons were serving in the armed forces; one son was recovering from wounds at the time of registration. William Levy was a 'clothier' by trade and had six children. All six sons were serving in the armed forces according to the returns.[16] One of his sons was killed serving with the 2nd York and Lancaster Regiment in March 1918. Pte. Henry Levy is commemorated on the Arras Memorial to the Missing. He was 30 years of age.[17]

There are around forty-five men listed in the returns for the Leeds Borough. However, not all have marked connections to Leeds, suggesting that some of the men and their families were either forced to move or had relocated. This may have had something to do with the prohibited areas which were enforced in many of the coastal towns and seaports. Robert Ketterer, Frederick Metzler and Christian Schreiner each had previous connections to Newcastle-upon-Tyne, Liverpool and Middlesbrough.

Metzler's profession or trade is given as pork butcher, Robert Ketterer was a watchmaker's dealer and Christian Schreiner an engine driver.[18] It needs to be noted, however, that many of the men listed on the borough returns were over military age and thus considered less of a threat. Amongst some of the other occupations listed in the Alien Register for the Leeds Borough are the following trades and professions:

Artist	Baker
Clerk	Clockmaker
Commercial Traveller	Cut Worker
Engine Driver	Foreman (Labour)
Hairdresser	Hotel Manager
Jeweller	Joiner
Machiner	Manager
Rag Auctioneer	Tailor
Boiler Worker	Butcher
Cloth Finisher	Clothier
Draper	Draughtsman
Foundry Worker	Glass Merchant
Independent	Iron Worker
Journalist	Litho-Artist
Motor Launchman	Photographer
Teacher (Languages)	Watchmaker

TNA HO 144/11720. Date: 1918-1930. ALIENS.

In terms of further legislation, a new order came into effect in February 1916 under the Defence of the Realm Act which required all alien residents to register themselves. Those unable to write their names or make their 'mark' were told to leave a left thumb-print on the page of the registration book and the paper they took with them from Leeds Town Hall.[19] Although largely concerned with the re-registration of Russian and Polish Jews on this occasion, the restrictions imposed on those thought to have been undesirable aliens had increased considerably by the middle years of the war.[20]

Nor was it uncommon to find applications for citizenship refused in this period, with at least eleven applicants being rejected between the start of the war and the end of 1915.[21] This was not without precedence: fifteen aliens had been deported from Leeds between 1905 and 1914 under the 1905 Aliens Act. Eleven men were deported to Russia, two to Austria, one to Italy and one to the United States. Two aliens were deported under the terms of the same Act in 1919 and another under the powers of the Aliens Restriction (Amendment) Act in the same year. Yet the end of the war also saw a rise in the number of applications for British nationality being granted, with 45 applications being approved in Leeds in 1919. The reason for the rise in successful applicants can be accounted for by the Government granting naturalisation to aliens who had served in the British Army during the war.[22]

Another interesting aspect of alien registration concerns the number of aliens who had been released on licence to work in the community in 1917 and 1918.[23] Documents held at the Manx Heritage Museum on the Isle of Man show that at least 75 men were transferred from Douglas and Knockaloe camps to work in the clothing industry in Leeds. Isaac Altmann, Max Becker and Max Bicker were amongst a number of German and Austrian-Hungarian internees released to work for Burton and Burton, the Premier Clothing Company and the St Albans Manufacturing Company at this time. A list of the businesses and the internees transferred to Leeds under licence accompanies this chapter.

One of the men released from Douglas Camp in August 1918 was Eduard Bohensky, an Austrian Jew. He is named on a prisoner of war list with the recommendation that he was 'not to be released at the expiration of war' but deported instead.[24] It is not known if Eduard Bohensky was deported after the war, but it would be a cruel twist of fate if this is the same Eduard Bohensky who perished in one of the Nazi death camps when he was deported from his home town in Austria in May 1942.[25]

APPENDIX B.
Return of Aliens Registered in Leeds.

NATIONALITY	MALES.	FEMALES.	TOTAL.
American	57	52	109
Armenian	1		1
Austrian	83	81	164
Belgian	31	35	66
Bulgarian	1		1
Chinese	18	2	20
Columbian	2		2
Czecho-Slovak	7	5	12
Danish	20	16	36
Dutch	19	16	35
Egyptian	5		5
French	47	61	108
Georgian	1		1
German	82	115	197
Greek	5	4	9
Hungarian	15	11	26
Italian	124	82	206
Japanese	6		6
Lithuanian	2		2
Latvian	1	1	2
Luxemburger	1	1	2
Norwegian	7	7	14
Pole	56	32	88
Portugese		1	1
Roumanian	12	12	24
Russian	2,058	2,304	4,362
Serbian	5		5
Spanish	3	4	7
Swedish	19	13	32
Swiss	40	27	67
Turkish	9	9	18
Ukranian	1		1
TOTALS	2,738	2,891	5,629

Fig. 24.2: Return of Aliens Registered in Leeds 1920.

The local response to the Aliens Restriction Act in August 1914 was swift and drew on a number of interconnected themes. These included the use of military and judicial powers to enforce the Act and the adoption of subsequent legislation which lent itself to one of the most repressive measures imposed on a small section of the civilian population during the First World War. It was a policy which would repeat itself twenty years later for those who found themselves in the 'wrong place at the wrong time' at the start of the Second World War.

Leeds Clothing Companies and Civilian Internees Released on Licence 1917-1918

Company Name	Civilian Internees
A. Benedict & Co., Clay Pit Lane	Jacob Browhood; Davies Crown; Leo Cutler; William Feather; Sandor Goldman; Max Knoll; Hersh Krebbs; Issak Krebs; Max Mandall; Maurice Nightingale; Ruben Nightingale; Charles Nightingale; Moses Pukatsch; Joseph Schaffer; Shoye Sler; S. Tannenbaum; Harry Wilder.
Burton & Burton, Concord St. Mills	Max Beckel; M. Bickel; Jacob Letzter; Jechiel Meyer; Harry Shrage; Kalmann Weissenberg.
Clifton Clothing Company, 41 Camp Road	Benjamin Emer; Victor Reich; Max Wolfisch; Aron Wolfram.
Gardam & Sons, Byron Street	Joseph Podherzer.
Hipps Ltd., Hipsley Works, Grace Street	Samuel Balon; Julius Beno; Abraham Brummer; Max Garfunkel; Max Haringer; Louis Kaiser; Rubin Mashal; Jack Ochsenberg; Simon Rosenberg; Lipa Shumer; David Schwartz; Morris Schwartz; Robert Seiler; Lewis Turkel.
D. Joseph & Sons, Grove House Lane, Camp Road	Isaac Altmann; Maurice Gross; Gerschon Halpern; Harry Halpern; Louis Ring.
Joseph May and Sons Ltd., Spring Well Street, Whitehall Road	Isaac Falk; Albert Hazenschnour; Elic Katz; Max Koenig; Simon Schlanger.

Lubelski and Sons, Hillidge Road, Hunslet	Ksieski; Alexander Liban.
St. Albans Manufacturing Co., 34 Trinity Street	Eduard Bohensky.
The Premier Clothing Co., 13 Cross Harrison Street	Joseph Abrahams; Barnet Alpong; Salomon Bell; Max Bicker; Herrmann Buch; Shye Fink; Sam Franklin; Henry Gordon; Simon Lerner; Moses Perzinck; Charles Schwartz; Sam Schwartz; Samuel Segal; Samuel Slainoff. Locations at Vicar Lane and Hanover Street also.
The Wholesale Bespoke Tailoring Company, St. Peter's Buildings	Salamon Pfeffer.
Wood & Silk, Woodhouse Lane	Morris Baum.
In addition	Goldman Capmakers. Mrs. J. Goldman, Saville Street, Leeds, and St. Albans Manufacturing Co., 34 Trinity Street – including Mendel Gertler, Nathan Jowitz, Nathan Kron, Morris Michnik, Isidor Rosenburg and Leon Schwartzfeld.

Sources:

Katrina Honeyman. *Well Suited: A History of the Leeds Clothing Industry 1850-1990*. Oxford: Oxford University Press, 2000.

i-Museum. Manx National Heritage, https://www.imuseum.im

Kelly's Directory (Leeds)

Death, Burial and Reburial: The Dead of Lofthouse Park

David Stowe and Claudia Sternberg (Leeds)

Civilian Internees

There were eight known civilian deaths at Lofthouse Park between April 1915 and July 1918. In addition to the eight, two German officers died in November 1918. Leutnants Wilhelm Georg Bade and August Dippold succumbed to pneumonia in the 2nd Northern General Hospital in Leeds and were buried in the nearby Lawnswood Cemetery. The first civilian death was Herman Krauss in April 1915. Krauss had cut his throat in the lavatories at Lofthouse Park Camp and died about eight minutes after being found at ten to one on the afternoon of Saturday, 10 April. An inquest held at the camp a couple of days later found that he had committed 'Suicide during temporary insanity'.[1]

Herman Krauss was a 39-year old married man with three children from Manchester. Before the war he had been a waiter at the Midland Hotel. He had been interned on 21 October 1914 and came to Lofthouse Park with around 200 other men from Manchester. Claude Schlichting and Alexander Gordon had both known the deceased and were called to give evidence at the inquest. Schlichting, who was also a waiter, had known Herman Krauss for seventeen years. In his evidence he said that Krauss had always been very quiet and reserved, but had been more depressed since his internment and would not talk about anything.

In giving his evidence, Alexander Gordon told the inquest that he had seen Krauss taking something out of a box on the Saturday morning, but had not been aware it was a razor. He added that Herman Krauss had acted as a paid steward to some of the wealthy internees, but the breaking up of the group of stewards he had worked with may have preyed on his mind when his friends had moved into better accommodation in another part of the camp, and he could not afford to go with them. Gordon had also spoken with Krauss shortly before his death and at the time thought the latter was in good spirits. The brief conversation was reported in the *Yorkshire Evening Post*:

> Krauss: 'I am practically tired of this occupation, and am thinking about chucking it up. I don't feel altogether well.' Then, tapping witness on the shoulder he said. 'Good bye old chappie.' Witness said: 'Are you released?' Krauss replied: 'Yes, a very good release, too, as you will see eventually.'[2]

Herman Krauss was buried in Manchester Southern Cemetery. His wife, Margaret Krauss, placed a notice in the *Manchester Evening News* thanking all friends and members of the Geneva Club for their sympathy and floral tributes during the family's sad bereavement.[3]

There was a second suicide at the camp when Walter Adolph Drautz hanged himself in July 1918.[4] Among the other deaths at Lofthouse Park were Johannes Deistel, who had died of heart failure in March 1916, John Henry Brickmann who suffered a cerebral haemorrhage in September 1916, and Karl Gustav Bauck, whose cause of death in November of the same year was due to a stomach tumour.[5] Johannes Deistel had taken part in a match on the skittle ground in the South Camp just before his death. He had also suffered from the effects of malaria, having spent some time in the Cameroons and Togoland before being interned. According to the *Rothwell Courier and Times* from March 1916. Deistel's post-mortem was carried out in the presence of a number of German doctors at the camp, who had agreed that his death was caused by the bursting of an aneurysm in the aorta.[6] His death was registered at Wakefield.

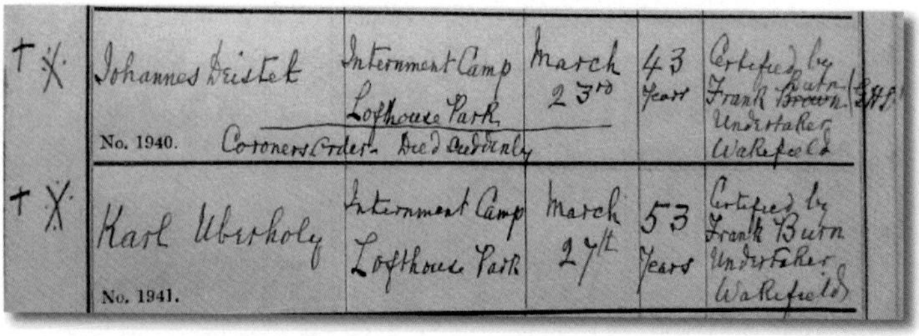
No. 1940. Johannes Deistel — Internment Camp Lofthouse Park — March 23rd — 43 Years — Certified by Frank Burn Undertaker Wakefield
Coroners Order. Died suddenly
No. 1941. Karl Uberholz — Internment Camp Lofthouse Park — March 27th — 53 Years — Certified by Frank Burn Undertaker Wakefield

Fig. 25.1: Lofthouse Burial Register and entries for Johannes Deistel and Karl Uberholz in March 1916 (West Yorkshire Archives Service, Leeds. RDP 116/4/1).

With the exception of John Henry Brickmann and Herman Krauss, the deceased were buried in the local churchyard at Lofthouse Christ Church, less than a mile from the internment camp where they had died. John Henry Brickmann was buried at Linthorpe Cemetery, Middlesbrough. A summary of the names of the deceased and cause of death where known may be found below:

Name	Cause	Burial	Cemetery
Herman Krauss	Suicide	14-4-1915	Manchester Southern
Paul Walbert	Not Known	6-5-1915	Lofthouse Churchyard
Otto Volley	Not Known	29-5-1915	Lofthouse Churchyard
Johannes Deistel	Heart Failure	23-3-1916	Lofthouse Churchyard
Karl Uberholz	Not Known	27-3-1916	Lofthouse Churchyard
J.H. Brickmann	Cerebral Haemorrhage	25-9-1916	Linthorpe Cemetery
Karl Bauck	Stomach Tumour	14-11-1916	Lofthouse Churchyard
Walter A. Drautz	Suicide	29-7-1918	Lofthouse Churchyard

Fig. 25.2: Lofthouse Christ Church Cemetery where six Loft-house Park civilian internees were buried. (Outwood Community Video, Ref. L11).

Military Prisoners

Leutnant August Dippold was captured at Ledegem, Belgium, on 14 October 1918. He was initially interned at Bevois Mount House at Southampton before being transferred to Lofthouse Park. Dippold was admitted to the 2nd Northern General Hospital on 15 November, where he died several days later. He was 34 years of age. Other admissions included Alfred Amreihn, Hans Kollberg, Carl Schindler, Herbert Schneider and Paul Schulz. Records also show a further five prisoners of war admitted to hospital suffering from influenza between 15 and 25 November 1918.[7]

Born in the fishing village Schlutup (near Lübeck) in February 1885, Leutnant Wilhelm Georg Maniluis Bade was serving as *Postsekretär* with the Prussian Reserve Infantry Regiment 221 when he was taken prisoner at Niergnies on 8 October 1918. He arrived at Lofthouse Park eleven days later. Bade's home address is given as Marienthalstrasse, Hamburg, according to ICRC records.

Further contact details for 'Frau Margarethe Bade' are given at the side of his name.[8] Standing at six feet seven inches (2.01m), the funeral of Wilhelm Georg Bade in November 1918 was covered in some detail in the local press – including images of the funeral service, which were published in the *Leeds Mercury*. Bade, who had been wounded in the field in 1916 and 1917, died from bronchial pneumonia. The inquest into his death was reported in the *Yorkshire Evening Post* on 23 November as follows:

> The Leeds City Coroner held an inquest today on the body of George [*sic*] Wilhelm Maniluis Bade (33), a lieutenant in the 221st Infantry Regiment of the German Army, who was a prisoner of war at the Lofthouse Park internment camp, and died at Beckett's Park Military Hospital from bronchial pneumonia. It was stated that Lt. Bade, who was a man of giant stature, being 6ft. 7in in height, did not report sick to the medical officer, but was seen by the medical officer when he inspected the huts on Monday. On Wednesday evening the deceased became very ill and was taken to the hospital at the camp, but the following day his condition became so serious that he was removed to the hospital at Leeds. When admitted to Beckett's Park he was conscious, but delirious, and he died on Friday.[9]

An account of the funeral service accompanies this chapter at the end.

Cannock Chase[10]

For geographical and political reasons, the graves of the six civilians at Lofthouse Christ Church Cemetery and the two military officers at Lawnswood Cemetery in Leeds were difficult places to reach for family and friends of the deceased. It cannot be known whether the graves were visited at all during or after the war years, or if local people looked after them. Large-scale repatriations of Germans took place from the end of the war to October 1919,[11] and it would take time over the course of the 1920s for British German relations to normalise. Both countries faced high numbers of military deaths on the battlefields abroad; it became a priority to respond to pressing logistical, psychological and cultural needs relating to searches, burials, reburials and remembrance. Only a few decades later, the Second World War multiplied the figures of civilian and military casualties and posed even greater challenges for dealing with the wartime dead.[12]

The catastrophic nationalism of Nazi Germany with its armed and genocidal destruction led to defeat, occupation and the post-war construction of two separate states, the Federal Republic of Germany in the West and the German Democratic Republic in the East. From the mid-1950s onwards, the (then West German) war graves charity *Volksbund Deutsche Kriegsgräberfürsorge e.V.* (VDK) was commissioned by the government to care for German war graves and remains abroad in accordance with bilateral agreements with other countries.

On 16 October 1959, the Federal Republic of Germany reached such an agreement with the British government; this differed from others of its kind because it included the dead of both world wars.[13] In February 1962, the VDK established an office at Dorney Reach near London to pursue the creation of a cemetery and organise the reinterment of First and Second World War German dead whose graves were not already maintained by the Commonwealth War Graves Commission (CWGC). Between April 1962 and April 1963 the VDK worked with 38 German and British staff and 16 vehicles across 687 locations in 75 counties.[14]

Among the bodies to be moved were Lofthouse Park prisoners of war Wilhelm Georg Bade and August Dippold. They were exhumed in Leeds and reinterred in Plot 4 of Cannock Chase War Cemetery in Staffordshire

(Fig. 25.3). The reburials of Bade and Dippold were two of 58 reinterments that, according to the CWGC, took place in 1963,[15] but the cemetery had already been used for military burials since 1917.

Cannock Chase was the location of the Brocton and Rugeley camps from the autumn of 1914. First used for transit, they became training facilities for 500,000 troops and also functioned as the base for the New Zealand Rifle Brigade. A hospital with 1,000 beds was established in 1916 to serve the soldiers in training, convalescents from the front and POWs held at Brocton Prisoner of War Camp. Those who died in the hospital or in the camps were put to rest in the local burial ground.[16] Bade and Dippold are buried at Cannock Chase War Cemetery alongside 255 other Germans from the period of World War One; 254 of them were soldiers and one was a civilian.[17]

Fig. 25.3: Gravestones of Lt. August Dippold and Lt. Wilhelm Bade, Cannock Chase War Cemetery (Photograph: David Stowe).

Karl Bauck, Johannes Deistel, Karl Drautz, Karl Ueberholz, Otto Volley and Paul Walbert – the six civilian internees who died at Lofthouse Park – were reinterred at
Cannock Chase German Military Cemetery. The site for
the cemetery, which is near but separate from Cannock
Chase War Cemetery, was cleared with the help of German
youth groups in the context of the VDK's *Aktion
Versöhnung über den Gräbern* (Reconciliation over the Graves
Initiative).[18] The cemetery was consecrated on 10 June
1967, containing 4,939 First and Second World War graves
(2,143 and 2,796 respectively). Many of the dead had died
in prisoner-of-war and internment camps and hospitals,
but some had been washed ashore as naval casualties. 73
had lost their lives as crew members of four World War
One zeppelins; a large number of men were airmen from
the Second World War who had been shot down or
crashed during the *Luftschlacht um England* (Battle of
Britain) and the Blitz in 1940-41.[19]

In the summer months of 1962, the VDK's *Fliegende
Gruppe 14*, a mobile operations team, was repositioned
from Manchester to Leeds to tackle the dispersed graves
of the West and North Riding, Cumberland and West-
morland.[20] The reinterments were undertaken by experienced *Umbetter* (reburial specialists), 'a post-war profession, which occupied at times more than one hundred
experts.'[21] Reburial teams followed guidelines which regulated how to ensure the '*volle Wahrung der Würde des Todes*'
('*full preservation of the dignity of death*'); this entailed careful
excavation, respectful handling of remains, screening for
privacy, avoiding contamination, fast onward transmission
and documentation of the entire process from exhumation
to reburial.[22] For known graves, the guidelines stipulated:

> If the grave location is on a regular cemetery with
> impeccable records and the details of the person to be
> reinterred are already known, it suffices to collect legacy
> objects, identity tag etc. found with the body in the

reburial bag, attach a reinterment number and then proceed to prepare the deceased in a reinterment case with reinterment number for transportation to the new cemetery. (translated from German)[23]

Despite some practical issues and cultural differences, the many reburials of 1962/63 were made possible by the close collaboration between the VDK, the CWGC, medical officers and a skilled workforce. Further support was received from the Home Office as well as local and religious authorities;[24] among the latter were those of Wakefield and Lofthouse Christ Church.

Fig. 25.4: Gravestones of civilian internees Karl Ueberholz, Otto Volley, Paul Walbert, Walter Drautz, and Karl Bauck at Cannock Chase German Military Cemetery. The grave of Johannes Deistel is on the reverse side of this row (Photograph: David Stowe).

The removal of six bodies from a small churchyard in Yorkshire in 1962, buried there under adverse circumstances in the 1910s, was a consequence of the British

German agreement of 1959 and the earlier German *Gesetz über die Sorge für die Kriegsgräber* (War Graves Act) of 27 May 1952. The focus of the legislation had been the Second World War, but through Section 1(2) it absorbed an earlier act, the *Gesetz über die Erhaltung der Kriegergräber aus dem Weltkrieg* of 29 Dezember 1922, thus incorporating any recognised war graves of World War One.[25]

The six civilians from Lofthouse Park, including the Manchester waiter, family man and suicide Herman Krauss, were just a footnote in the bigger story of displaced wartime fatalities and their posthumous removals. It is not without irony, however, that a German *Soldatenfriedhof* in England became the men's final resting place, despite the fact that they had never taken part in any of the military actions that accounted for the majority of the dead around them.

Funeral of Wilhelm Georg Maniluis Bade

Article from
The North Leeds News
Friday, 29 November 1918

'Fifty German Officers Sing Hymns at a Brother Officer's
Funeral: Unusual Scene at Lawnswood Cemetery'

A strange scene was witnessed at Lawnswood Cemetery on
Monday morning when military honours were accorded at
the funeral of the German officer Lieut. Wilhelm Maniluis
Bade, who died of pneumonia in Beckett's Park Hospital
last Friday.

Fifty German officers were released on parole from
Lofthouse Park where Bade, who was a regimental adjutant in the German Army, had been interned after the recent fighting on the Western Front. The half hundred
compatriots – three of whom were in the undress uniform
of the Prussian Guards – were conveyed by a special car
from the Internment Camp to Beckett's Park Military
Hospital.

The coffin, covered with a German flag, arrived on a
gun-carriage and was carried by six of the Germans to the
wheeled bier on which it was conveyed to the graveside
which was on the east side of the cemetery not far from
the boundary wall and at a distance of about a hundred
yards from the last resting places of the graves of about
forty British soldiers – Colonials, Irish, Scotch and Welsh.
The coffin was covered with wreaths and according to
German military custom, the soldiers took precedence in
the procession. First came the firing party – a company of
men from the Honourable Artillery Company at Chapel-
town Barracks – followed by the bier with an escort of
German officers on either side and afterwards the unarmed British escort. These were followed by a clergyman

of the Church of England, Captain D.C. Wingate (who accompanied the prisoners) and Sergt. Major Dobson, R.G.C.

At the graveside, the Germans – most of them wearing 'field grey' overcoats – lined up in two sections. The service was that prescribed by the English Book of Common Prayer and was read by the Army chaplain in surplice and hood. After the coffin had been lowered, a choir, selected from amongst the German officers and conducted by one of their number sang in German the hymn *Der Herr ist Mein Hirte (The Lord is My Shepherd)*. Following the firing of three volleys over the grave by the firing party, a British soldier sounded the 'Last Post.'

As the final note died away, the senior German officer, standing at the head of the grave, stooped and threw three handfuls of earth upon the lowered coffin. This was repeated by every German officer in turn, each of them giving the military salute before he returned to the ranks. When the British party had marched away, an address was delivered in German by Capt. Schmidt, a Protestant clergyman who had been with the late Lieut. Bade during the whole of the four years that he had been fighting in France.

The party also sung *Ich hatte einen Kamerade (I had a Comrade)*, after which the German officers departed. Thus ended this singular episode in the history of the Great War.

***

GIANT GERMAN OFFICER BURIED AT LAWNSWOOD—Lieut. G. W. Bade, a German officer, six feet seven in height, was buried at Lawnswood Cemetery, Leeds, yesterday. Our picture shows a choir composed of the deceased officer's comrades singing at the graveside. (Leeds Mercury.)

Images of Wilhelm Bade's funeral at Lawnswood Cemetery, Leeds, from *Leeds Mercury*, Tuesday, 26 November 1918, p. 12.

Headstone of Wilhelm Bade, Cannock Chase War Cemetery (Photograph: David Stowe).

Notes and Sources

Introduction (Claudia Sternberg and David Stowe)
Pages xii-xxxii

1. For more detail on *In the Wrong Place at the Wrong Time* see https://ruhlebenlofthouse.com
2. For the Liddle Collection see https://library.leeds.ac.uk/special-collections/collection/723.
3. On the study visit to Yorkshire see https://ruhlebenlofthouse.com/2017/02/14/study-visit-to-yorkshire-berlin-pupils-on-ruhleben-part-i/. A professionally curated exhibition on the *Engländerlager* Ruhleben and war captivity, entitled *Nachbarn hinter Stacheldraht* (Neighbours behind Barbed Wire), is presented at the Museum Alte Kaserne Zitadelle from 4 May until 25 November 2018.
4. Peter Wood's article in Kate Taylor, ed. *Aspects of Wakefield: Discovering Local History* 3 (Barnsley, 2001), 150-62, Liddle Collection LIDDLE/WW1/DF/GA/CIV/16.
5. Berchasi/Berchesi in Liddle Collection LIDDLE/WW1/TR/01/051 and LIDDLE/WW1/DF/GA/CIV/12.
6. Internment data from TNA NA/WO394/5, Statistical Abstract, November 1917. As quoted in Panikos Panayi, 'Prisoners of War and Internees (Great Britain)' in: *1914-1918-online. International Encyclopedia of the First World War*, ed. by Ute Daniel et al., Berlin 2014, DOI: 10.15463/ie1418.10296.
7. See the Further Reading section in this book.
8. For Manx Heritage and Knockaloe Camp see and https://manxnationalheritage.im/, http://www. knockaloe.im/ and http://www.knockaloe.org.uk/.
9. More on Stobs Camp can be found here http://www.stobscamp.org/.
10. For the Anglo-German Family History Society see http://www.agfhs.org/site/index.php.
11. Paul Cohen-Portheim, *Time Stood Still: My Internment in England, 1914-1918* (Duckworth: London, 1931).

12. Exhibition *Hinter Stacheldraht: Die Kriegsgefangenenlager in Celle 1914-1918* at Bomann-Museum Celle, 26 May – 11 November 2018.
13. See, for example, the headline 'Forget Brexit, It's how we mark the Somme centenary which will define us as a nation' in the *Yorkshire Evening Post* online, 29 June 2016, https://www.yorkshireeveningpost.co.uk/your-leeds/ forget-brexit-it-s-how-we-mark-the-somme-centenary-which-will-define-us-as-a-nation-1-7987780/amp (accessed 4 July 2017).
14. A sample selection: Christopher Hope, 'Three million EU citizens in the UK could be deported if Britons vote for a 'Brexit', Home Office suggests', *The Telegraph* online, 15 May 2016, https://www.telegraph.co.uk/news/2016/05/15/three-million-eu-citizens-in-the-uk-could-be-deported-if-britons/ 15 MAY 2016; Lord Lamont on 2 March 2017 in *Daily Politics* (BBC Two Television), https://www.facebook.com/ BBCPolitics/videos/1694400777243440/(accessed 1 March 2018); Chancellor of the Exchequer Philip Hammond in a Sky News interview during his visit to Washington on 13 October 2017, http://www.bbc.co.uk/news/business-41608243; Daniel Boffey and Lisa O'Carroll, 'UK plan to register EU citizens would be illegal, say MEPs', *The Guardian* online, 23 October 2017, https://www.theguardian.com/ politics/2017/oct/23/uk-plan-to-register-eu-citizens-would-be-illegal-say-meps; on registration and 'settled status' for EU citizen see the Home Office information at https://www.gov.uk/guidance/status-of-eu-nationals-in-the-uk-what-you-need-to-know.
15. For Theresa May's speech at the Conservative Party conference in Birmingham on 5 October 2016 see https://www.independent.co.uk/news/uk/politics/theresa -may-speech-tory-conference-2016-in-full-transcript-a73461 71.html; for her follow-up on the use of the phrase, see her speech at the Charity Commission Annual Meeting of 9 January 2017:

https://www.gov.uk/government/speeches/the-shared-society-prime-ministers-speech-at-the-charity-commission-annual-meeting (accessed 28 March 2018).

16. On British Army deployments in Germany see https://www.army.mod.uk/deployments/germany/ (accessed 10 April 2018)

17. British Council in partnership with the British Embassy Berlin, Goethe Institute, Deutscher Kulturrat, UK-German Connections and Deutsche Welle, https://www.britishcouncil.de/en/uk-germany-2018/about (accessed 28 March 2018).

1 From Pleasure to Detention (David Stowe)

Pages 1-32

1. *The Leeds Mercury*, 23 June 1906. p. 6; *The Yorkshire Evening Post*, 2 June 1908. p. 3; *The Yorkshire Evening Post*, 6 May 1909. p. 1; *The Yorkshire Evening Post*, 8 September 1908. p. 3. The forerunner of the Yorkshire (West Riding) Electric Tramways Company was the Wakefield and District Light Railway Company until it was taken over in April 1905. Herbert Charles Metcalfe was appointed Chief Constable in 1901 at a salary of £800 per year. See *Yorkshire Post and Leeds Mercury*, Saturday 20 January 1940. p. 8.

2. *The Era*, 25 April 1908. p. 31.

3. *The Yorkshire Evening Post*, 24 April 1922. p. 7.

4. *The Yorkshire Evening Post*, 2 June 1908. p. 3.

5. *Ordnance Survey* (OS) *Map*: CCXXXXIII.7. Edition of 1908 (Lofthouse); Re 'large house', see Ref. 6 below for 'private carriage way' on Block Plan; Rhodes, Ronald P. *Going Back a Bit: A Resume of the Village of Lofthouse Gate in the Early 1900s. Supplement on Lofthouse Park. Book 2.* Publisher Unknown: Undated. pp. 1-7.

6. Block Plan: *Lofthouse Park Limited - Proposed Pavilion & Premises.* c. 1906. Ref. A14. Wakefield Library Services.

7. See Rhodes, Ronald P. *Going Back a Bit, Supplement on Lofthouse Park* (not paginated). Rhodes also mentions a Helter Skelter, House of Mirrors, and a 'Kelly's Cottage', which was

something similar to a Ghost Train, with cobwebs, rattling skeletons, and unexpected gusts of wind.

8. *Yorkshire Evening Post*, 8 September 1908. p. 3.

9. *Sheffield Independent*, 12 July 1909. p. 9.

10. *Leeds Mercury*, 2 June 1914. p. 7.

11. *Yorkshire Evening Post*, 29 August 1910. p. 6.

12. *Sheffield Daily Telegraph*, 2 June 1908. p. 5.

13. *The Yorkshire Post*, 2 August 1910. p. 9; See also *Yorkshire Post*, 6 August 1910. p. 1. Advertisement: "Lofthouse Park - Flying Exhibitions and 'Tram Fares' from Thwaite Gate, Sandal, Ossett, Horbury and Agbrigg".

14. *Flight*, 24 May 1913. p. 570.

15. *The Era*, 13 May 1914. p. 27.

16. *The Leeds Mercury*, 13 June 1914. p. 3; See also *Leeds Mercury*, 2 June 1914, p. 7, and *Leeds Mercury*, 20 May 1914, p. 4, for cancellation of the 'Animal Congress' and change in ownership of Lofthouse Park. Eg. Advertisement: "The Greatest Amusement Park in the World, Under London & Continental Management, New to England and Entirely Novel."

17. *Leeds Mercury*, 20 June 1914, p. 3

18. *Leeds Mercury*, 8 September 1914, p. 4.

19. *Yorkshire Evening Post*, 22 October 1914.

20. *Ibid.*

21. The National Archives, Kew (TNA hereafter), FO 383/162, *Reports of Visits to Camps in UK*, 8 January 1916.

22. Paul Cohen-Portheim, *Time Stood Still: My Internment in England 1914-1918* (London, Duckworth, 1931).

23. Panikos Panayi, *Prisoners of Britain: German Civilian and Combatant Internees during the First World War* (Manchester and New York: Manchester University Press, 2012), pp. 92-3.

24. TNA, FO 383/360, *Report on Inspection of Lofthouse Park*, 10-12 May 1918 (June 1918); *Yorkshire Evening Post*, Wednesday, 21 April 1915, p. 5.

25. See FO 383/360 above.

26. *Yorkshire Post*, Saturday 22 May 1920, p. 3.

27. *Ibid.*

28. TNA, FO 383/33, *Reports on German Prisoners' Camps in UK*, July 1915; See Reports of visits to camps in UK, 8 January 1916.
29. *Leeds Mercury*, 9 March 1915, p. 4; *Yorkshire Evening Post*, 15 March 1915, p. 3.
30. Anon, *Naval Attaché's Reports* (Office of Naval Institute, February 1915), p. 24.
31. *Yorkshire Evening Post*, Tuesday 27 July 1915, p. 5.
32. TNA, *Reports on German Prisoners' Camps in UK*, July 1915.
33. TNA, *Reports of visits to camps in UK*, 8 January 1916.
34. Panayi, *Prisoners of Britain*, p. 44.
35. *Ibid.*
36. TNA, *Report on Inspection of Lofthouse Park*, 10-12 May 1918.
37. iMuseum: Manx National Heritage – First World War Internment. http://www.imuseum.im/
38. *Ibid.*
39. TNA, *Reports of Visits to Camps in UK*, 8 January 1916.
40. *Yorkshire Evening Post*, Thursday, 14 May 1914, p. 7.
41. (The) *Pittsburg Press*, Sunday, 16 January 1916. Trove Newspaper Archive.
42. International Committee for the Red Cross (hereafter *ICRC*, Geneva), Ref. D. 184-1. Date accessed 27 July 2017.
43. TNA, CO 323/746/51, *Gibraltar. Prize court proceedings relating to claims for wages by Messrs (Ernst) Glahn and Max Klein*, 24 March 1917.
44. See *ICRC*, Geneva, D. 186-4 to 6. Transfer to Holland.
45. TNA, FO 383/162, *Germans Brought from Africa in UK*, Letter dated 13 January 1916 (No. 74).
46. TNA, FO 383/34, *Treatment of Germans Brought to UK from Africa*, Letters dated 12 and 22 November 1915.
47. See *Treatment of Germans brought to UK from Africa*, Letter dated 8 October 1915.
48. *Ibid.*
49. See *Germans brought from Africa in UK*, Letter dated 22 January 1916 (No. 158).
50. See *Germans brought from Africa in UK*, Letter dated 13 January 1916 (No. 74).
51. TNA, FO 383/360 (1918), *Report on Wakefield Camp* (Swedish Legation), 20 June 1918.

52. Cohen-Portheim, *Time Stood Still*, pp. 78-79; 90-91.

53. *Ibid.*, p. 78

54. TNA, FO 383/162 (1916), *German Prisoners at Wakefield*, Letter dated 22 December 1915.

55. TNA, *G.S. Haines* WO 374/30046; TNA, *George T. Cattell* WO 374/12880; TNA, *R.W.H. Ronaldson* WO 374/58984. See also Ruth Allison's chapter on Commandant Haines.

56. Hansard 1803-2005. *House of Commons Debate*, 26 July 1915. Vol. 73. cc 1962-63. Site accessed 25 August 2017. See also *HC Debate*, 15 May 1916. Vol. 82. cc 1111-2 where questions were raised about an internee called Hitner who was able to order two dozen pocket flash-lamps from a London firm, and the goods duly delivered to Lofthouse Park Camp.

57. *The Times* (Digital), Tuesday 29 June 1915, p. 5; *The Times* (Digital) Wednesday, 2 June 1915, p. 6.

58. R.P. Rhodes, *Going Back a Bit: A Resume of the Village of Lofthouse Gate in the Early 1900s*. Supplement to Lofthouse Park. Book 2 (Publisher Unknown, Undated), pp. 7-8.

59. Graham Mark, *Prisoners of War in British Hands during WWI: A Study of Their History, the Camps and Their Mails* (Great Britain, The Postal History Society, 2007), p. 140.

60. Cohen Portheim, *Time Stood Still*, p. 65.

61. Oscar Froitzheim, (The) *Pittsburg Press*, Sunday, 16 January 1916, p. 3. Date accessed 30 July 2017.

62. *Yorkshire Evening Post*, Thursday, 13 April 1916, p. 5; *Nottingham Evening Post*, Friday, 14 April 1916, p. 3.

63. See *Report on Wakefield Camp*, Exhibit A. Surviving accounts show that £47 18 shillings was paid to the Rothwell Gas Company for the supply of gas used for cooking in the South Camp in the first quarter of 1918.

64. Rhodes, *Going Back a Bit*. Gill's Dividend Stores also advertised in the local press. See *The (Wakefield) Express*, Saturday, 19 December 1914, p. 4

65. See Chapter 12 on the camp journal *Lager-Bote*.

66. I am grateful to Paul Stowe for the information.

67. *Yorkshire Evening Post*, 21 June 1915, p. 3. The provisions in this case had been intended for the camp guard.

68. *Yorkshire Evening Post*, Monday 8 March 1915, p. 5. 'Eating their heads off.' The comments were made by members of the local government board at Rothwell.

69. Matthew Stibbe, *British Civilian Internees in Germany: The Ruhleben Camp, 1914-18* (Manchester: Manchester University Press, 2008), p. 97; John Yarnall, *Barbed Wire Disease: British and German Prisoners of War, 1914-19* (Stroud: The History Press, 2011), p. 163.

70. ICRC Database, Geneva, D151-8, D158-7, D170-8, D208-11; see also TNA FO 383/442 for Leonard Holman and his claim for the return of his property on repatriation.

71. See also Chapter 25 on deaths at Lofthouse Park, including those of Herman Krauss and Walter Drautz.

72. TNA, FO 383/360 (1918), *P/W Camp at Lofthouse Park, Wakefield*.

73. *Ibid.*

74. TNA, FO 383/119 (1916), *Petitions from Prisoners Interned at Lofthouse Park Camp, Wakefield, Yorkshire, Wakefield: Letter to Walter Hines Page from Lofthouse Park Camp*, 8 January 1915. Second letter in file, with names, 12 November 1915.

75. *ICRC*, Geneva, AUT 1-VIII, AUT 3-IX, AUT 5-IX, AUT 11-VIII, AUT 12 - VII, AUT 13-VII, AUT 14-VII, AUT 15-VII, AUT 16-VII, AUT 17-VII.

76. *Ibid.*

77. *Ibid.*

78. TNA, FO 383/360 (1918), *Report on Wakefield Camp* (Swedish Legation), 20 June 1918.

79. TNA, FO 383/246, *Austrians in Australia claiming to be officers.* See *ICRC*, Geneva, Anton Gerl, Hong Kong. Date 20-4-1916. Also Appendix IV 'Prisoners of War Released from Internment', Ref. *1996.

80. TNA, FO 383/246, *Rank of Anton Woisetschlager, interned at Alexandra Palace*; See also *Report on Wakefield Camp* (June 1918) where rank is given as 'Verpflegsakzessist Stellvertreter' of the Imperial and Royal Army.

81. TNA, FO 383/246, *Interned Austrians Claiming to Be Officers.*

82. TNA, FO 383/246, *Treatment of Aspirant Officers in Austrian Army who are P/W in UK.*

83. TNA, FO 383/249, *Anton Gerl, Interned at Wakefield.*

84. TNA, FO 383/246 (1917), *Rank of Max Krausz, interned at Alexandra Palace*; TNA, FO 383/7 (1915), *Detention of Paul Reiser, Ensign*. See Treatment *accorded to Paul Reiser*, and *Paul Reiser detained at Wakefield*, October 1915; See also *Report on Wakefield Camp*, 20 June 1918.

85. See *Report on Wakefield Camp* (June 1918)

86. TNA, FO 383/276 (1917), *Visits to Camp in UK. Transcribed copy of report by Dr Vischer on visit to Detention Camp at Douglas.*

87. See *Report on Wakefield Camp* (June 1918).

88. See Paul Cohen-Portheim, *Time Stood Still*, p. 107.

89. TNA, FO 383/360 (1918), *Repatriation or Transfer to a Neutral Country of A.H. p/w at Wakefield.*

90. *Ibid.*

91. *Ibid.*

92. TNA, FO 383/360 (1918), *Army Council Instruction No. 623 of 1918* (2 June 1918).

93. TNA, FO 383/360 (1918), *Abolition, or Better Cooking, of Horse Flesh at Present Served to A.H. P/W in UK*. Count Wrangel to the Court of St. James, dated 25 June 1918.

94. *Ibid.*

95. TNA, FO 383/360 (1918), *P/W Camp at Lofthouse Park, Wakefield*. Report on visit by Lt. Col. Lundbled, 26 & 27 October, 1918.

96. *Ibid.* See also Panayi, *Prisoners of Britain*, pp. 141-146, and section on scale of rations and 'Food'.

97. TNA, FO 383/360 (1918), *Extension of Visiting Hours at Wakefield*. See also, Visits to P/W interned at Wakefield, Letter dated 1 August.

98. See *Report on Visit by Lt. Col. Lundbled*, 26 & 27 October 1918.

99. See *ICRC*, Geneva, for individual names and further details.

Part I: Family Narratives

2 Family Ties (Carol Wright)

Pages 33-39

1. Census of England and Wales, 1911.
2. *Ibid.*
3. Yorkshire Marriages, 1907. Find My Past. Site accessed 24 August 2017.
4. Census of England and Wales, 1911.
5. Census of England, Wales and Scotland, 1871.
6. Rothwell and District Record, 'Early Recollections of Rothwell'. July 2002, p. 8.

3 Richard Cornelius Bechtel (Eberhard Haering)

Pages 40-47

1. Christmas Concert Programme, 1914 (not reproduced in this chapter): Commander P.M. Wotton (*HMT Royal Edward*), Commandant de Cordes, Captain (Adjutant) McCulloch (POWs); Committee: Baron von Nettlebladt, Baron Von Horst, Herr Richard Heckmann and Herr F. Kalhof; Management: Hans Altman (General Manager and Musical Director), Bruno Jablonsky (Manager), and Carl Bertram (Choir Diregent). The Christmas Concert was performed on the evening of Thursday, 24 December 1914. (Bechtel Family Archive). Lieutenant-Colonel Ernest de Cordes was later Commandant at the Prisoner of War Camp at Frimley, Berkshire. See *1911 Census* for full name Ernest Lucas de Cordes.
2. See Chapter 19 on Commandant G.S. Haines for more on Baron von Horst and a later inquiry in 1918. Nettlebladt was repatriated from Lofthouse Park to Holland in 1918. See Appendix 6.
3. Anon. *Naval Attaché's Reports*. Office of Naval Intelligence, February 1915. p. 10.
4. *Ibid.*
5. *Ibid.*

6. The *Royal Edward* later embarked a large number of infantry soldiers and men of the Royal Army Medical Corps at Avonmouth on 28 July 1915; on 13 August 1915 it was torpedoed on its way to Gallipoli by the German submarine *UB-14* and sank with considerable loss of life. Commander Peter M. Wotton, who is named on the 1914 Christmas programme, was among the casualties. See note 1.

7. *Sheffield Daily Telegraph*, 13 April 1915, p. 4.

8. Richard Bechtel did not make his own drawings, but it was common practice to obtain camp views from fellow internees who drew well. Some of them advertised their talent and services in the Lofthouse Park camp magazine. See Chapter 8 on the artist-internee Max Schnös and Chapter 12 on the camp journal *Lage-Bote*.

4 Richard Oswald Siebenhüner (Richard Oswald)

Pages 48-51

1. John Walling, *The Internment and Treatment of German Nationals during the 1st World War* (Grimsby: Riparian, 2005), and *Coming Home* (Grimsby: Riparian, 2008) by the same author.

5 John Henry Brickmann (Alan Muddiman)

Pages 52-58

1. 1901 Census England and Wales, Brickmann.

2. ICRC, Geneva, Brickmann, John Henry. Ref. DCVI - 5. Accessed 29 June 2017.

3. *North Eastern Daily Gazette*, Friday, 4 September 1914.

4. *North Eastern Daily Gazette*, Monday, 7 September 1914.

5. For books mentioned in this part of the text, see John Walling, *The Internment And Treatment of German Nationals during the 1st World War* (Grimsby, 2005), John Walling, *Coming Home* (Grimsby, 2008), and Ronald P. Rhodes, *Going Back a Bit: A Resume of the Village of Lofthouse Gate in the Early 1900s. Supplement to Lofthouse Park. Book 2* (Publisher Unknown, Undated).

6. *North Eastern Daily Gazette*, Friday, 22 September, and Tuesday, 26 September 1916. The death notice shows that

John Henry Brickmann was known also as 'Harry' to his friends.

7. The National Archives, Middlesbrough Constabulary to Home Office, 1916. Form 14. 322011/2.

Part II: Case Studies

6 Case Studies I (David Stowe)

Pages 59-65

Dr Gerhard Bartram: S.M.S. *Kronprinz Wilhelm* and S.S. *Hellig Olav*

1. Anon, *Review of German Cruiser Warfare 1914-1918*, H.M. Government, 1940. p. 12.
2. TNA, FO 383/143 (1916), *German medical officers interned in UK.*
3. TNA, FO 383/143 (1916), *Internment of German Medical Personnel in UK.*
4. TNA, FO 383/143, *German civilian doctors detained at Stratford.*
5. See *German medical officers interned in UK.*
6. See *German civilian doctors detained at Stratford.*
7. *Ibid.*
8. See *German medical officers interned in UK.*
9. *Ibid.*
10. ICRC, Geneva, Ref. DH-7. Date accessed 30 July 2017.

1st Officer H. Brammer: *Eleonore Woermann* and 'Neutral' Territory

11. TNA, FO 383/143 (1916), H. *Brammer, detained at Wakefield.*

Professor Gustav Adolf Bredow: Sculptor

12. TNA, FO 383/143 (1916), Re. *G.A. Bredow: His petition for his release.* See also *Detention of G.A. Bredow in UK.*
13. ICRC, Geneva: Bredow, Gustav Adolf (Index Card).

P.W. Brünger: Director of Niger-Berne Transport - Warri, Nigeria

14. TNA, FO 383/162 (1916), *Interned German prisoners at Wakefield.* See also ICRC Database, *Brünger, Paul Wilhelm.*

15. TNA, FO 383/305 (1917), *German subjects taken prisoners in Nigeria* (June 1917.)
16. *Ibid.*
17. TNA, FO 383/ 162, *Letter dated 7 January 1916.*
18. TNA, FO 383/305 (1917), *German subjects taken prisoners in Nigeria* (July 1917).

Ludwig Lichtenstadter
19. TNA, FO 383/143 (1916), *Ludwig Lichtenstadter, interned at Wakefield.*

7 Case Studies II (David Stowe)

Pages 66-72

Otto Froitzheim: Tennis Player
1. *Commonwealth War Graves Commission* (CWGC) Database.
2. (The) *Pittsburg Press*, Sunday 16 January 1916, p. 3. Date accessed 30 July 2017.
3. *Ibid.*

Guido von Georgevits: Aviator
4. TNA, FO 383/118 (1916), *Austria-Hungary: Prisoners, including Georgevitch, Austro-Hungarian aviator.*

Count Eginhard Beissel von Gymnich: *S.S.* Caserta and Gibraltar Camp
5. TNA, FO 383/143 (1916), *Count Eg. Beissel von Gymnich, interned at Wakefield.*
6. *ICRC*, Geneva, date accessed 30 July 2017.

Dr Karl Hoch: S.S. *Hellig Olav* and Report from Boarding Officer
7. TNA, FO 383/143 (1916), *Documents taken from three Germans from 'Hellig Olaf'.*

Frederick Wiener and Alfred Klapproth: Escapees
8. *The Times*, Tuesday 29 June 1915, p. 5. Date accessed 30 July 2017.

9. TNA, FO 383/121 (1916), *Austrian subject, who escaped from camp at Wakefield, and served with Austrian forces.*
10. *Ibid.*
11. *Ibid.*

8 Max Schnös: Artist and Illustrator (Franz Götz)

Pages 73-77

1. The quotation is taken from autobiographical material by Max Schnös held at the Heimatmuseum Baunach. Thi material also forms the basis for the information in this chapter, together with a letter by Schnös to Studienrat Dr. And. Fehn, dated 9 July 1934.

9 Gustav Wiesener, No. 1639 (Corinna Meiß)

Pages 78-85

1. Goslarer Stadtarchiv: Melderegister Gustav Georg Wiesener.
2. The credit information agency Creditreform was founded in Mainz, Germany, in 1879, and had 336 Vereine and 277 branches in 1914. It is still providing its services today, operating internationally with offices across Europe and in China. For the Goslar branch, see also Corinna Meiß, *Chronik Creditreform Goslar 1879-2014* (Goslar, 2014).
3. The National Archives, Kew: HO 405/57968: WIESENER, L A A aka WEISSENER, A L A aka RABE; WIESENER, G G, Years of birth 1880; 1870.
4. The German Hospital in Dalston (Hackney) was established in 1845, initially offering a dozen beds for underprivileged German immigrants and non-German local poor. By the end of the 19th century, the hospital had grown to over 140 beds and was extended further in 1911 and 1912. During the First World War, it remained in operation and its German staff in place. In the Second World War, the German personnel was interned on the Isle of Man and the hospital was run by British staff.
5. ICRC Historical Archive, Geneva: Gustav Georg Wiesener's index card and entries in the POW lists.

10 German Pork Butchers (Karl-Heinz Wüstner)
Pages 86-93

1. Friedrich Naumann, 'Die amerikanische Neutralität' in *Die Hilfe: Wochenschrift für Politik, Literatur und Kunst, Vol. 22* (1916), pp. 125-6.
2. Ernest G.F. Vogtherr, *No Regrets* (Napier, 1965), p. 10. The author explains that his grandmother, at her wedding in Germany, resolved that if she had a son he would be sent to England as soon as legally possible to avoid mandatory military service.
3. Panikos Panayi, *German Immigrants in Britain during the 19th Century, 1815-1914* (Oxford: Berg, 1995), p. 7.
4. John S. Roberts, *Little Germany* (Bradford: City of Bradford Metropolitan Council, Art Gallery and Museums, 1977), p. 21-2.
5. Sue Gibbons, *German Pork Butchers in Britain* (Maidenhead: Anglo-German Family History Publications, 2001), p. 9.
6. *Ibid.,* p. 11. See also Louis Schonhut (chapter 1), note 11.
7. Robert Roberts, 'The Classic Slum: Salford Life in the First Quarter of the Century' [1971], in George Dowey Smith, Daniel Dorling and Mary Shaw, eds. *Poverty, Inequality and Health in Britain 1800-2000: A Reader* (Bristol: The Policy Press, 2001), p. 309.
8. Richard M. Ford, *From Belsenberg to Britain: A Case Study* (Huddersfield-Netherton, unpublished family chronicle, 2010), p. 9.
9. See Sue Gibbons, p. 11.
10. Karl-Heinz Wüstner, 'New Light on the German Pork Butchers in Great Britain (1850-1950)'. Conference Diasporas, Migration and Identities: Crossing Boundaries, New Directions, 11-12 June 2009, University of Surrey, Guildford, UK: http://www.surrey.ac.uk/cronem/files/conf2009papers/Wuestner.pdf (accessed on 12 August 2017), p. 3.
11. Louis Schonhut, *And Then the Sun Shone: A Family Chronicle of the Schonhut Families in England* (Grange over Sands, unpublished family chronicle). See Chapter 4.

12. John Grund of Altrincham was a member of a canine society and went to shows with his dogs. He won top prizes for his Great Dane puppies and novice dogs. The *Manchester Courier*, Monday, 18 January 1909, p. 9. I thank Mrs. Gillian Schuler-Owen for this information.

13 See Sue Gibbons, pp. 35-7.

14. The *Yorkshire Post*, Tuesday, 18 May 1915. p. 9; 'GF. Ziegler. To The Public of Wakefield and District', in *The Wakefield Express*, October 1914.

15. See ICRC Database, Geneva, Andrassy, Carl (Heinrich), and Andrassy, Paul (accessed 30 August 2017).

16. Georg Kuch was born on 11 November 1867 at Alkertshausen. I thank Mrs. Dorothy Ramser for this information. See also http://grandeguerre.icrc.org/en (accessed on 29 August 2017).

17. Karl Rohn was born on 14 June 1890 at Dörrenzimmern. Kind information by Mrs. Patricia Richardson in an email of 20 April 2016.

18. See Waldman, Frederick, on ICRC Database, Geneva, and *Künzelsau Civil Registry*, Vol. 1. p. 54.

19. *Ibid.*

20. *Ibid.*

21. *Ibid.*

22. Waldman, Frederick, ICRC Database, Geneva, Ref. D. 204.4 (accessed 30 August 2017).

23. Patricia Richardson in an email to the author on 20 April 2016.

24. Patricia Richardson in an email to the author on 30 July 2017.

25. Georg Friedrich Ziegler in a letter to his father.

26. *Wakefield Express*, Saturday, 3 July 1965.

11 Paul Cohen-Portheim (Claudia Sternberg)

Pages 94-100

1. Paul Cohen-Portheim, *Time Stood Still: My Internment in England, 1914-1918* (New York: E.P. Dutton & Co., 1932) [first published London: Duckworth, 1931], p.8. Quotations are taken from the 1932 American edition of *Time Stood Still*.

2. Cohen-Portheim, *Time Stood Still*, p. 14.

3. Cohen-Portheim, *Time Stood Still*, p. 29.

4. Cohen-Portheim, *Time Stood Still*, p. 30.

5. Cohen-Portheim, *Time Stood Still*, p. 63.

6. Cohen-Portheim, *Time Stood Still*, p. 63.

7. Cohen-Portheim, *Time Stood Still*, p. 65.

8. Cohen-Portheim, *Time Stood Still*, pp. 65-6.

9. Cohen-Portheim, *Time Stood Still*, p. 148.

10. Cohen-Portheim, *Time Stood Still*, p. 184.

11. Paul Cohen-Portheim, Untitled. *Proofs for autobiographical sketch* [not dated, probably 1930], p. 1a (translated from German). Held at Berlinische Galerie, Werner Hegemann Archive, Berlin; Document ID: BG-AS 1584.28.1-6.

12. *Ibid.* (translated from German).

13. Cohen-Portheim, *Time Stood Still*, p. 166.

14. Cohen-Portheim, *Time Stood Still*, p. 82.

15. Cohen-Portheim, *Time Stood Still*, p. 83 (italics in original).

16. Paul Cohen-Portheim, *England, The Unknown Isle*. Trans. by Alan Harris. (London: Duckworth, 1930), pp. 220-21.

17. International Tracing Service/Digital Archive Bad Arolsen: See Siegbert Lachmann - Section: 1.2.1.1, Document ID: 11192220; Section: 1.1.42.2, Document ID: 5052188; Paula Mühsam - Section: 1.2.1.1, Document ID: 11192067; Section: 1.1.42.2, Document ID: 5066939; and Heinrich Mühsam - Section: 1.2.1.1, Document ID: 11192067; Section: 1.1.42.2, Document ID: 5066938.

18. Cohen-Portheim, *Time Stood Still*, p. 81.

Part III: Camp Life and Culture

12 *Lager-Bote* (Emily Bagshaw)
Pages 101-108

1. This chapter is based on Emily Bagshaw, 'Wie haben die Internierten in *Lofthouse Park* ihre Lagergemeinschaft strukturiert, welche Bewältigungsstrategien haben sie angenommen, um mit ihrer Gefangenschaft fertig zu werden, und wie haben sie ihre Erfahrungen in der Gefangenschaft dargestellt?' Unpublished B.A. Dissertation (University of Leeds), June 2017. Supervisor: Professor Ingrid Sharp.

2. Paul Cohen-Portheim, *Time Stood Still: My Internment in England 1914-1918* (London: Duckworth, 1931), p. 90.

3. Author 'Hi'. 'Stacheldrahtkrankheit'in *Lager-Bote*, Zweites Heft (Issue Two), 1 March 1916, pp. 8-10, here p. 9.

4. Author 'Dr. B.''Aus meinem Skizzenbuch'in *Lager-Bote*, Erstes Heft (Issue One), 15 February 1916, pp. 6-7, here p. 7. The article continues in *Lager-Bote*, Zweites Heft (Issue Two), 1 March 1916, pp. 10-12.

5. Cohen-Portheim, *Time Stood Still, p.* 151.

6. Fritz Draeger. 'Wert gymnastischer Koerperkultur' in *Lager-Bote. Lager-Bote*, Zweites Heft (Issue Two), 1 March 1916, pp. 4-6, here p. 5.

7. Cohen-Portheim, *Time Stood Still,* p.104-5.

8. Rainer Pöppinghege, *Im Lager unbesiegt: Deutsche, englische und französische Kriegsgefangenen-Zeitungen im Ersten Weltkrieg* (Essen: Klartext Verlag, 2006), p. 215.

9. Schriftleitung (Friedrich H. Thoele, F. Grah, Hugo Schoeman). 'Geleitwort!' in *Lager-Bote*, Erstes Heft (Issue One), 15 February 1916, p. 3. Original text: 'so bleibt doch die schmerzliche Tatsache bestehen, dass kostbare Jahre, wer weiss wie viele, unseres Lebens mit so geringem aeusseren Erleben erfuellt sind, dass sie uns nicht mehr wert sind, als wenige Wochen in Freiheit.'

10. Fritz Grah. 'Probleme'in *Lager-Bote*, Erstes Heft (Issue One), 15 February 1916, pp. 4-5.

11. Author 'H.T.' 'Huetten' in *Lager-Bote*, Erstes Heft (Issue One), 15 February 1916, p. 3. NB: The German *Umlaute* ä, ö and ü are spelled ae, oe and ue in the poem and throughout the two issues of *Lager-Bote* because respective German letters for typesetting were not available to most British printers. The camp magazine was printed by 'The Eagle Press, Wakefield', located on Wood Street, as indicated on p. 12 of the first issue.

12. Dr. Busse. 'Arbeiten und nicht verzweifeln!' in *Lager-Bote*, Zweites Heft (Issue Two), 1 March 1916, pp 3-4, here p. 4.

13. Authored by 'Paulchen, Goenner und Abonnent'. 'Dem Leser!' in *Lager-Bote*, Erstes Heft (Issue One), 15 February 1916, p. 5. Original text: 'Und wenn sie frohe Stunden / Uns bringt in Wort und Bild / Dann schweiget, boese Zungen / Dann ist ihr Zweck erfuellt.'

13 Hermann J. Held (Henning Ibs)

Pages 109-119

1. The chapter is based on Klaus Henning Ibs, *Hermann J. Held (1890-1963): Ein Kieler Gelehrtenleben in den Fängen der Zeitläufe* (Frankfurt/M. etc.: Peter Lang, 2000), and archival sources held at Archiv der Rechtswissenschaftlichen Fakultät der Universität Kiel, Landesarchiv Schleswig, Privatarchiv Klaus Held and The National Archives (Kew).

2. Hermann Held, 'Zivilgefangenschaft', in *Wörterbuch des Völkerrechts und der Diplomatie*, edited by Karl Strupp (Berlin and Leipzig: De Gruyter, 1929), Volume III, pp. 663-743, here p. 690. The designated ports were: Aberdeen, Dundee, West Hartlepool, Hull, London, Folkestone, Falmouth, Bristol, Holyhead, Liverpool, Greenock, Dublin and Rosslare.

3. *Ibid.*

4. In May 1916, the local Hon. Secretary of the Friends' Emergency Committee for the Assistance of Germans, Austrians and Hungarians in Distress had approached Michael Sadler, Vice-Chancellor of the University of Leeds, on behalf of students and professors interned in Lofthouse Park. They enquired whether the University might extend

them library privileges and lend books for purposes of study and teaching in the camp. Sadler agreed in principle, provided explicit military approval was obtained. (TNA FO 383/189 [1916]: *Germany: Prisoners, including: Loan of educational books to civilian prisoners at Lofthouse Park, Wakefield, Yorkshire.*
5. Letter from *Regierungsräte* (state councillors) P. Hermans and Dr. Rosenberg of 25 September 1916 (Privatarchiv Klaus Held VI./462).
6. *Vorlesungsverzeichnis* Lofthouse Park 1918, p. 4.
7. Letter (Privatarchiv Klaus Held).

14 Postal Lifelines (Postal Historian)
Pages 120-136

1. Panikos Panayi, *Prisoners of Britain: German Civilian and Combatant Internees during the First World War* (Manchester and New York: Manchester University Press, 2012), p. 147.
2. John Yarnall, *Barbed Wire Disease. British and German Prisoners of War, 1914-19* (Stroud: The History Press, 2011), pp. 8-12.
3. Graham Mark, *Prisoners of War in British Hands during WWI: A Study of their History, the Camps and their Mails* (Exeter: The Postal History Society, 2007); see Chapter 6, 'Conduct, Discipline, Facilities, Etc.', pp. 31-32, in which Mark summarises the main points of the regulations governing the 'Correspondence of PoWs and Internees' as found in Army Council Instructions 49, dated 16 January 1918.
4. *Ibid.*.
5. *Ibid.*. pp. 23-25
6. See Chapter 7 for further information on Wiener and Klapp-roth.
7. The National Archives, Kew (TNA), FO 383/162, *Reports of visits to camps in UK*, 8 January 1916. See also complaints about the delay of letters and parcels. These complaints were not uncommon and feature in a number of petitions and reports.
8. Destinations for outgoing mail, based on the postal collection, included Ashton-under-Lyne, Berlin, Birmingham, Brad-ford, Brighton, Budapest, Dortmund, Glanerbrug (Nether-lands), Glasgow, Gütersloh (redirected to Friedrichsfeld),

Hamburg, Hanover, Kidderminster, Cologne (Köln), Leeds, London, the US consulate at Manchester, Munich (München), Oxford, Shipley, Spandau and York. Editors' note: Names are transcribed from handwritten letters and may contain errors.

15 Religion and Faith (David Stowe and Claudia Sternberg)

Pages 137-142

1. The *Yorkshire Evening Post*, 'German Pastor and Lofthouse Camp', 26 November 1914, p. 4.
2. *Ibid.*
3. Cd. 7817, Miscellaneous No. 7 (1915), *Correspondence Between His Majesty's Government and The United States Ambassador Respecting The Treatment of Prisoners of War and Interned Civilians in The United Kingdom and Germany Respectively.* London: HMSO, April 1915, pp. 73-74. See Enclosure in No. 3. Sir Edward Grey to Mr Page, United States Ambassador in London, 13 March 1915.
4. *The Board of Deputies of British Jews. 63rd Annual Report.* Session 5673 to 76 – 1913 to 1916. London. 1915. See Google BJPA Berman Jewish Policy Archive (Stanford). p. 25; 36. Appendix.
5. *The Jewish Chronicle*, 21 August 1914, p. 12.
6. See Note 4 in Henning Ibs's chapter on Hermann J. Held for more information.
7. The *Yorkshire Evening Post*, 'Religious Services at Lofthouse Park', 7 July 1917.
8. See Cd. 7817. Miscellaneous No. 7 (1915).
9. *The Yorkshire Evening Post*, 'Religious Services at Lofthouse Park', Saturday, 7 July 1917, p. 3.
10. TNA, FO 383/339, *Treatment of Turkish P/W in UK*, 27 September 1917.
11. TNA, FO 383/339, *Treatment of Turkish P/W in UK*, 17 September 1917.
12. TNA, FO 383/339, *Ottoman P/W in British Hands*, August 1917.

13. FO 383/432 (1918). Visits of inspections to prisoners' camps in UK. The reports on visits by Dr Sturler to Wakefield and Alexandra Palace, 11 February 1918. See also Stowe and Section II in Chapter 1, 'From Pleasure to Detention'.

14. Khedouri Shasha was transferred from Lofthouse Park to the Isle of Man in October 1918 when the camp closed to civilians. See Manx National Museum i-Museum for the length of stay at the Isle of Man. See also *1911 Census* (Manchester, Great Britain), and Sarah Stein Abrevaya, *Extraterritorial Dreams: European Citizenship, Sephardi Jews, and the Ottoman Twentieth Century* (Chicago and London: Chicago University Press, 2016), p. 91, 174 and Note 68 for further details on background and internment.

15. Biographical information on Hans Schmidt from Martin-Luther-Universität Halle-Wittenberg: http://www.catalogus-professorum-halensis.de/schmidthans.html (accessed 14 March 2018).

16. Hans Schmidt. *Aus der Gefangenschaft: Predigten gehalten im Offiziers-Gefangenenlager Lofthousepark bei Wakefield in England* (Göttingen: Vandenhoeck & Ruprecht, 1919).

17. Schmidt, *Aus der Gefangenschaft*, p. 5.

16 Music and Theatre (Claudia Sternberg)

Pages 143-154

1. Lofthouse Park programmes for concerts, plays, crafts shows and sporting events have been digitised by Staatsbibliothek zu Berlin – Preußischer Kulturbesitz and can be accessed online via: http://digital.staatsbibliothek-berlin.de/

2. Paul Cohen-Portheim, *Time Stood Still: My Internment in England, 1914-1918*. New York: E.P. Dutton & Co., 1932 [1931], pp. 146-58.

3. *Lage Bote*, Issue Two, 1 March 1916, p. 15.

4. Reviewer 'R.', 'Aus Unserem Musikleben' in *ibid.*, p. 12-3, here 12.

5. *Ibid.*, p. 13.

6. *Ibid.*, pp. 12-13.

7. Wilhelm Friedrich and Lockroy were pseudonyms for Wilhelm Friedrich Riese and Joseph Philippe Simon, respectively.

8. Reviewer 'R.', 'Deutsche Theater-Verein', in *Lage-Bote*, Issue One, 15 February 1915, pp. 7-8, here 7.

9. Cohen-Portheim, *Time Stood Still*, p. 146.

10. *Ibid.*, p. 147.

11. Lofthouse Park production titles have been compiled from the theatre programmes held at State Library Berlin, see note 1. The performance dates for the three compounds were: *Raub der Sabinerinnen* (11, 12 and 13 March 1916), *Die wilde Jagd* (12, 13 and 14 Feburary 1916), *Der Biberpelz* (2, 3 and 4 February 1918), *Alt-Heidelberg* (1916, dates not known), *Im Klubsessel* (26, 27 and 28 February 1916), *Moral* (22, 23 and 24 January 1916) and *Die Sorina* (18, 19, and 20 May 1918).

12. Katja Krebs, 'German Theatre in the West End, 1900-1914: A History of the Deutsches Theater.' In *Im Spiegel der Theatergeschichte/In the Mirror of Theatre History*, edited by Paul S. Ulrich, Gunilla Dahlberg and Horst Fassel (Münster: LIT Verlag, 2015), pp. 255-82.

13. Ibsen's *Der Volksfeind* was performed on 1, 2, and 3 April 1916, Bernstein's *Bakkarat* on 3 and 4 December 1916 and Gauvault and Charvay's *Fraeulein Josette – Meine Frau* on 16, 17, and 18 June 1917.

14. The programmes for *Sei Ernst!* (performed 21, 22 and 23 April 1917) and *Der Fächer der Lady Windermere* (performed 16, 17 and 18 March 1918) can be accessed via the persistent URLs of State Library Berlin:

http://resolver.staatsbibliothek-berlin.de/SBB0000E0BF00000000
http://resolver.staatsbibliothek-berlin.de/SBB0000E0D200000000

The family of Leo Kunodi had written to the authorities in Vienna in April 1916 with a request for intervention in Kunodi's favour. His relatives claimed that he had been left partially paralysed in the right arm after a severe attack of malaria, and was thus unfit for military service. Kunodi had been invalided from the Imperial and Royal Army in 1904 due to a hernia. The request was forwarded to the US Embassy in London asking if the embassy would 'kindly use its good offices with British authorities' in order to secure a medical examination. Records are inconclusive about the success of the intervention. Source: The National Archives, Kew (TNA), FO 383/115 [1916], Leo Kunodi. Dr Straube is possibly Dr. Reinhold Straube, who was transferred to Holland from Wakefield on 22 February 1918. Source: ICRC Database, Geneva, Straube, Reinhold Dr., Ref. D. 186-4.

15. Reviewer 'F.R.', 'Zur Theater-Vorstellung im Nordlager am 1. Februar 1916' in *Lager-Bote,* Issue One, 15 February 1916, pp. 8-9, here 8.

16. Reviewer 'R.', 'Zur Theatervorstellung im Westlager vom 11. Februar 1916' in *Lager-Bote,* Issue Two, 1 March 1916, pp. 13-14.

17. Cohen-Portheim, *Time Stood Still,* p. 152.

18. Reviewer 'R.', 'Zur Theatervorstellung im Suedlager vom 12. Februar 1916' in *Lager-Bote,* Issue Two, 1 March 1916, p 14.

19. Reviewer 'R.', 'Zur Theatervorstellung im Suedlager vom 12. Februar 1916', *op. cit.*

20. L. von der Decken is listed in the records of the ICRC Database as 'Leonard', but it is possible that the entry contained an error and referred to Leopold (and not Leonard) von der Decken. Leopold Wolfgang von der Decken, born in 1895, had lived in London before the war and worked in the theatre. If 'Leonard [v.d.] Decken' was indeed Leopold Wolfgang, then the Lofthouse Park visual artist would later take on the name John Decker and migrate to the USA, where he worked as a caricaturist and painter in New York and later in Hollywood until his death in 1947. Like other Lofthouse internees, L. von der Decken was moved to Knockaloe on the Isle of Man before his release in 1919. On Decker see Stephen C. Jordan, *Bohemian Rogue: Life of Hollywood Artist John Decker* (Lanham, MD: Scarecrow, 2005).

20. *Die von Hochsattel* was performed on 27, 28 and 29 October 1917 and *Taifun* on 27, 28 and 29 September 1918.

21. The small orchestra played, for example, in the intermission for *Die von Hochsattel.* The overture and potpourri accompanied *Der Haeuptling* on 31 August and 1 and 2 September 1918.

22. Tammy Proctor, *Civilians in a World at War, 1914-1918* (New York and London: New York University Press, 2010), pp. 230-31..

23. Benjamin Suchoff, *Bartók's Mikrokosmos: Genesis, Padagogy, and Style* (Lanham, MD, and Oxford: Scarecrow, 2002), p. 14.

24. *Liebelei*, performed at 17, 18 and 19 August 1918.

25. Fest Programm zur Feier des Geburtstages SM des Kaisers, Sued Lager, 27 January 1916. URL of State Library Berlin: http://resolver.staatsbibliothek-berlin.de/SBB0000DB7600000000

26. Christoph Jahr, '"Mr. Goodhind, the prima donna of Ruhleben": Theater- und Geschlechterrollen im Engländerlager Ruhleben 1914-1918.' In *Mein Kamerad – Die Diva. Theater an der Front und in den Gefangenenlagern des Ersten Weltkriegs*, edited by Julia B. Köhne, Britta Lange and Anke Vetter (Munich: Edition Text + Kritik, 2014), pp. 91-9, here 91.

27. Cohen-Portheim, *Time Stood Still*, p. 146.

28. *Ibid.* p. 137.

17 Arts and Crafts (Claudia Sternberg)

Pages 155-160

1. Kunst- und Handfertigkeits-Ausstellung des West-, Nord- und Suedlagers: Im Zelte des Westlagers vom 20-23 September, 1917 (programme). State Library Berlin, PPN746319851, URL: http://resolver.staatsbibliothek-berlin.de/SBB0000D8AD00000000

2. See note 20 in the previous chapter.

3. Paul Cohen-Portheim, *Time Stood Still: My Internment in England, 1914-1918*. London: Duckworth, 1931.

4. On Max Schnös, see Chapter 8.

Part IV: Military Life and Culture

18 National Reserve and Royal Defence Corps (David Stowe)

Pages 161-172

1. TNA, WO 32/18622, *Re- Organisation of R.D.C.*, Statement B. Dated 27-8-1918.
2. William Herbert Scott, *Leeds in the Great War, 1914-1918: A Book of Remembrance* (Leeds: Leeds Libraries and Arts Committee, 1923). See Roll of Honour at the end of Scott and men who served/died with R.D.C. The names were cross-checked with the Commonwealth War Graves Commission Database and place of burial in Leeds. See also *Supplement to the London Gazette*, 28 June 1916, pp. 6423-6431, for a list of officers who had been transferred to the Protection Companies shortly after the Royal Defence Corps was formed. The officers were transferred from the Territorial Force (T.F.) Reserve (General List). The list also includes officers transferred to the Observer Companies.
3. *Leeds Mercury*, 20 March 1916, p. 3.
4. *Yorkshire Post*, 18 December 1911, p. 4
5. *Yorkshire Post*, 2 February 1912, p.5
6. *Yorkshire Post*, 26 February 1912, p. 3.
7. *Ibid.*
8. *Yorkshire Evening Post*, 13 August 1914, p. 2.
9. *Yorkshire Evening Post*, 2 December 1917.
10. Robert Brown's service documents are found on Ancestry and Find My Past.
11. See *Yorkshire Evening Post*, 2 December 1917.
12. *Yorkshire Evening Post*, Tuesday 17 October 1939, p. 6. 'On The Home Front in the War of 1914-18'.
13. Matthew Marley, *Lofthouse Diaries*, 1911-1919. West Yorkshire Archive Services (Wakefield). Ref. Z203.
14. *Yorkshire Evening Post*, 3 September 1946. p. 3; See also the service documents for Charles Dobson on Ancestry and Find My Past.
15. *Ibid.* re service documents for Pte. Henry Braginton.
16. *Ibid.* for James Patrick Gillen.

17. *National Roll of the Great War* (Leeds), Pte. J. Gillen, p. 128.

18. See Note 2 and W.H. Scott, *Leeds in the Great War*; also CWGC Database.

19. TNA, WO 332/18622, *War Establishment of one company*, Ref. 2D. The figures given are for October 1917.

20. TNA, WO 332/18622, *Present Distribution of Provisional and Reserve Companies R.D.C., by Command.*

21. See TNA, WO 32/18622, Statement 'B', and numbers guarding POW Camps. The figures given in July actually show an increase of nearly a thousand men from the figures given for April of the same year (27,000). The difference is accounted for by miscellaneous duties and the use of reserve protection companies, according to Statement B. The figures for Vulnerable Points and those for Special Military areas and M.I.5 may be found in the same document.

22. TNA, WO 32/18622, *Memorandum dated 27 July 1918*. Ref. 115.

23. See Statement 'B', 22-7-1918.

24. The number of civilians interned at Lofthouse Park in May 1918 was 1063. See Report on Inspection of Lofthouse Park, 10-12 May 1918 (June 1918).

25. TNA, WO 32/18622, *Memorandum dated 27 July 1918*. Ref. 115. H.

26. TNA, WO 374/32401, *Lt. G.C. Hebden*. See also *Supplement to the London Gazette*, 22 March 1916, p. 3158. Gazetted Lieutenant, Territorial Force Reserve, March 1916.

27. TNA, WO 374/28808, *Lt. T.E. Gray*. Thomas Edmondstone Gray was a chemist and was a general manager in a Manufacturing Business (Chemicals) before the war.

28. TNA, 374/31830, *Major H.S. Hassall*. Harry Hassall died eighteen months after he discharged.

29. *Yorkshire Evening Post*, Wednesday, 21 January 1920, p. 7. 'Revised Version of the Barnbow Incident. The Soldier's Statement.' Billed as the 'Barnbow Incident' in the press, this concerns the story of a sentry who was wounded in the hand after shots had been fired on the evening of 17 January 1920. The Commandant at Lofthouse Park was asked to

investigate the shooting. A revised version of the incident was later submitted.

30. TNA, WO 374/58984, *Colonel R.W.H. Ronaldson.* The camp was officially closed on 13 March 1920.

19 Gregory Sinclair Haines (Ruth Allison)

Pages 173-181

1. Gregory Sinclair Haines, "'Punishment" as Applied to Soldiers and Sailors', in Ralph Earle, ed. *United States Naval Institute Proceedings.* Vol. 38. March, 1912. Whole No. 141. U.S. Naval Institute: Annapolis, Maryland, p. 69.

2. See above. Note, p. 69.

3 *GS Haines*, WO 374/30046. The National Archives (TNA hereafter).

4. See TNA, *GS Haines.*

5. 'Prisons Bill'. House of Lords Debate, 29 July 1898. Vol. 63. Columns 404-415, *Hansard 1803-2005* (website); TNA, *GS Haines*; 'History of the MPS' (Military Prison Service), *British Army* (website); Lieutenant-Colonel G. Haines, 'Reformatory Treatment of Soldiers and Sailors under Sentence of Detention', in Ralph Earle, ed. *United States Naval Institute Proceedings*, Vol. 38, March, 1912, Whole No. 141. U.S. Naval Institute: Annapolis, Maryland, p. 1390.

6. See TNA, *GS Haines.*

7. *Ibid.*

8. *Ibid.*

9. *The London Gazette*, 3 December 1909, Issue: 28314, p. 9235; TNA, *GS Haines.*

10. See Ralph Earle, ed., *United States Naval Institute Proceedings*, p. 69; pp. 79-86.

11. *The London Gazette*, 3 May 1912, Issue: 28604, p. 3180; TNA, *GS Haines.*

12. See TNA, *GS Haines.*

13. See *Hansard*, 20 November 1919.

14. 'Newbury, Berkshire: Racecourse Turned into War Camp.' BBC website *World War One at Home*, 13 February 2014.

15. Anon. *Naval Attaché's Reports.* Office of Naval Intelligence, February 1915, p. 14.

16. TNA, *GS Haines.*
17. *Ibid.*
18. See *Naval Attaché's Reports,* p. 10; Thomas Boghardt, 'A German Spy? New Evidence on Baron Louis von Horst,' *The Journal of Intelligence History* Vol. 1, No. 2 (Winter 2001), pp. 101-127, here p. 120.
19. *Ibid.,* p. 107, p. 124: 'Miss Lillian Scott Troy (Deportation)', House of Commons Debate, 20 November 1920, Vol. 121, Column 1167, *Hansard 1803-2005* (website).
20. 'The German Prisoners of War Camp at Jersey, During the Great War, 1914-1918'. *The Channel Islands and the Great War* (website), pp. 5-6.
21. Panikos Panayi. *The Enemy in Our Midst: Germans in Britain During the First World War* (Oxford: Berg, 1991), p. 103.
22. *The Yorkshire Post,* 16 December 1916, p. 5.
23. 'MP's Wife and German Prisoners'. *The Times* (Digital), Wednesday, 19 June 1918, p. 7.
24. *Ibid.*
25. *Ibid.*
26. 'Mrs Leverton Harris's Reply: Letter to the Editor of The Times', *The Times* (Digital), Thursday, 20 June 1918, p. 7.
27. TNA, *GS Haines.*
28. *The Times,* Wednesday, 19 June 1918, p. 7.
29. TNA, *GS Haines.*
30. *Ibid.*
31. *Ibid.*

NB: The following sites were accessed on 12 July 2017: BBC World War One at Home; British Army; Hansard 1803-2005; Journal of Intelligence History; London Gazette; The German Prisoners of War Camp at Jersey; The Times (Digital).

20 Prisoner-of-War Camp (Oliver Wilkinson)

Pages 182-188

1. A potential transfer had been indicated to the German Government in June 1918. Graham Mark, *Prisoners of War in British Hands during WW1: A Study of their History, the Camps and their Mails* (Exeter: Short Run Press, 2007), p. 140.

2. The National Archives, Kew (hereafter TNA), FO 383/505, *Report on the transfer of those at Lofthouse Park Camp*; Also see Mark, *Prisoners of War*, pp. 140-1.

3. *Aberdeen Daily Journal*, 13 January 1919, p. 6.

4. ICRC Database, Geneva, A 38370-72, 'List No.220 of German Prisoners of War. Appendix IV'.

5. Heinz H.E. Justus, 'An Unconducted Tour of England', Joe Randolph Ackerley (ed.), *Escapers All: Being the Personal Narratives of Fifteen Escapers from War-time Prison Camps, 1914-1918* (London: John Lane, 1934), p. 205.

6. TNA, FO 383/506, Reports *on visits to officers' prisoner of war camps by Dr F Schwyzer, Dr A.L. Vischer and Dr A de Sturler, February and March 1919: Ripon, Skipton & Lofthouse Park.*

7. TNA, FO 383/506, *Reports on visits to officers' prisoner of war camps.*

8. TNA, FO 383/505, *Report on the transfer of those at Lofthouse Park Camp.*

9. TNA, FO 383/419, *Condition of Prisoner of War Camps at Wakefield & Ruhleben.*

10. TNA, FO 383/506, *Reports on visits to officers' prisoner of war camps.*

11. *Nottingham Evening Post*, 13 November 1919, p. 1.

12. Hermann Pörzgen, *Theater ohne Frau: Das Bühnenleben der kriegsgefangenen Deutschen 1914-1920* (Königsberg etc.: Ost-Europa-Verlag, 1933), p. 187.

13. See Mark, *Prisoners of War*, p. 170.

14. TNA, FO 383/508, *Treatment of Members of Germany Navy Now Interned at Wakefield* (1919), pp. 267-8.

15. See Oliver Wilkinson, *British Prisoners of War in First World War Germany* (Cambridge: Cambridge University Press, 2017), pp. 34-9; Brain K. Feltman, *The Stigma of Surrender: German Prisoners, British Captors and Manhood in the Great War and Beyond* (Chapel Hill: University of North Carolina Press, 2015), pp. 45-6.

16. Panikos Panayi, *Prisoners of Britain: German Civilian and Combatant Internees during the First World War* (Manchester: Manchester University Press, 2012), pp. 278-9.

17. Three inmates from the camp died during the influenza epidemic of November 1918. TNA, FO 383/506, *Reports on visits to officers' prisoner of war camps.*

18. Justus, 'An Unconducted Tour of England', pp. 206-15; ICRC Database, Geneva, A 28875 'List No.221 of German Prisoners of War. Appendix A'. Also see Feltman, *The Stigma of Surrender,* pp. 102-5.

19. Feltman, *The Stigma of Surrender,* pp. 90-1 & 143.

20. *The Times,* 24 March 1919, p. 9; *Yorkshire Post,* 25 March 1919, p. 6.

21. Name sometimes listed as Leroe, Lewe or Leroi. *The Times,* 21 July 1919, p. 12; *The Manchester Guardian,* 23 July 1919, p. 14.

22. *The Times,* 12 August 1919, p. 12; *The Times,* 1 September 1919, p. 7.

23. *Aberdeen Daily Journal,* 13 November 1919, p. 6; *Courier and Argus,* 13 November 1919, p. 5; *Devon and Exeter Daily Gazette,* 13 November 1919, p. 1; *The Times,* 13 November 1919, p. 9; *Manchester Guardian,* 13 November 1919, p. 7.

24. *Nottingham Evening Post,* 13 November 1919, p. 1. Note this report also differs by indicating that the tunnel was discovered following a 'tip-off' by a fellow POW.

25. On such anxieties see Oliver Wilkinson, 'A Fate Worse Than Death? Lamenting First World War Captivity', *Journal of War and Culture Studies,* 9, 1 (2015), pp. 24-40.

26. Feltman, *The Stigma of Surrender,* pp. 142-47.

27. *Manchester Guardian,* 22 December 1919, p. 3.

28. Panayi, *Prisoners of Britain,* pp. 273 and 8. Also see A.L Vischer, *Barbed Wire Disease: A Psychological Study of the Prisoner of War* (London, John Bale, Sons & Danielson Ltd., 1919), passim.

29. Justus: 'An Unconducted Tour of England', pp. 201-18; *The Listener,* 22 July 1931, p. 148; 'Flight from England Foiled by Flu', *Evening Telegraph and Post,* 23 May 1933, p.2.

30. ICRC Database, Geneva, 40241 & 40770, 'List No. 253 of German Prisoners of War. Appendix I'.

31 Vischer, *Barbed Wire Disease,* p. 83.

32. *Aberdeen Daily Journal,* 13 January 1920, p. 6.

33. Panayi, *Prisoners of Britain,* p. 277.

34. TNA, WO 374/58984, *Colonel R.W.H. Ronaldson.*

21 Albert H. Brugger (Claudia Sternberg)
Pages 189-199

1. For more on Lofthouse Park POWs and escape attempts, see Chapter 20.
2. See Chapter 7 for the Wiener/Klapproth incident.
3. All quotations from Brugger's text are translated from the German original, i.e. Albert Hermann Brugger, *Meine Flucht aus dem Kriegsgefangenen-Lager Lofthouse Park near Wakefield* (Berlin: Hans Siep, n.y. [1937]), here p. 9.
4. Brugger, *Meine Flucht*, p. 11.
5. Brugger, *Meine Flucht*, p. 12.
6. Brugger, *Meine Flucht*, p. 13.
7. *Ibid.*
8. Brugger, *Meine Flucht*, p. 16.
9. Brugger, *Meine Flucht*, p. 19.
10. Brugger, *Meine Flucht*, p. 24.
11. Brugger, *Meine Flucht*, p. 25.
12. *Ibid.*
13. Brugger, *Meine Flucht*, p. 27.
14. Brugger, *Meine Flucht*, p. 39.
15. Brugger, *Meine Flucht*, pp. 58-9.
16. Brugger mistakenly calls Ofenheim 'Oppenheim' (pp. 61-2). Ofenheim had participated in the International Economic Conference, called by the Fight the Famine Council, on 4-6 November 1919.
17. Brugger, *Meine Flucht*, pp. 69-70.
18. Brugger, *Meine Flucht*, pp. 81-2.
19. Preface to *Meine Flucht*, p. 7. The *Sturmabteilung* (SA), 'Storm Troopers' or 'Assault Division', was a paramilitary organisation of the National Socialist German Workers' Party (NSDAP). Still in existence in 1937, it had lost considerable power after the 'Night of the Long Knives', a leadership purge that took place in 1934.
20. Brugger, *Meine Flucht*, pp. 51-4.
21. This was made possible by the *Erlass zur Ergänzung der Offiziere während des Krieges* of 29 September 1914.

22. Brugger, *Meine Flucht*, p. 55.
23. Brugger, *Meine Flucht*, p. 51.
24. *Ibid.*

22 Celler Schloss (Hilke Langhammer)
Pages 200-205

1. A wider discussion of the Celler Schloss can be found in Hilke Langhammer, 'In Celle interniert: Das Schloss als Kriegsgefangenenlager im Ersten Weltkrieg', *Celler Chronik* 22 (2015), pp. 157-202.
2. Federal Archive Freiburg/Military Archive, RM 5/2551: 'Karte mit den Stammlagern der Kriegsgefangenen. Aufgestellt Januar 1916.' The camp description can be found in a US-American inspection report ('chiefly civilians of the better class') and in a Danish Russian report ('Leute aus höheren Ständen'): United Kingdom, Parliament: Reports by United States Officials on the Treatment of British Prisoners of War and Interned Civilians at Certain Places of Detention in Germany. Miscellaneous No. 11 (1915), London: His Majesty's Stationery Office, 1915, p. 21; Berichte der dänisch-russischen Kommissionen zum Besuch der Gefangenenlager in Deutschland, Kopenhagen 1915, p. 33.
3. Duncan Heaton-Armstrong. *The Six Month Kingdom: Albania 1914.* Edited by Gervase Belfield and Bejtullah Destani (London, New York: I.B. Tauris, 2005).
4. Auguste Vierset. *Adolphe Max* (Brussels: Imprimerie industrielle et financière, 1934).
5. Robert A. Reddie, however, was successful with a further attempt in July 1917 and reached the Netherlands after a few days. TNA WO 161/96/23.

23 Dismantling Lofthouse Park Camp (David Stowe)
Pages 206-211

1. TNA MUN 5/141. 'Surplus': *The Official Organ of the Surplus Government Property Disposal Board – Ministry of Munitions.* Director of Publicity: Ministry of Munitions, No. 2, 16 June 1919, p. 4.

2. *Yorkshire Post*, 22 May 1920, p. 3.

3. *The Yorkshire Post*, 26 May 1920, p. 6.

4. *The Yorkshire Evening Post*, 25 May 1920, p. 3.

5. *The Yorkshire Post*, 22 May 1920, p. 3.

6. TNA MUN 5/141. *Ministry of Munitions. Disposal of Surplus Government Property: Memorandum by the Surplus Government Disposal Board on the work carried out by them from the time of their appointment in January, 1919, to the end of May, 1920.* p. 29, p. 42.

24 Leeds and the Alien Register (David Stowe)

Pages 212-223

1. A version of this chapter was presented at the conference *Beyond the Western Front: The First Global War,* Albert Hall Conference Centre, Nottingham, 1 and 2 July 2016 ('The Domiciled Other as Enemy Alien: Leeds and the Alien Register, 1914-1919').

2. *Yorkshire Post*, 10 August 1914, p. 4.

3. *Yorkshire Evening Post*, 14 August 1914, p. 3.

4. *Ibid.*

5. *Yorkshire Evening Post*, 25 August 1914, p. 2.

6. *Yorkshire Post*, 11 September 1914, p. 8.

7. *Yorkshire Evening Post*, Wednesday, 2 September 1914, p. 3

8. ICRC Database: Julius Radl. Re-interned Handforth.

9. *Yorkshire Post*, 14 October 1914, p. 7.

10. *Yorkshire Post*, 2 January 1915, p. 8.

11. *Yorkshire Post*, 14 October 1914, p. 7.

12. *City of Leeds. Report on the Police Establishment and the State of Crime with Tabulated Returns for the Year Ended 31 December, 1916.* Appendix B: 'Returns of Enemy Aliens registered in Leeds, 31 December 1916', p. 43. Similar returns for the numbers of Belgian refugees registered in Leeds at this time were compiled in the same way.

13. *Yorkshire Post*, 28 February 1916, p. 6.

14. *Ibid.*

15. The National Archives, Kew, HO 144/11720 (ALIENS).

16. *Ibid.*

17. CWGC Database. Further information relating to Pte. Henry Levy may be found on Ancestry and Find My Past.
18. See HO 144/11720 (ALIENS).
19. *Yorkshire Evening Post*, 14 February 1916, p. 3.
20. See *Report on the Police Establishment*, Appendix B: Return of Alien Enemies registered in Leeds, 31 December 1916, p. 43
21. See *Report on the Police Establishment*, 31 December, 1914, p. 15. See also *Report from 1915*.
22. See *Report on the Police Establishment*, 31 December, 1918, p. 43.
23. *i-Museum*: Manx National Heritage, https://www.imuseum.im
24. *Ibid.*
25. Eduard Bohensky (Lackenbach). *Holocaust Yizkor, Jewish Gen.* (Yohanan Loeffler, 2009).
http://kehilalinks.jewishgen.org/Lackenbach/html/Holocaust _Yizkor.html. See also Eduard Bohensky, ICRC Database.

25 Death, Burial and Reburial (David Stowe and Claudia Sternberg)

Pages 224-237

1. *Yorkshire Evening Post*, Monday 12 April 1915, p. 5.
2. *Ibid.*
3. *Manchester Evening News*, Friday, 16 April 1915, p. 4. Acknowledgments Page.
4. *Burial Records, 1858-1924.* Parish of Lofthouse (Lofthouse Churchyard). Ref. West Yorkshire Archive Service. RDP 116/4/1, p. 257
5. *Ibid.*, Karl Gustav Bauck, p. 247. See also Chapter 5 on John Henry Brickmann.
6. The *Rothwell Courier and Times,* 25 March 1916, p. 5.
7. ICRC Database, Geneva, Dippold, August. See also 'A' 25920, 'A' 30998, 'A' 32261 and 'A' 32263.
8. ICRC Database, Bade, Wilhelm Georg. See also 'A' 28963, 'A' 4447, 'A' 27223, 'A' 27565, 'A' 28951.
9. *Yorkshire Evening Post*, Saturday, 23 November 1918, p. 5. See also *Leeds Mercury*, 26 November 1918, p. 12.
10. The authors would like to thank Peter Päßler at the Volksbund Deutsche Kriegsgräberfürsorge e.V. for his

support in sourcing and sharing material from the VDK archive in Kassel. We would also like to thank Alan Roberts (Skipton POW Project) for the information he shared on burials at Cannock Chase.

11. According to Panikos Panayi, of the men interned at the time of the Armistice, 84 per cent were repatriated; overall, the pre-war German community of 57,500 people had been reduced to 22,254 in 1919. See Panikos Panayi, *Prisoners of Britain: German Civilian and Combatant Internees during the First World War* (Manchester, New York: Manchester University Press, 2014 [2012]), p. 279.

12. WWII recoveries and reburials are still ongoing in Eastern Europe; see, for example, David Crossland, 'New Cemetery in Russia: Germany Still Burying Eastern Front Dead.' *Spiegel Online* 31 July 2013,
http://www.spiegel.de/international/europe/germany-to-open-last-wwii-war-cemetery-in-russia-a-914093.html
(accessed 13 March 2018).

13. After Luxembourg, Norway, Belgium, France, Italy and Egypt, the United Kingdom was the seventh country to establish a formal agreement with the Federal Republic of Germany.

14. V.D.K. G. England. 'Schlussbericht' (Final Report), 3 typescript, dated 31 May 1963, signed by office manager Schenkel (VDK Archive).

15. CWGC historical information for Cannock Chase War Cemetery at
https://www.cwgc.org/find-a-cemetery/cemetery/2000401/Cannock%20Chase%20War%20Cemetery (accessed 13 March 2018). The VDK 'Schlussbericht' (*op.cit.*, p. 1) states that the North of England reburials took place in summer and autumn of 1962.

16. Cannock Chase War Cemetery information panel, CWGC (2013),
http://media.cwgc.org/media/239358/cannock_chase_war_cemetery.pdf (accessed 13 March 2018).

17. CWGC Database for Cannock Chase War Cemetery, https://www.cwgc.org/find/find-war-dead (data as of 13 March 2018).

18. Volksbund Deutsche Kriegsgräberfürsorge. *Deutsche Soldatenfriedhöfe im Ausland: Cannock Chase Großbritannien.* Kassel: VDK, n.d., p. 4. On the initiative: 'Versöhnung über den Gräbern,' *Sonderdruck* (special edition) of *Westermanns Monatshefte,* Issue 11 (1963).

19. *Deutsche Soldatenfriedhöfe (op.cit.,* p. 3) and 'Schlussbericht' *(op. cit.,* p. 2). Of the 4,939 dead at Cannock Chase German Military Cemetery, 4,769 had been exhumed and moved by the VDK between 1962 and 1963.

20. Excerpt from 'Bericht zur Dienstreise von Herrn Dr. Seifert nach Großbritannien in der Zeit vom 11. bis 19. Juni 1962' ('Report on Visit to Britain by Dr Seifert, 11-19 June 1962'), p. 2 (VDK Archive).

21. 'Versöhnung über den Gräbern' *(op.cit.,* pp. 73-4, our translation).

22. 'Umbettungsrichtlinien des Volksbundes Deutsche Kriegsgräberfürsorge e.V. für Umbetter' (Reinterment Guidelines), typescript, dated 19 June 1952 (VDK Archive).

23. 'Umbettungsrichtlinien,' *op.cit.,* pp. 1-2.

24. 'Schlussbericht,' *op.cit.,* pp. 2-3.

25. The German war graves act has undergone several revisions since 1952, working towards an inclusive understanding of war graves in light of genocide and dictatorship and accommodating political changes such as Reunification. The first modifications to the 1952 act were made in the renamed *Gesetz über die Erhaltung der Gräber der Opfer von Krieg und Gewaltherrschaft* (Act for Maintaining the Graves of the Victims of War and Tyranny) of 1 July 1965

Further Reading

Bird, John C., *Control of Enemy Alien Civilians in Great Britain, 1914-1918* (London, 1986).

Cesarani, David, and Kushner, Tony, eds., *The Internment of Aliens in Twentieth Century Britain* (London, 1993).

Cohen-Portheim, Paul, *Time Stood Still: My Internment in England 1914-1918* (London, 1931).

Cresswell, Yvonne M., ed., *Living with the Wire: Civilian Internment in the Isle of Man during the two World Wars* (Douglas, 1994).

Denness, Zoë. *"A question which affects our prestige as a nation": The History of British Civilian Internment, 1899-1945.* PhD thesis, University of Birmingham 2012.

Dove, Richard, ed., *'Totally un-English?' Britain's Internment of 'Enemy Aliens' in Two World Wars* (Amsterdam, 2005).

Feltman, Brian K., *The Stigma of Surrender: German Prisoners, British Captors & Manhood in the Great War and Beyond* (Chapel Hill, 2015).

Field, Charles, *Internment Mail on the Isle of Man* (Sutton Coldfield, 1989)

Harris, Janet, *Alexandra Palace: A Hidden History* (Stroud, 2005)

Jones, Heather, *Violence against Prisoners of War in the First World War: Britain, France and Germany, 1914-1920* (Cambridge, 2011).

Jones, Heather. 'The Great War: How 1914–18 Changed the Relationship between War and Civilians.' *The Royal United Services Institute Journal* 159 (2014): 84–91.

Manz, Stefan. *Constructing a German Diaspora: The "Greater German Empire", 1871-1914* (London, 2014).

Manz, Stefan. '"Enemy Aliens" in Scotland in a Global Context, 1914–1919: Germanophobia, Internment, Forgetting', in Hannah Ewence and Tim Grady, eds. *Minorities and the First World War.* (London, 2017).

Mark, Graham, *Prisoners of War in British Hands during WWI: A Study of their History, the Camps and their Mail* (Exeter, 2007).

Mosse, George L., *Fallen Soldiers: Reshaping the Memory of the World Wars* (Oxford, 1990).

Murphy, Mahon. *German Prisoners of War and Civilian Internees from the German Colonies in Captivity in the British Empire, 1914–1920.* PhD diss., London School of Economics, 2015.

Murphy, Mahon. *Colonial Captivity during the First World War: Internment and the Fall of the German Empire, 1914–1919* (Cambridge, 2017).

Nachtigal, Reinhard. 'The Repatriation and Reception of Returning Prisoners of War, 1918–1922.' *Immigrants and Minorities* 26 (2008): 173–4.

Noschke, Richard, *An Insight into Civilian Internment in Britain during WWI: From the Diary of Richard Noschke and a Short Essay by Rudolf Rocker* (Maidenhead 1998).

Panayi, Panikos, *The Enemy in Our Midst: Germans in Britain during the First World War* (Oxford, 1991).

Panayi, Panikos, 'Sausages, Waiters and Bakers: German Migrants and Culinary Transfer to Britain, c1850-1914', in Stefan Manz, Margrit Schulte Beerbühl and John R. Davis, eds., *Migration and Transfer from Germany to Britain, 1660-1914* (Munich, 2007), pp. 147-159.

Panayi, Panikos *Prisoners of Britain: German Civilian and Combatant Internees during the First World War* (Manchester, 2012).

Panayi, Panikos, ed. *Germans as Minorities during the First World War: A Global Comparative Perspective.* Farnham: Ashgate, 2014.

Proctor, Tammy, *Civilians in a World at War, 1914-1918* (London, 2010).

Rhodes, Ronald P., *Going Back a Bit: A Resume of the Village of Lofthouse Gate in the Early 1900s.* Supplement to Lofthouse Park. Book 2 (Undated).

Sargeaunt, B.E., *The Isle of Man and the Great War* (Douglas, 1922).

Smith, Leslie, *The German Prisoner of War Camp at Leigh, 1914-1919* (Manchester, 1996).

Stent, Ronald, *A Bespattered Page? The Internment of His Majesty's 'Most Loyal Enemy Aliens'* (London, 1980).

Stibbe, Matthew, *British Civilian Internees in Germany: The Ruhleben Camp, 1914-18* (Manchester, 2008).

Walling, John, *The Internment And Treatment of German Nationals During The 1st World War* (Grimsby, 2005).

Wilkinson, Oliver, *British Prisoners of War in First World War Germany* (Cambridge, 2017).

Wood, Peter, 'The Zivilinternierungslager at Lofthouse Park'. In: Kate Taylor, ed. *Aspects of Wakefield: Discovering Local History*, 3 (Barnsley, 2001), 150-62.

Yarnall, John, *Barbed Wire Disease. British and German Prisoners of War, 1914-19* (Stroud, 2011).

Appendix 1

Report on the transfer of those at Lofthouse Park Camp near Wakefield Yorkshire to the Isle of Man

(January 1919)

On 11 October 1918 a notice was exhibited in the Camp in which the prospect of the evacuation of the camp was dealt with. That evening the 14 October was given out as being the date fixed upon for the journey.

The Camp Captains telegraphed the War Office asking that this order should be cancelled, at the same time asking to be allowed to enter into correspondence with the competent authorities in London. This request was refused. The Camp Commandant gave the prisoners permission to take down the partitions from their rooms and use the wood for the construction of boxes etc in which to pack up their belongings, especially the numerous books they had collected during their long internment.

On 13 October an order came through from the War Office limiting the amount of luggage to 100lbs heavy and 20lbs hand luggage.

The Commandant, recognizing its hardship, endeavoured to have this order rescinded.

At 5.00pm confirmation of the order was received and as part of the baggage had already been loaded up for transport it had to be unloaded and repacked as speedily as possible, so that only what was absolutely necessary had to go.

Everything else had to remain behind such for example as a quantity of provisions, in part dearly acquired by the prisoners and the kitchen personnel. Numerous presents sent to the prisoners through the Red Cross from all parts of the Globe. All the vegetables in the camp which had been raised at great expense – notably cabbages. [...]

Numerous small tables and chairs as also carpenters and mechanics tools as well as countless books to the various inhabitants of the camp.

All these had to be left behind without receipts and in part not even packed up owing to lack of time.

Apart from the loss of their provisions, that of their books particularly to be deplored as amongst these were educational works required by the interned for their preparations for examinations for voluntary one year course of military service etc.

The evacuation commenced at 3.00am on 14 October (1918).

Prior to embarkation the police confiscated all dogs. Many of these had been sent to their owners from home. Some had even been in their possession at the camp, where dogs had never been forbidden, and to this day many dogs are to be found in the camp at Knockaloe

On their arrival at Douglas on the East coast of the island all the prisoners luggage had been taken from them and they were then taken by rail to Peel on the West coast whence they had to walk a couple of miles to their new place of internment.

All the prisoners were sent to Camp 4 Compound 4 where arrangements for their reception had been made by the Senior Camp Captains Kanert and Unde who had been sent on in advance for that purpose.

At the same time the Camp Commandant forbade these captains to communicate in any way with those at Wakefield on the subject of these arrangements. On the contrary he ordered them to fill straw sacks and told them to remember they were prisoners. The Captains consequently made arrangements with a man who contracted to put the camp in some sort of order provisionally.

Three days after their arrival the prisoners received their luggage, but only to the extent of 100lbs of weight because a new order at this camp decreed that limit. In most cases the hand baggage containing the more valuable property was simply retained.

I would point out that prior to 12 October i.e. the time of the transfer from one camp to the other, no orders had ever been issued at Wakefield as to a limit being placed on the amount of luggage.

Source: The National Archives, FO 383/505 (1919). [There are a number of syntactical and other errors in the original text.]

Appendix 2

Treatment of Members of German Navy at Scapa Flow and Nigg Camp (Scotland) Now Interned at Wakefield

(1919)

Lofthouse Park, Wakefield. 2 July 1919

To His Excellency, The Swiss Minister, London

I beg to bring the following to the notice of your Excellency.

After the sinking of the German ships and Torpedo boats at Scapa Flow on 21-7-19 the German officers and crews were taken to the Battleships *Revenge, Royal Sovereign, Royal Oak*, and *Ramilles* in British drifters and destroyers and partly in German boats which conveyed them to Nigg in Scotland, where they were interned at Nigg Camp. I with twenty other naval officers and a paymaster were transferred thence to Lofthouse Park.

I beg to make complaint of the treatment accorded us, subsequent to the sinking of the German Fleet, by the crews of British ships and destroyers, as also of our treatment by the Scottish guards who accompanied from Nigg to the prisoner of war camp, a complaint which is the more serious seeing that the events occurred several months after the conclusion of the Armistice.

Complaints:

Leutnant Zaeschmar: The Life Boat in which I and the crew of torpedo boat *V.126* left our ship rowed off in the direction of the Flotilla and where so doing were subjected to rifle fire from a Drifter. Something was shouted to us from the Drifter, but being unable to understand what was said I immediately ordered the oars to be taken in, and replied to this effect. The cutter was hotly fired upon at short range both by a Destroyer, a Drifter and by British who were on board another German boat (*V.45*), civilians on the Drifter taking part in the shooting. I called out several times that we were defenceless and had no ill intentions and also asked what we were required to do. After repeated enquiries we were told to return to *V.126* which we at once did, notwithstanding that we continued to be fired upon. In view of the position and conduct of the Life boat it could not be assumed that an attempt to escape was contemplated.

Leutnant W. Meisel *VII Flotilla*: On landing at Nigg I was struck in the back with a rifle in the hands of a British seaman while British officers looked on laughing.

Leutnant F. Plath *VII Flotilla*: I saw German officers and men carrying kit bags or heavy trunks when landing at Nigg pushed into the water by British sentries near the landing stage.

Leutnant R. Junker *VI Flotilla*: On landing at Nigg I found one of my kit bags in a damaged condition. I wished to take it along with me but a Scotchman with a bayonet prevented me from doing so. I saw nothing more of this bag or any other portion of my belongings which contained all my belongings.

On *24 VI* (24 June), I, together with 21 other German officers was transferred by train to Wakefield. We were guarded by a Scotch officer and two men who, whenever the officer was absent, behaved in the most unseemly manner, more particularly while the train was stationary at York during the night. Threatened with the bayonet, my laurel badge was taken from my cap, and the ribbon of an order from my coat. We were also forced to perform humiliating acts and the populace threatened us in an insulting manner at various railway stations.

Oberleutnant A. Hoffmann *VI Flotilla*: A British officer accompanied by a soldier removed the stars from the should strap of an overcoat I was wearing, attempts to resist being prevented by threats of the bayonet. The officer boasted to the people on the platform that he had already shot a German officer in consequence of his refusing obedience.

Leutnant R. Junker *VI Flotilla*: Threatened with force of arms when attempting to prevent a Scotch sentry from taking the laurel badge from the cap of a sleeping German officer.

Leutnant W. Meisel *VII Flotilla*: 'Robbed in a similar manner' and told that his laurel badge was intended for an officer.

Leutnant F. Plath *VII Flotilla*: Besides having his laurel badge confiscated, was also deprived of the crowns on his jacket sleeves and this also happened to Oberleutnant Nordmann, Fuhrmann, Terfloth.

Witnesses Named in Original Text
Scapa Flow and Wakefield

Lt. W. Hennecke VII Flotilla	Lt. L.H. Hinselmann III Flotilla
Lt. W. Meisel VII Flotilla	Lt. W. Giesler I Flotilla
Lt. F. Plath VII Flotilla	Ober-Lt. L.H. Tillessen,
Ober-Lt. L. Burkner	Lt. R. Tauber VI Flotilla
Lt. W. Rogge I Flotilla	Ober-Lt. A. Hoffmann VI Flotilla
Ober-Lt. C .Behr I Flotilla	Lt. R. Junker VI Flotilla
Oberleutnant Nordmann	Lt. Adami
Lt. Glaser	Lt. Overbeck
Lt. Kluber	Lt. Zaeschmar

Your Excellency will see from the foregoing statements, which each individual officer is prepared to substantiate on oath, that the defenceless German officers and crews were subjected by the British officers, crews and guards to the most unwarrantable and illegal treatment, notwithstanding that the former offered no resistance whatever inasmuch as they had no arms available for the purpose.

These statements further prove that British officers not only made no efforts to restrain their men, but that they encouraged, and in several cases even abetted them, leading, as in the case of *Flotilla VI* to the death of excellent senior warrant officers and the wounding of numerous other German seamen. The officers were either unwilling or unable to restrain their men at critical moments from making use of their weapons against defenceless men.

Casualties Named in Original Text
Scapa Flow

Engineer Mark Graf. V.126	Killed
Engineer Beike. V.126.	Killed
Engineer Pankrath. V.126	Seriously wounded
Engineer Maehle	Slightly wounded in hand
Engineer Hebel	Slightly wounded, head
Fireman Schroder	Slightly wounded, arm
Fireman Muller	Slightly wounded, left hand
Torpedo Machinist Peil	Wounded. Shot in the knee
Torpedo Fireman Funk	Wounded. Shot in the stomach
Torpedo Fireman Hilbig	Wounded. Two fingers shot away

In the absence of the officers even more undisciplined acts took place which, however, it would take too long to enumerate specifically.

I beg of Your Excellency, in the name of the so hardly used German officers, to prefer against the British Government a claim for compensation, and I would further ask you to lay this report before the Competent British Authority and to transmit the enclosed copy of same to the German Government.

Statement. Captain Lieutenant [name unclear] in Command of Torpedo *Flotilla VI*. POW 1271 Lofthouse Park Camp, Wakefield.

Source: TNA FO 383/508 (1919). Treatment of Members of German Navy Now Interned at Wakefield [Abridged and amended text].

Appendix 3

Curriculum for Different Subjects:
Classical Schools and Polytechnic and High Schools

Lutheran Religion	a) History of Religion from the Reformation to the present day with a short survey of developments before the Reformation; b) Instruction to enable an understanding of the religious contemporary conditions; c) Instruction in belief and morals in connection with the writings of the New Testament with a view to facilitate a proper understanding of the world and the life of the present day.
Roman Catholic	a) Relief; b) Instruction about God and Providence; c) Instruction in the Godliness of Jesus Christ; d) The teachings of the Church and her authority and Commandments; e) Moral Instruction; f) Instruction on the subject of conscience; g) Teaching about the State, the family, and socialism; h) Instruction about receiving the Holy Sacraments (Penance, Eucharis, Marriage); j) The history of the Church; k) The most important events since the division of faith in the 16th Century.
German	Some compositions, of which in each half year at least one must be done in class. As a rule several subjects are to be given to choose from, also the wishes of the young men re subjects, may be followed.

	Occasional lessons in language and the history of language. Study of some classical and poetical works.
Latin – Classical Schools	a) Repetition of construction and parsing; b) Reading of selections from Livy, Cicero's easier philosophical writings, Germania and the Annals of Tacitus; c) Practice in unprepared translation; c) Selections from Horace.
Latin – Polytechnic Schools	a) Repetition of construction and parsing; b) Reading of selections from Caeser's Civil War, Livy, and the Germania of Tacitus.
Greek	a) Repetition of construction and parsing; b) Reading of selections from Plato and from Herodotus and Thucydides; c) One tragedy by Sophocles or Euripedes; d) Selections from Homer.
French: Polytechnic/High	a) Repetition of construction and parsing; b) Practice in writing and speaking the language; c) Translations from the German or free expositions of what has been previously read as exercises; d) Reading of interesting Prose and Poetry.
English: As Above	The same as French.
History	a) German History from the year 1806 to the present day; b) Review of former development; c) The relations of Germany with other civilized states, especially considering the World's War[1] d) Expositions connected with agriculture and commercial politics;

	e) Repetitions in Geography, Geology, and Physical Geography (General Knowledge of the Earth); f) The young men must be incited to read important works.
Mathematics: Classical	a) Repetitions of the earlier parts of Geometry, Stereometry, and Trigonometry; b) First divisions of arithmetic and geometry, with the practice of compound interest and percentage; c) Enlargement of the conception of numbers through algebra from whole and positive numbers to complex numbers; d) Continuation of exercises in Trigonometry and Stereometry; e) The principle of co-ordination; f) Selected parts of Physics.
Mathematics: Polytechnic/High	The same as in Classical Schools. Added thereto – Exercises in Maximum and Minimum. Analytical Plane Geometry. Foundations of Geometry.
Natural Science[2]	The lessons indicated by the general curriculum in selected sections.

[1] It was recommended that this part of the curriculum be omitted in subsequent approval of the course.

[2] This includes Physics and Chemistry.

Source: TNA FO 383/304 (1917). Germany: Prisoners, Educational Facilities for German P/war, June 1917

Appendix 4

Sample List of German Civilian Internees

Approximately two million civilians were interned globally during the First World War. The International Prisoners of War Agency was established in Geneva on 21 August 1914 partly as a response to keep track of the increasing number of civilian and military personnel taken prisoner. The Agency was established by the International Committee of the Red Cross (ICRC). It was also a means by which warring nations could submit lists of prisoners. These lists contained names, age, residence, place of birth, profession, and place of capture in some instances. Additional data might include dates and information on transfer between camps or the release and repatriation of internees where found.

It is estimated that the Agency received more than 40,000 pages and documents in total – including many requests from families. The following list of civilian internees held at Lofthouse Park Camp has been drawn up from such documents. Documents held at the Manx Museum on the Isle of Man have been put to similar use. The ICRC Database proves equally useful for researching civilian internees at camps such as Ruhleben in Germany. Thanks are due to Matthew Stibbe for drawing attention to the possibilities of the database.

The list on the following pages includes the names of almost 350 German civilians who had been interned at Lofthouse Park Camp between 1914 and 1918. The number also includes men of the German Reserve Army.

German Civilian Internees

Abel, Karl

Ackermann, George

Albert, Frank

Arnold, Alexander

Auperle, John Daniel

Balluder, Walter H.C.

Bardelben von, Herman A.

Basserman, Hans (Dieter)

Baumann, J.

Beck, Franz

Beck, Frederick

Becker, Leo

Becker, Max

Beissell, Eginhard Graf

Beneke, William

Bente, Ewald

Bernhard, Otto Heinrich C.

Bernstorff, Werner F.B. Graf

Berr, E

Bever, Wolfgang Friedrich

Bissinger, L.

Bley, A.

Blumberg, H.

Bohn, Carl Frederick

Bornemann, W.

Bower, John George

Bowler, Georg

Braun, Ludwig

Brenner, Johann

Brown, Solomon

Bruhns, M.

Busch, Wilhelm Adolf F.G.

Carle, Henry

Caspar, C.

Cheim, Alfred Walter

Clemens, Hans

Clemens, K.

Clemens, Theodore

Conta, H.

Cretius, O.

Dahms, Hermann

Davids, A.

Decken, Leonard

Dell, Fritz

Dell, Louis

Dierolf, Friedrich

Donath, Reinhold

Donges, John George

Dunkel, Max Hermann

Duwe, Carl Gustav

Ehrenbrand, Friedrich

Ehret, Joseph

Elies, Willy J.C.K.

Feege, William

Fehling, Otto

Filboy, J.

Firnkorn, Ernest

Fisher, Frederick

Fisher, Leonard
Freytag, P.
Frohmüller, Walter
Froitzheim, Otto
Fuchs, Adolf
Gaertner, K.
Gaih, H.
Gildemeister, A.
Glahn, Ernst A.E.L.
Goldner, O.
Goldschmidt, W.
Gottschalk, A
Groedel, W.
Grossman, Walther
Grossman, Wil.
Gschwind, Frederick
Gunther, C
Haag, Frederick
Haas, R.
Haase, H.
Haeuseler, Adolf Franz G.
Hamburger, E.
Hannemann, Charles
Hansen, A.
Hartmann Charles L.
Heinig, Rudolf
Held, Hermann
Hellman, Fritz
Helms, P.V.
Hemmen, H.
Hemmersbach, Bern'd

Henschel, P.
Hermann, P.
Hermans Peter Heinrich
Hesse, Frederick
Heydemann, Ewald R A.P.O.
Hickisch, Kurt Oskar
Hinrichs, Wilhelm J.H.
Hoch, Emil
Hochheimer, Carl R. Jr
Hochheimer, Carl R. Jr.
Hoffman, G.
Hofman, Julius
Hofman, Philip
Hohenleitner, Wilhelm
Hollman, Leonard
Hots, J.
Huenecke, R.
Istel, Fritz
Jacob, George
Jaede, W.R.
Jaeger, Hans Frederick
Jaeger, Ph.
Jahn, Walter Heinrich
Janowski, Nathan D.
Jansen, Charles
Joseph, Hans Erich
Joseph, Morris
Jung, Otto
Karle, August
Karle, Henry
Kiel, L.

Kirschstein, C.

Kleinenbroich, Wilhelm

Klinemann, M.

Klinger, A.

Klinger, Andreas

Knoth, A.

Koch, Conrad

Kraaft, Ewald H.M.F.

Krahmer, Franz Felix

Kramer, Rudolf

Kranter, Ernst Hugo

Krauss, Hermann

Krauss, M.

Kress, Karl Christian

Kretzschmar, Heinrich Emil

Kruskop, Theodore A.

Kuensemueller, R.

Kullmer, G.

Lahann, A.

Lamberts, R.

Lange, A.E.

Lange, Heinrich Albin

Langer, Joseph

Langerfeld, Hans

Laubender, John H.

Lebrecht, Otto

Leister, W.

Leitlof, Georg Friedrich

Lepique, Karl H. A. W

Lesk, Emil Vienzenz

Lindenborn, P.

Lindermann, Wilhelm

Lippold, Fdk George

Lippold, Herbert F.H.

Lohmann, O.

Lueb, H.

Luerssen, Heinrich

Lungenmuss, A.

Luth, J.

Lutz, J.

Maltzahn, H.

Marschhausen, W.

Martin, Wilh. Emil W.

Marz, H.

May, E.

Mayer, Herman

Meier, Kurt Alfred

Meinecke, Alwin HAW

Melber, Frederick

Metzenthin, Theodor W.

Meyer, J.

Meyer-Riefstahl, RA

Miescke, F.

Miles, Gott.

Millar, Ch.

Miller, John

Mirow, Paul F.K.

Molls, Clemens Engelbert

Morisse, J.

Motsch, Fritz

Mueller, J.G.

Müller, Eduard Gerhard

Müller, Engelbert

Müller, Otto

Müller, Wilhelm

Nauber, Otto

Neser, Wilhelm

Nettlebladt, N.V.

Neu, Harry

Neuhaus, O.

Neukircher, H.

Niederprüm, Wil. Adam P.

Nietzsche, H.

Nirschl, Joseph Georg

Oczipka, G.

Paetz, H.

Pagenstecher, L.

Passlack, Daniel Carl L.P.

Peterman, Alfred Kurt

Philipkowski, Ewald

Pinske, Hermann

Plucinski, Stanislaus

Quoss, Fritz

Raetz, Hermann Moritz R.

Reineeke, E.

Reis, Alois

Rentzell von, Werner

Richus, F.

Riedel, Friedrich Curt

Riedelsberger, Fritz G.

Ringwald, R.

Roehner, H.

Rohde, Walther F.W.

Rohleder, Willie

Rohr, Friedrich Wilhelm

Roll, Arno Kurt

Ross, Charles

Rottschalk, G.

Sadewasser, K.

Salmon, Ernst

Saloman, Frank

Salomon, Salli

Sander, Otto

Schaefer, C.

Schamberger, W.

Scherhag, F.

Schick, Chr.

Schiller, C.

Schindge, P.

Schlentker, E.

Schmidt, Carl Freidrich

Schmidt, Hans Freidrich

Schmidt, Kurt

Schmidt, Peter

Schmidt, Vincent

Schnabel, F.

Schneider, H.

Schrader, Paul

Schraeder, Walter

Schreiber, Karl

Schrimpff, Rudolf

Schuenemann, E.

Schuenemann, H.

Schulze, Paul

Schwarz, Friedrich E.W.

Schweitzer, H.

Selb, E.

Senff, Alfred

Sieben, M.

Siebt, H.

Siemers, Martin

Silberberg, L.

Simon, H.

Smith, Joseph Richard

Solbisky, H.

Söll, Fiedele

Sommerkamp, Friedr.

Stede, P.

Steinhorst, Franz A.

Stelter, Johann Willy E.

Stermann, Henry

Steuer, W.

Stier, Curt

Straube, R.

Stunder, Frederick

Summerman, G.

Tomczyk, H.

Trilk, Henry

Trilk, Louis

Trilk, William

Trotha von, Wolf Dietrich

Tugendheim, B.

Unger, Bruno Carl

Viehweg, Max Edwin

Vogelman, Georg

Vogt, Charles John J.

Vogtlaender, M.

Volker, Frederick

Voss, E.

Wagelein, Carl

Wagner, Louis

Wahl, L.

Waldman, Frederick

Wallrabenstein, Ph.

Warncke, A.

Warnecke, Hermann

Warnecke, Julius M.

Wascher, Carl

Wauer, William

Weis, Frederick

Weisenbach, William

Weiss, Ch.

Weisse, W.

Wellen, Frank

Wellen, Wilhelm

Wennrich, L.

Werthauer, F.

Wickert, H.

Wilms, Robert

Winkelmann, Johann

Woeffle, Franz

Wontropka, J.

Worlitzer, Johann Emil Dr

Zaubitzer, Herman

Zelle, Carl Heinrich

Ziegenbein, Erich August

German Reservists

Barth, Carl Otto

Berberich, Franz

Bergel, Paul Julius

Beving, Fritz Wilhelm

Boernert, Carl Hermann

Elsässer, Franz

Falkenthal, Ernest Wilhelm

Feigel, John Leonhardt

Fuchs, Johann Leonhard

Gorner, Herman Karl

Grober, Ferdinand Gustav T.

Heil, George

Hybbenoth, Paul

Johannson, Oscar Henry A.

Käppner, Henry

Kastenbauer, Ernest

Kleyer, Ferdinand

Klotscher, Walther R.T.

Kolnig, Philip Charles Henry

Mozer, Fritz

Ochman (von) Josef

Panzer, Charles

Pfeifer, Frederick

Pfeil, Hermann Rudolf W.

Pickert, Rudolf

Rauner, Johann

Rossknecht, Carl

Sigel, Andrew

Steiger, Alfred

Stein, Reinhold

Tischer, Johann

Zettler, Max

Zwick, Albert Robert

Sources:
The Archives of the International Prisoners-of-War Agency
http://grandeguerre.icrc.org/Content/help/Introduction_en.p
df
ICRC Database (Geneva): 1914-1918 Prisoners of the First
World War ICRC Historical Archives
http://grandeguerre.icrc.org/en/File/Search
Knockaloe Virtual Museum and Website: Holland List II
http://www.knockaloe.org.uk/documents

Appendix 5

Sample List of Austro-Hungarian Civilian and Military (Reservist) Internees

Allweiss, Barnett	Flank, Aron
Allweiss, Rubin	Flash, David
Alpong, Berkowicz	Fonor, Maxwell William
Apfelbaum, Henry	Franzl, Joseph
Bach, Abraham	Freedman, Maurice
Balcar, Charles	Freh, Antonic
Barsh, William	Freidman, Lazarus
Baum, Morres	Frengl, Antonic
Bell, Solomon	Fuccik, Maxim
Benes, Anton	Getzels, Harris
Berger, Meyer	Getzels, Harris
Black (Schwartz) Harry	Goldman, Jacob
Black, Benson	Halpern, Joe
Böhm, William Rudolf	Halpern, Levi
Borodynski, Prekop.	Hecht, Simon
Bratspies, Sam	Heilpern, Herschell
Charczyszya, Michal	Hempling, Saloman
Cohen, Barnett	Hilgarth, Charles
Cohen, George	Hirschfeld, Nathan
Cohen, Luis	Hoffmann, Rudolf Franz
Diner, Joseph	Hunger, Salomon
Fabish, Joseph	Izenberg, Osiaz
Fedorski, Miecryslaw	Kainzmeyer, Hubert
Feldman, Bernard	Kandler, Max
Finder, Lambert	Kleimunz, Leon
Fischler, Isaac	Klein, Harry

Klinghoffer, Hyman

Klinghoffer, Soloman

Kolar, Charles

Kuhnberg, Max

Labinski, Basil

Lader, Sam

Landman, Charles

Lemberger, Naftali

Lesniowski, Josef

Mayer, Jechiel

Michaly, Ignacz

Mintzer, Harry

Monath, Sam

Nyder, Frank

Parnes, Victor

Petoritz, Jacob

Pytlowany, Wladyslaw

Pytrycia, Andrew

Quell, Joe

Rabensteiner, Erwin

Rabl, Leo

Radiwanz, Abraham

Reece, Israel

Retter, John

Roitner, Adolf

Roniz, Eric

Rosmarin, Harry

Runge, Frederick

Scharf, Jacob

Schenk, Edmund

Shumer, Lipa

Shusman, Isaac

Sinnreich, Dr Joseph

Skidoniak, Martin

Slezer, Harry

Slotwiner, Hari

Sogeder, Gustave

Solar, Stefan

Solar, Wasyl

Stern, Levy

Stern, Phillip

Stross, Abraham

Summerfield, Moses

Szuszanski, Nicolaj

Tarnawski, Peter

Teitelbaum, Israel

Teitelbaum, Mendel

Tritschel, Francis

Vater, Abe

Vrtal, Constantine

Waldman, Morise

Warunek, Jan

Waxenblatt, Robert Morris

Whelan or Szuslow, Michael

Woolf, Isaac

Zamzer, Mendel

Reservists

Baller, Alexander   Malauschek, Englebert Josef
Därmstadter, Hyman   Petryszyn, Stanislaw
Kandal, Pincas   Zimmerman, Leopold
Kuszej, Ignatz   Cohen, Lazarus
Nussbaum, Nathan   Helfer, Haymann (Chaim)
Vozab, Albert   Kitzmüller, Franz
Chlupac, Francois   Nimand, Morris
Habitswallner, Auguste   Steinbrecher, Charles
Kitzmüller, Franz

Source: International Committee for the Red Cross (ICRC) Database. Refs. AUT 1-VIII, AUT 3-IX, AUT 5-IX, AUT 11-VII, AUT 12 - VII, AUT 13-VII, AUT 14-VII, AUT 15-VII, AUT 16-VII, AUT 17-VII.

Appendix 6

Sample List of German Internees
Repatriated to Holland

Lofthouse Park

Name	Age	Occupation	Place Arrested
Becker, Max	35	Merchant	Leicester
Caspar, C	38	Doctor	Kirkwall
Filboy, J	33	Merchant	Lagos
Gaih, H	30	Clerk	Plymouth
Goldschmidt, W	37	Merchant	Albany St.
Gottschalk, A	36	Merchant	Albany St.
Gunther, C	42	Merchant	Blackheath
Hamburger, E	38	Merchant	'V' Division
Henschel, P	32	Musician	Douala
Hoffman, G	43	Missionary	Cameroon
Jung, Otto	32	Clerk	'V' Division
Klinemann, M	38	Merchant	'X' Division
Knoth, A	25	Farmer	Falmouth
Krauss, M	27	Clerk	Muswell Hill
Marz, H	27	Clerk	Manchester
May, E	44	Film Agent	Walton St.
Miles, Gott.	35	Merchant	Albany St.
Millar, Ch.	39	Farmer	Hull
Nettlebladt, NV	42	Director	-
Neuhaus, O	40	Engineer	Douala
Nietzsche, H	28	Clerk	Kirkwall
Oczipka, G	37	Merchant	Douala
Richus, F	43	Merchant	Togo
Ringwald, R	27	Clerk	Falmouth
Salomon, Salli	40	Independent	Norwood
Schick, Chr	41	Butcher	Wakefield
Schindge, P	43	Merchant	Manchester
Schiller, C	32	Merchant	Brixton
Schlentker, E	32	Merchant	South Africa

Name	Age	Occupation	Place Arrested
Schmidt, Kurt	33	Planter	Gibraltar
Schmidt, Peter	32	Merchant	Manchester
Schmidt, PL	33	Merchant	Brixton
Schoenebeck	40	Merchant	Kirkwall
Schuenemann, H	32	Merchant	Douala
Schweitzer, H	21	Student	Brixton
Selb, E	38	Watchmaker	Ely
Sieben, M	25	Waiter	Sheffield
Stede, P	36	Planter	Buea
Straube, R	34	Barrister	Falmouth
Wahl, L	40	Engineer	Birmingham
Weiss, Ch	31	Merchant	Albany St.
Wickert, H	32	Baker	Camden Town

Source: Holland List II. Knockaloe Documents
http://www.knockaloe.org.uk/document